Unravelling Management

Unravelling Management

Its Institutions, Practices and Beliefs

Edited by
James G. Carrier

berghahn
NEW YORK • OXFORD
www.berghahnbooks.com

First published in 2025 by
Berghahn Books
www.berghahnbooks.com

Library of Congress Cataloging-in-Publication Data
A C.I.P. cataloging record is available from the Library of Congress
Library of Congress Cataloging in Publication Control Number:
2024046828

British Library Cataloguing in Publication Data
A catalogue record for this book is available from the British Library

ISBN 978-1-80539-692-5 hardback
ISBN 978-1-80539-693-2 ebook
ISBN 978-1-80539-694-9 web pdf

https://doi.org/10.3167/9781805396925

Contents

Preface

This volume is an attempt to scratch an intellectual itch, and as its title indicates, the itch is about management.

In different ways, I have been close to managers and management most of my life. When I was a child in Washington, DC, my parents ran a business that had two or three drugstores, and my father went to work every morning to manage them. After they sold the last of their stores, his attempt to retire turned into his setting up a small financial firm in New Hampshire. My brother got an MBA degree at Columbia. After I finished my doctorate and conducted a year of fieldwork in Papua New Guinea, I taught at the university there and had a spell as department head, which entailed managing it.

This exposure, however, was not the thing that I had read about in the newspapers or in books like William Whyte's *The Organization Man* (1956) and Rosabeth Moss Kanter's *Men and Women of the Corporation* (1977); nor was it what I saw lampooned in movies like *Office Space* (Judgemental Films 1999) or in comic strips like *Dilbert* (dilbert.com). Equally, it was not what my fellow academics were referring to when they complained about the administration of their universities, which is to say their management, and nor was it what, I imagined, was taught in business schools. Those all were less a concrete set of people doing concrete things and more a conceptual category, albeit one that had significant influence in the world. This is the basis of that intellectual itch.

My efforts to scratch that itch did not help much, because the more I thought about management the more I realised that it seemed to be everywhere but was, at the same time, opaque. So I decided to see if I could find other people who could help in the scratching. The result is the chapters that follow.

What I have said indicates that this volume does not reflect a particular argument or intellectual perspective. Rather, it is exploratory – an attempt to see how we might think about management and where that thinking might lead us.

As I read through the draft chapters as this volume was coming together, I saw that there is a range of ways of approaching management, managers and their contexts. I found that stimulating, and I hope that others will feel the same.

References

Judgemental Films. 1999. *Office Space*. [nc]: Judgemental Films.

Kanter, Rosabeth Moss. 1977. *Men and Women of the Corporation*. New York: Basic Books.

Whyte, William H. 1956. *The Organization Man*. New York: Simon & Schuster.

Introduction

Seeing Management Abstractly

James G. Carrier

Management is everywhere. Firms and government agencies need it. Schools teach it and companies consult about it. Books and articles are written for managers, and about them. People are told to apply it to themselves, and they talk about it when they gossip about the idiocies and virtues of their managers. There is even a *Management for Dummies* (Pettinger, Nelson and Economy 2011), now in its second edition, and a subfield called critical management studies. In the face of all this, what is the point of another work about management?

Perhaps because it is everywhere, management has, as Marie-Laure Djelic (2016: 1) puts it, 'reached a status of taken-for-grantedness, a kind of naturalness that makes it essentially transparent and invisible to us'. This invisibility would seem to be belied by all those schools and consulting firms, books, articles and talk, but they are about good and bad managers, about management systems and styles, and about the company policies that managers implement. For instance, anthropologists have been interested in audit culture (e.g. Shore and Wright 1999; Strathern 2000), but they have approached it as a type or technique of management. With rare exceptions, then, those schools and articles, and that talk, are not about management in the abstract as a thing in itself that needs to be analysed and understood. In that sense Djelic is correct to say that management is invisible.

The purpose of this volume is to encourage the naive consideration of management. One way to do that is to try to think about management in general rather than about specific sorts of management, such as financial management or the work that human relations departments do. Another and related way to do that, at least at the outset, is to construe 'management' broadly, rather than offer a precise definition of it. Doing so is the first step in questioning the assumptions and elisions that adhere to it and that make it seem familiar and ordinary, and so seeing management abstractly. Clearing those away will make it easier to think about what management is and what managers are, and how they came to be that way; about the differences that they might make in the world, and the differences that the world might make in them. It also will help us to explain why management takes the form that it does as a social institution, with its associated set of beliefs and practices, and as a cultural phenomenon as revealed in those books and articles, newspaper stories and everyday talk. As this may suggest, although particular managers, the work they do and the places they do it, appear in this volume, they are not its ultimate concern. Rather, they are a way to study management both as an abstract entity and as a common institution.

Because it is intended to encourage that naive consideration, this volume makes no pretence of being thorough, much less definitive. Rather, it is meant to be exploratory, in the hope that it will stimulate others to think afresh about that ubiquitous and taken-for-granted phenomenon. The same applies to this Introduction. In it, I do not seek to survey the different ways that people have approached or might approach management, for that task would be too large.

One reason for this is that 'management' is a complex term. For instance, Stefan Leins (2019: 91) sees it as pervasive, covering everything from corporate management to risk management and asset management, 'a mode of governing people or things in accordance with economic ideas and rationales'. Commonly it refers to the oversight of organisations, especially firms. More narrowly it can refer to a structured set of positions such as a bureaucracy, or to the function of managing an organisation. More narrowly yet, it can refer to the specific set of people who are the managers of an organisation. In the first part of this Introduction, I will be concerned primarily with the structured set of positions and functions, and to a lesser extent with the oversight.

In the pages that follow I lay out what seem to be important aspects of common understandings of what management is, the form that it takes and why it does so. Some of these are taken for granted and rarely articulated, while others have been formally laid out. One reason to consider these common understandings is to see the assumptions on which they rest and their limitations. Doing so allows us to see the partiality of those common assumptions, which makes it easier to pose more general questions about management: What is it? What is distinctive about it? How did it get here? What are its advantages and disadvantages, it benefits and costs, for what and for whom? What does it say about the world around us and about the ways that we think about that world?

I need to stress that the common understandings are about management in general, rather than the particular aspects and techniques of management that feature in specialist literature and the curricula of schools of management. Those who know that literature or studied in such schools, then, will need to step back from the particularities of what they know, and instead think of management in general, abstractly.

I begin by viewing management as a concept, an institution and a set of practices intended to perform certain functions. In common with the literature on management and the common uses of the term, I refer primarily to business management. I hope to make clear, however, that seeing management as particularly characteristic of companies can lead us to misunderstand both the nature of management and the nature of companies.

Management Structure

According to Weber (1946: 204), management-like structures have existed in specific places and periods for many centuries. However, management in its present form arose and became widespread in the second half of the nineteenth century.

Weber's (1946: 196–244) description of ideal-typical bureaucracy is the most influential rendering of management structure, as widely manifest in employment and company law and on organisational charts. It is important to remember, however, that Weber's ideal type is intended to be a conceptual tool that is useful for thinking about the real world rather than a description of it or guide for it. As he said, an ideal type 'cannot be found empirically anywhere in realty' (Weber 1949: 90).

For Weber, management is a hierarchical, structured set of positions, what he calls a bureau. Those positions, and hence their occupants, share certain attributes. A key one is having some degree of control over a set of subordinate positions, and hence over the people who occupy them and the resources associated with them. The subordinates and resources that their superiors control are employed or owned by the entity rather than the superiors. As well, superiors themselves are creatures of the entity. They have no rights to their position or the resources associated with it other than what is laid out in the terms of their employment. Further, their control is based on no personal authority or charisma, but springs from the rules of the entity, which include the rights and duties of superiors and subordinates with regard to each other. In this sense, then, both superiors and subordinates are impersonal beings who are expected to act according to the rules, and to consider their activities in terms of those rules. As Weber (1946: 198) put it, 'the authority to order certain matters by decree ... does not entitle the bureau to regulate the matter by commands given for each case, but only to regulate the matter abstractly'.

While all who fit this definition are people whom we would call managers, not all management positions, and hence not all managers, are alike. Particularly, the positions vary in the degree of their control over subordinates and resources, and in the degree of judgement that occupants can exercise in that control. For Weber (1946: 196–201), those who occupy positions of greater control and judgement do so because of their specialist training and the experience that they have acquired as they pursue their managerial careers.

This ideal bureaucracy resembles a government department, though Weber (1946: 196–97) said that it occurs in private enterprises in advanced capitalist systems. A government department is a body of civil servants who interpret and carry out the instructions of their political masters, whether government ministers or legislatures. This is echoed in a common term for the head of a corporation: CEO, chief executive officer. That is the officer whose job it is to oversee (the 'chief' part) the carrying out (the 'executive' part) of the decisions of the board of directors, which corresponds to those ministers and legislatures.

What I have described is a common conception of management bureaucracy, but it is important to remember that it is an ideal type. It reflects Weber's interest in legal-rational authority, which he said developed especially in modern Western societies (see Bendix 1962: 391–416). As its name indicates, that type of authority rests on rules and formal qualifications, and leaves no place for sentiments or values. In it, then, subordinates obey their superiors because that is what is in their terms of employment. However, a firm or any other organisation is a social body, for in it a set of people interact with each other repeatedly. As Keith Hart (2005) argues, one aspect of that sociality is that people want, and develop, more personal reasons to justify their different positions in the bureaucratic hierarchy.

There is one further thing to be noted about Weber's model: it is directed inward rather than outward. That is, it is concerned with the constituent parts of the organisation and their relationships with each other as the organisation goes about its business. This orientation is appropriate given Weber's interest in legal-rational authority. However, it can reduce the tendency to situate the organisation and its bureaucracy in its larger context. This can be unfortunate if that larger context affects the organisation and its management, for that inward orientation can lead us to construe these contextual effects as the consequence of pressures and processes internal to the organisation, further conceptually isolating management from external influences.

The Spread of Modern Management

Two things are commonly held to account for the emergence and spread of modern management, and it is worth noting that they were described initially for firms in the United States. Those initial descriptions implied that the US is the heartland of management and management thinking – an implication that reverberates into the present.

One of those two things is what Adolf Berle and Gardiner Means (1932) described, the separation of the ownership of commercial enterprises, what they called the modern corporation, from control of them, which became common late in the 1800s (for some of the complexities of this, see Haan 2022: 573–601). Hitherto, enterprises were generally run by those who owned them, whether an individual or a group. Moreover, routinely those enterprises were not fully separate from their owners, who were personally liable for the debts of the enterprise and, if there was a group of owners, could not withdraw from the enterprise without the consent of the other members of the group. Gradually, however, joint-stock companies developed, in which a company would sell stock or shares to investors.

These companies were much more separated from those who had invested in them than had been the case before. For one thing, increasingly these were limited-liability companies, which means that investors were not liable for the debts of the company, but instead could lose no more than the amount of money that they had put in. In addition, investors were free to sell their shares if they wanted, regardless of the wishes of other investors. With the limited-liability joint-stock company, then, businesses could be approached in terms that were more impersonal and financial than before.

Share owners have claims on the company. For one thing, they normally have a say in the important decisions of the company, formalised in the election of company directors that is a part of periodic shareholder meetings, though company management may see that as interference (Pratley 2024). As well, they have a claim on company profits, in the form of dividends. Often, they see themselves – as they are seen more generally – as those who direct the company's overall strategy or orientation, which Means (1931) called 'control'. They employ managers to oversee the operation of the company to ensure that it carries out those directions, which Means called 'management'.

This growing separation of ownership and control is thus seen to have triggered the need for specialist managers. Appropriately, it was around the middle of the nineteenth century that schools of business and commerce began to appear in Europe and North America, although the modern graduate school of business first appeared around the end of the century in the United States. That growing separation was shaped to a significant degree by changes in corporate law and finance, changes that reflected political and economic pressures and interests arising outside of firms and enterprises rather than internal to them.

The other thing that is commonly thought to account for the spread of management in its present form also reflected events external to enterprises rather than their internal operation. It is what is described in perhaps the most influential history of management in the United States, Alfred Chandler's *The Visible Hand* (1977), which describes what the book's subtitle calls a managerial revolution (for commentary, see John 1997). He said that before that revolution, which is to say up to about 1840, businesses in the US were overwhelmingly fairly small enterprises operating in a single premises. Their relationships with each other, and thus the operation of the economy, were dominated, he said, by the market – Adam Smith's invisible hand.

Beginning in the 1840s, however, firms began to become larger and more complex. As part of this, they developed corporate and management structures that resemble what is common today, with divisions or subunits often dispersed geographically, which also entailed the need for a body of employees who would carry out the functions of management. Chandler said that when this company form became widespread, Smith's invisible hand of the market gave way to the visible hand of management.

Chandler said that in the United States this change in firms and the associated emergence of the new form of management followed from a set of technological changes: in transportation, with the spread of railroads, in communication, with the spread of the telegraph, and in power, with the increasing use of anthracite as fuel. As he described it, together they fairly naturally led to large corporations with central management that were involved in mass production and marketing, which were more efficient than the smaller, older firms. This illustrates Djelic's (2016: 8) observation that management commonly 'presents itself as preoccupied only with efficiency questions, not power issues'.

Chandler's materialist and economistic account of the growth of firms and modern management naturalises that growth, in the sense that it strips out the social and political forces that shaped it. What Charles Sabel and Jonathan Zeitlin (1985) say about production in various parts of Europe and the US raises questions about this naturalisation. Their concern is what they call industrial districts, which might be better thought of as industrial 'ecologies', a label that implies the interaction of entities that exist in an ecological system. They describe things ranging from silk production in Lyon, through edge-tool and speciality steel in Sheffield, to a range of textiles in Philadelphia. As they explain, well into the twentieth century, and thus well after the emergence of large firms and modern management in the second half of the nineteenth, these were areas of substantial production and technological innovation of the sort that is supposed to be characteristic of modern corporations, but carried out without unified management. Rather, these industrial ecologies were comprised of small, independent workshops that interacted with each other in a combination of competition and cooperation. Moreover, '[f]irms were not enduring units of production but rather temporary combinations of machines and skills directed to the achievement of particular tasks: the "constant" in the Philadelphia textile industry was the "mill building rather than the firm"' (Sabel and Zeitlin 1985: 149, quoting Scranton 1983: 50).

From what Sabel and Zeitlin say, it is not clear that large-scale production and marketing by integrated firms with central management, made possible by railroads, telegraphs and anthracite, had spread because such firms were more efficient than smaller ones, much less the industrial ecologies of Lyon, Sheffield and Philadelphia. As well, it is not clear that mass production was as ubiquitous as Chandler's model implies: 'In the 1970s roughly 70 per cent of all production in the metalworking sector in the United States consisted of small batches' (Sabel and Zeitlin 1985: 137). This offers further reason to doubt Chandler's explanation of the rise of modern management, resting as it does on technological drivers and an economistic rationale based on a presumed efficiency.

Similarly, Mark Granovetter (1984) investigated the size and nature of firms and their constituent establishments in the US in the twentieth century, and ended up questioning the widespread assumption that firms were getting larger and hence more in need of a substantial management structure. He found that large manufacturing firms were getting larger, but that manufacturing was employing a declining proportion of the labour force. In 1920, manufacturing firms employed 42.7 per cent of those in the private sector, but in the following decades that figure declined. Especially after 1950, employment grew significantly in the services sector, where firms and establishments were much smaller than in manufacturing: 'An historic watershed was reached in 1982, when the proportion of the labor force in services, 25.7%, first overtook that in manufacturing' (ibid.: 324).

Granovetter (1984: 327) concluded by saying that in the United States 'at least one in four private-sector workers find themselves in establishments with less than 20 employees, one in two in those with less than 100, and more than four in five in those with less than 1,000'. An establishment where a thousand people work may fit Chandler's vision of the large modern corporation with its modern management; a firm of less than a hundred is unlikely to do so, and one of less than twenty almost certainly does not. The situation has changed since Granovetter wrote: by 2019 establishments had become larger. Even so, in that year one in five people worked in establishments with less than twenty employees, a bit over a third in establishments with less than a hundred, and about one in two worked in establishments with less than a thousand employees (Census Bureau 2022).

It is not clear, however, what these changes might tell us about Chandler's argument and the assumptions on which it rests. The technological changes that concerned him may have allowed firms to get bigger, to need more complex management, and consequently to drive smaller and perhaps less efficient firms out of business. However, those smaller firms remain numerous in the United States well into the twenty-first century. Moreover, according to Sabel and Zeitlin, Chandler's technological changes did not have the expected effects in many industries in Europe and the US.

Some factors other than technological change and the supposed efficiency associated with it also seem to be important for the emergence of modern management. One obvious factor, external to firms and their operations, is governments and their policies. Writing around 1980, and focused especially on Italy, Suzanne Berger (1981: 71) describes the prevailing view of government and important economic associations: they 'all proclaim that the future of Italy has no room for the small-scale'. The view seemed to be that bigger is better, because it is more efficient, and hence more competitive. Also, of course, a government that has to deal with a small number of large firms is likely to have an easier job than one that has to deal with a large number of small ones. For various reasons, then, government policies would encourage firms to grow larger.

Management Functions

Chandler held that the increasing size and scope of companies made managerial direction and coordination – what Means called control and management – more necessary. They are the focus of much of the literature on management, though it is important to recognise that they are functions that can be served in a number of different ways and that can have a number of different names.

What I call 'direction' is deciding what the organisation or some part of it should be doing, which may not differ from what it is already doing. This can relate to small things or large, from deciding if a division's letterhead should be changed to deciding if a financial firm ought to get out of retail banking and concern itself only with investment banking. What I call 'coordination' is seeking to ensure that the various parts of the organisation, and hence the people and things that are part of them, act in ways that mesh with each other so that the organisation as a whole operates appropriately in a given direction.

Direction and coordination have long been seen as the two key purposes or functions of management, whether carried out by those called managers or those called leaders. If we take them seriously, however, we find that they tell us little that is distinctive about the nature of modern management or even of companies. Let me try to explain.

I bake sourdough bread. A few days ago I noticed that we were down to our last loaf, so I decided that it was time to start another batch. In the evening, I took the sourdough starter out of the refrigerator and refreshed it, which means adding water and flour to it and letting it sit for the yeast to work. I refreshed it again the next evening. The following evening I refreshed it for the final time, but in a larger container with much more flour and water. The next morning I put a small part of the mixture back into the refrigerator to be a starter for the next batch. To the rest I added more water, flour and other ingredients, and kneaded the dough for the first of three risings. For the last rising I put the dough into loaf tins, and after it had risen I put the tins in the oven and baked the bread.

I have described how I make bread to show the direction and coordination that it entails. The first direction was the initial decision to make bread. That, of course, led to subsidiary directions, the decisions about what to do at each step over the next few days. Each act of direction required its own coordination: the timely gathering and appropriate use of the necessary ingredients and equipment, as well as my own body and its movements.

Making bread illustrates my more general point. If a common assumption is that management entails direction and coordination, that assumption, while correct, is pretty much meaningless, as any purposeful human activity entails them. That is why I said that seeing these as the central purposes of modern management actually tells us little of interest. As Martin Parker (2018: 105) puts it, it is wrong to think that 'there is a distinct set of activities which can be called "management", and that these are different from the sort of things that ordinary people do in coping with most of their lives'.

If what I have argued is correct, a question arises, one that this volume tries to address. Management is a distinct social phenomenon seen as different from ordinary life. However, if the functions that are used to explain and justify management are, as Parker put it, 'the sort of things that ordinary people do in coping with most of their lives', then what makes it different from that ordinary coping and what are we to make of those explanations and justifications? To begin to address that question we need, as I have said already, to approach management naively – that means to try to identify the institutions associated with management and their attendant practices, beliefs and consequences.

Managers

I described Weber's ideal type of bureaucracy, attending particularly to the structure of bureaucratic relationships. The core of that type is reflected in the common assumption that management entails managerial positions occupied by people who oversee their subordinates, whether as portrayed in the organisational chart, in movies like *Office Space* (Judgemental Films 1999) or in comic strips like *Dilbert* (dilbert.com). However, that assumption appears to be less accurate than many seem to think.

For instance, there are substantial commercial enterprises that operate without management bureaucracy, such as the British cooperative food enterprise Suma (described in Parker 2018: 116–19). In it, managerial direction and coordination are distributed among the members of the enterprise: decisions about direction are made collectively; members rotate through all positions in the enterprise so that no distinct set of people form a management bureaucracy. Similarly, the Dutch enterprise Buurtzorg provides nursing care. Around 2015 it had a staff of about a thousand nurses, and aside from a small number of advisory and accounting personnel, it was made up of about eight hundred teams of twelve nurses each, who 'plan their own schedules and employ their own co-workers' (Bregman 2020: 275), and it has nothing that looks like a management structure.

As Richard Edwards (1979: chap. 7, 8) has argued, corporate direction and coordination can occur without managers who directly oversee subordinates in the way of an office manager or a shift manager in a coffee house. Michael Burawoy (1982) described how they can be carried out by means of an impersonal system of pay and bonuses that motivates employees to work hard and do what the company wants. The same is true of platform systems like Uber, in which a computer system directs drivers who to pick up and what route to take to the destination. A different sort of management without direct managerial supervision is what some call neo-management. This involves things like a corporate focus on teams and corporate practices that encourage teamwork and an orientation towards one's fellow team members, and induce people to monitor and control themselves in ways that the company wants (Røyrvik 2018: 80–82).

More strikingly, direction and coordination can occur in the absence of even the indirect supervision of Uber, neo-management and what Burawoy described. In 1913, the Highland Park plant of the Ford Motor Company began to operate with a moving assembly line. The line was designed to reflect what Ford engineers had identified as the sequence of operations involved in producing cars. Each of the tools and pieces of equipment on the line was designed to carry out the job appropriate to the different steps in that sequence and was put in the appropriate place in the plant, and needed only unskilled workers. In other words, direction and coordination were exercised by the layout of the plant itself and its moving assembly line (Hounshell 1984: chap. 6).

From what I have said in the preceding paragraphs, it seems that what are often taken to be the core functions of management can be carried out without a body of managers, and that carrying them out does not require the overseeing of subordinates. Like other aspects of the common rendering of corporate management, this one seems more problematic than it appears at first glance. If direction and coordination can take a range of forms and are not distinctive to companies or organisations, some questions arise: Why are they carried out in firms in the ways that they are? To begin to answer this we might want to look outward rather than inward. For instance, do financial institutions, intentionally or otherwise, induce firms to adopt particular forms of management? To further their own interests, do managers themselves collectively induce firms? Are particular management forms merely fashions that come and go in certain sectors?

Management and the Firm

I now turn to a pair of assumptions about management and the companies that they manage. Those assumptions are linked, as they seem to reflect the view of economic actors and actions that Smith laid out in *The Wealth of Nations* ([1776] 1976) and that have been influential ever since. For him, the economy is peopled by individual actors who are separate from and autonomous of each other, who own their own resources and pursue their own interests.

The first of this pair of assumptions is that the companies where managers do their managing are, like Smith's autonomous individual, distinct and bounded entities. This is fairly explicit in Chandler's view, for the small firms of the old order were independent entities that dealt with each other in market transactions, while modern management emerged to ensure, among other things, that large companies were coherent and self-directed. As well, it is implied in what Weber says about bureaucracy, which exists to further the activities that go on within the government department or modern corporation. More concretely, Uber drivers, Burawoy's co-workers and those on the assembly line at Highland Park are part of the firms that manage them. However, the nature of management suggests that the assumption that the company is a distinct and bounded autonomous entity need not be correct. As Marina Welker (2014: 2) put it: 'Problems with *Homo economicus* and the more generic liberal actor model become apparent when we try to figure out where a corporation begins and ends, where exactly its boundaries lie'. Let me illustrate the problem.

Over the past few decades many companies have decided to buy things that previously they had made or done for themselves, commonly called outsourcing. If those things were purchased in impersonal market transactions, as Chandler held was the case in the old order, they would conform to Smith's view of economic actors and have no particular implications for the relationship between management and the firm. However, the British retail firm Marks & Spencer (M&S) shows that the situation is not always this simple.

Through much of the twentieth century, M&S had a reputation for the good quality of what it sold, and its relationships with its suppliers were shaped by their desire to maintain that quality. In many cases, M&S staff collaborated with the staff of suppliers, suggesting and evaluating possible changes in the production process, at times to the point that they were located on the supplier's premises and helped to shape what the suppliers were doing. This has implications for the idea that the firm is a bounded entity that is directed and coordinated by its managers. That is because some of those being managed by M&S managerial staff were outside of M&S itself. This in turns raises the question of the autonomy of M&S and the boundary between it and its suppliers: Where does one firm end and some other firm begin?

The relationship between management and the boundary of the firm was complex as well in the case of the Italian clothing company Benetton in the 1970s. Then, almost two-thirds of the company's production was carried out by 'a large network of small local subcontractors' in and around Treviso, in the north-east of Italy (Pirone 2010: 76). To assure consistent quality, 'tight control was imposed on subcontractors, to whom raw materials and precise technical details to make the garment were sent' (ibid.). Again, where does Benetton end and a subcontractor begin?

M&S and Benetton raise questions about the Smithian assumptions that shape Chandler's explanation of the emergence of modern management. They also raise questions about the second of those intertwined assumptions about management and the companies that they manage. Chandler's assumption is that modern management emerged and spread because technological changes facilitated high levels of production, which in turn entailed having larger and more integrated companies, and the modern management they required.

Management Business

Thus far I have considered some of the common assumptions about how modern management emerged, about its structure, how it operates and what it does – assumptions that help to make management appear natural and taken for granted. I have argued that those assumptions are less self-evident and secure than many people seem to think, and hence that management itself may be less self-evident. This is not to deny that modern management exists or that it can have significant effects. It does, however, indicate that we might want to consider other things that make management seem self-evident. Here I want to suggest one such factor, but I do so only tentatively, for I have not been able to locate work that deals with it. That factor arises from an observation that management itself is an important industry or sector of the economy.

Because management is big business, it commands substantial resources and touches and benefits a lot of people. Some make a good living from management, such as consultants, those who teach in business schools and those who write successful books about management. It is reasonable to assume that they will be prone to thinking that management is important. There are also people for whom the benefit is smaller, such as those who work for a business journal or for a company that publishes management books. That benefit may not lead them to embrace management and its thinking, but it is likely to lead them to see management as something that is natural and taken for granted.

Probably the most visible part of the management sector is management consultancies, and although I refer blandly to consultancy firms it is important to recognise that they are not all alike. That is because they often specialise in different aspects of corporate life, perhaps how to set up and run a secure IT system, or how to deal with banks. While lots of firms do consultancy work, here I will describe only seven of them: the three biggest consultancy firms and the four largest accounting firms that do consulting. This list is hardly exhaustive, but it is enough to help us to see how big a business management is.

The consulting firms are McKinsey & Co., Boston Consulting Group and Bain & Co. Because what I say here is only speculative, it is reasonable to draw on Wikipedia for information on them for fiscal years (FY) 2019 or 2020, before the disruptions of Covid-19 and the invasion of Ukraine. Between them, these three firms had revenues of $23.6 billion (all figures are in US dollars) and had about 62,500 staff. The four accounting firms are somewhat more difficult to summarise, because consulting is only part of what they do. They are Deloitte, EY (Ernst & Young), KPMG and PwC (PricewaterhouseCoopers). Between them, for FY 2019 or 2020, they reported a total revenue of $164 billion, of which $61 billion was from consulting. Only EY reported the number of staff working in consulting: 72,000. If we assume that the proportion of total staff working in consulting matched the proportion of total income coming from consulting, then the other three would have had 344,000 staff in consulting (Deloitte 2021; EY 2021; KPMG 2021; PwC 2021). In all, then, these seven firms appear to have generated consulting revenue of some $84.5 billion and employed about 478,000 people in that work. To put this in perspective, in November of 2019 airlines in the United States employed just under 453,000 staff (BTS 2020).

Aside from consulting firms, the most visible part of the management sector is business schools, and there are a host of them. An informal search on Wikipedia indicates that there are about 430 in the United States, 140 in India, 88 in Canada, 65 in the UK, and 45 each in China and Pakistan. These are all businesses in their own right that employ large numbers of people. In addition to their more obvious teaching staff there are secretaries, administrators, examiners and the like. As well, there are the people and firms who prepare and print course materials and who maintain the lecture halls and buildings that the schools use, as well as their internet and remote-learning facilities, not to mention the plumbers, electricians, cleaners, and so on. All of this adds up, both in terms of those whom management touch, and the money that business schools generate and spend. In their annual report for 2019, one of the most prestigious business schools, at Harvard, reported an annual revenue of $860 million and expenses of $831 million (Harvard Business School 2020a), and in FY 2020 they had over 240 full-time equivalent faculty positions and just under 2,000 staff positions (Harvard Business School 2020b).

Beyond business schools, there are the more-or-less academic journals aimed at existing and aspiring managers, and the more prestigious business schools each have their own. In the US, Harvard has the *Harvard Business Review*, which reported 340,000 subscribers in 2019 (Harvard Business School 2020a), the Booth school at the University of Chicago has the *Chicago Booth Review* and the Massachusetts Institute of Technology has the *MIT Sloan Management Review*. There are also periodicals that publish scholarly research on management, although the boundary between them and the preceding titles is fuzzy. These include titles like the *Academy of Management Journal, Journal of Management and Organization, International Studies of Management and Organization, Management and Organization Review* and *Organization Management Journal*. All of these employ people like copy editors and proofreaders, as well as those involved in their printing and distribution, such as editors and typesetters, printers and those who maintain websites.

Magazines and journals are not the only media concerned with management. There are also books, the most famous of which is probably *In Search of Excellence* by Tom Peters and Robert H. Waterman, published in 1982. It sold 122,000 copies in the first two months and more than five million copies by 1998 (Clark and Salaman 1998: 140). While many firms publish management books, some specialise in them, and they are so numerous that there are web pages with titles like '18 Top Business Book Publishing Companies' (Som 2021).

The last aspect of the business that I want to mention is management events. That includes everything from the meetings of management organisations, such as the Institute of Management Consultants and the American Management Association in the US, and the Chartered Management Institute and the Chartered Institute of Personnel and Development in the UK, through the panels and conferences organised by management periodicals and consulting firms, to talks by management gurus and those who aspire to be one. These events charge fees to attend, often substantial ones. They also have associated commercial costs: venues have to be hired and staffed, events have to be advertised and catered, and so on.

I have said that my point is speculative, but I think it is worth pursuing by those with more wit and knowledge than me, as management is not just an activity, what managers do. In aggregate it is a big business, and as such it makes management real to many people in many ways. For some it may make management attractive and important, while for most others, as I suggested, it may make management simply something natural and taken for granted.

About the Chapters

I have said that this volume is intended to encourage people to see management abstractly, which means naively, free of the assumptions and elisions that make it seem familiar and ordinary. Doing so does not mean laying out the truth of management or discovering what management really is. Rather, it means showing some of the complexities of management, of its effects and of what people tell themselves about it. One way to do this is to treat management, and especially the management of the firm, as an important and influential institution. The first two substantive chapters in this volume consider features of that institution.

The first of these chapters is by Andrew Orta, 'The Production of Management and the Disappearance of the Manager in MBA Education'. Its focus is the relationship in the United States between management and another institution, management education, particularly MBA programmes in business schools. The two are in a symbiotic relationship. MBA programmes are the main way that new managers are produced, and they help to make the position of managers and of management more generally legitimate; this, in turn, helps to solidify the programmes' importance and thereby attract applicants.

As this chapter describes, the emergence of business schools paralleled the emergence of large corporations in the second half of the nineteenth century, and their graduates were seen as knowledgeable and skilled managers who were necessary for the operation of large, hierarchical corporations. Moreover, the consolidation of business education in the late nineteenth and early twentieth century was furthered by claims that much of our lives are linked to business, and that sound business sense, learnt in business schools, was essential in many areas of life beyond the halls of corporations.

The large corporations and corporate thinking that were the focus of business education produced some unfortunate effects, including those associated with work on relentlessly demanding assembly lines and the associated labour activism. Business schools responded to these challenges by presenting themselves as offering a solution, in the form of a shift away from economics and related areas in their curricula, and a shift towards the social sciences, especially industrial psychology and personnel management. The result was an increasing number of graduate schools of business, an increasing number of graduates, and the renewed claim that sound business education would alleviate many of America's ills.

This edifice rested on the foundation of the dominance of large corporations, a foundation that looked increasingly shaky as the twentieth century came to a close, so that the skills that business education had claimed to teach became less relevant. The growing importance of what was seen as market logic challenged the importance of the idea of stable firms with commitments to employees, community and customers. Increasingly, free-wheeling individuals such as corporate raiders and entrepreneurs, as well as the finance that buttressed them, were the focus of attention, and business education began to pivot in appropriate ways. Instead of managerial skills, it began to focus on leadership and innovation. The manager, then, was replaced by the innovative leader, ever alert to the wider environment and the advantages that can be gained by linking into it, producing successful enterprises and potential solutions to many of the country's problems.

Orta's chapter traces the evolution of business education as an institution that continued to claim its importance for both commercial success and national well-being. The next chapter considers something else that is important for the institution of management, because it helps to render legitimate the power of management and of individual managers – it is my own chapter, 'Management's Hidden Realm'.

Prior to the development of joint-stock companies in the nineteenth century, the predominant form of enterprise in the UK and the US was the artisanal workshop. In most areas, those who ran them had two important bases of authority over their subordinates: they were the employer and they were likely to be guild masters, recognised as knowing the technical, commercial and social aspects of their enterprise. With the separation of ownership and control, and with the increasing size of enterprises, these bases of authority weakened. Instead, managers increasingly claimed a new basis, which was the specialist knowledge that they possessed, taught in the growing number of business schools that Orta describes.

That knowledge constituted what I call a hidden realm of knowledge and skill. That realm is esoteric in the sense that acquiring it calls for specialist training; it is universal in the sense that it applies to all situations that come within its ambit; and it is efficacious in the sense that applying it will produce the desired results. A hidden realm is common in professions such as medicine, where people go to medical school to acquire knowledge that applies to all human bodies and that, if properly applied, will produce efficacious treatment. Claiming its own hidden realm buttressed the authority of management and individual managers.

As the chapter describes, however, it is not clear that there is such a hidden realm. In spite of this, belief in it has been important since early in the twentieth century, and the chapter suggests that the persistence of that belief rests on the occupational advantages it offers. For instance, the assertion that there is a hidden realm asserts as well the importance of management and managers, and the supposed content of that realm helps managers to make sense of the world they confront, and provides guides to action.

The chapter concludes by considering the way that the claim to a hidden realm helps management to occupy an important class position, but class in Weber's sense rather than Marx's: control over access to valuable positions in the economic realm, such as jobs in management. Those who seek to become managers need to go to business school, where they learn about that hidden realm and its supposed efficacy. Equally, assessment of the work of managers is in the hands of managers, either those who are their superiors in the firm where they work or, if they are near the top of their company's management in the United States, by compensation committees. The members of those committees are also managers, albeit in other firms, and they submit their recommendations to the firm's board of directors, which rarely challenges them. One consequence is that over the past few decades the income of those in higher management positions in the US has grown by a vast amount. While that growth is justified in various ways, it turns out that an important reason is that there is no consensus on how to evaluate senior managers. The result is that decisions about their pay tend to follow the pay of senior managers in comparable firms, which reflects the firm's desire to be seen as legitimate in the eyes of those other firms.

The next pair of chapters address a different question, which is why there is so little sign of an emerging anthropology of management; and the suggested answers centre on the way that anthropologists, especially in the United States, see management. The first of the chapters is by Michael M. Prentice, 'Writing Managers and Management: Anthropology's Last Repugnant Other?' In the second half of the twentieth century, anthropologists began to study Western institutions, such as law, medicine, education, religion and business corporations, analysing how these operate and how culture and subjectivity are constructed within them. Prentice observes that, while there have been numerous ethnographies of white-collar workplaces, an anthropology of management has not developed. One plausible reason for this is anthropology's long-standing critical orientation towards Western expansion into non-Western places, carried over into a critical orientation towards the introduction of capitalistic practices or regimes into non-capitalist places within the West.

Prentice points to a different factor, that management occupies a narrative position of the 'repugnant Other', particularly within American anthropology. Building on Susan Harding's (1991) argument about why certain Christians were not included within a developing anthropology of Christianity, Prentice shows that corporate managers occupy a position parallel to that of those excluded Christians, so that they also become repugnant Others. The fundamentalist American Christians that concerned Harding were not recognised as proper anthropological subjects, not because of the radical nature of their beliefs, but because they were culturally close to American anthropologists. Likewise, Prentice describes how management and managers are not treated as proper subjects in contemporary anthropological writing, in part because they are felt to be already culturally known and hence subject to critique rather than investigation. One effect of this is that managers and management occupy a relatively fixed narrative position as the embodiment of modernity without sociality.

The chapter considers three contemporary ethnographies of global capitalism to explore the ways that managers and management are cast as repugnant Others, and the consequences of that casting. Prentice shows a tendency to paint managers and management in one of two different lights. In one, management is a distant, asocial force premised on technical rationality and seeking profit at the expense of the environment, virtue or care, and the individuals who anthropologists encounter are treated as unscrupulous or deceptive. In the other, those individuals are reluctant participants in management hierarchies who harbour their own critiques of capitalism, resist higher levels of management, demonstrate care for their co-workers and, at times, even think like anthropologists. The consequence is to bifurcate managers and management into two simple sorts: one driven by greed and profit, the other attempting to resist it. This reflects anthropology's critiques of global capitalism, but it hinders our understanding of how the discourse and techniques of management have spread to many sectors of society (e.g. public-finance management, risk management), and of how certain kinds of subjects emerge from within these institutions and discourses.

A resistance to seeing managerial subjectivity as a particular historical formation worthy of investigation goes against many of the tenets of anthropology itself. The effects of this are particularly limiting on studies of management elsewhere, such as in East Asia, Europe, Africa and Latin America, where ethnographers tend to seek out extreme cases of Western management practices rather than explore what indigenous management might mean. The dominance of this American framing in anthropological work on management is particularly pronounced as scholars from other fields have explored postcolonial and indigenous approaches to management, and Prentice says that anthropologists would be well advised to take those approaches seriously.

Prentice's chapter indicates that anthropological work on management is shaped and constrained by disciplinary attitudes and orientations, so that culturally managers are difficult, even distasteful, subjects of study. The next chapter approaches this distaste in a different way, through Felix Stein's tale of his attempts to study the firm of management consultants where he was employed, describing both the practical and the ethical difficulties he encountered. His chapter is entitled 'Against Collaboration: The Ethics of Studying Corporate Management'.

During the past few decades many anthropologists have told themselves that they should change the way that they approach their research and writing. Instead of celebrating the heroic fieldworker that Malinowski described, alone on a tropical beach, those anthropologists talked in terms of collaboration with those among whom they carried out their research. Conventional fieldwork necessarily involves a degree of daily collaboration with those among whom one is living, the 'participant' part of 'participant observation' – but this was more than that. Many came to espouse collaboration in formulating and carrying out the research, analysing the results and writing them up, not least because it would expose the researcher to perspectives beyond those common in the discipline. For some, the failure to collaborate in this way was a sign of celebrating one's individual research and academic prowess, and even reinforcing neocolonial dominance over the places where they did their research. For such people, collaboration was not simply intellectually productive, but it was also moral, for it was a route to engaged anthropology, coming to take on the views and values of those with whom they were doing their research.

To a degree, albeit for different reasons, collaboration was coming to be important in the business world where Stein sought to carry out his research. What he found, however, is that anthropological advocacy of collaboration ignores the complexities and ethical divergences that field research, in this case in the corporate world, can entail.

His consultancy job was in what is called strategic managerial advice, which amounts to advising and assisting middle- and upper-level management in whatever they want to do, provided that it is legal and pays the consultants' salaries. The consulting firm was not, then, offering advice in any substantive area, like banking or the airline industry, but was simply advising on how to manage some aspect of the company that hired them. After about a year in the job, Stein decided to see if he could study the consultancy firm that employed him. He was motivated in part by the amoral orientation of the firm, which simply did what the client firm wanted, and in part by unease at the large amount of money he was being paid compared to the pay of those affected, often adversely, by his firm's advice. Turning the consultancy company into an intellectual object was a way of dealing with his unease. He sent a draft research proposal to the director of his office, and after a fair amount of effort and accommodation with those in the firm, it was accepted and he started his research.

In the process he came to realise that the idea of collaboration with those at the site of one's research can throw up contradictions. For instance, his research interests differed from the interests of the consultancy firm, and his work would not benefit the firm in any way that they considered important: for example, it would not generate new business or new and better ways of doing consultancy, but it would involve a slow, deliberative and questioning style of thought that was alien to consultancy work. Not only was he being employed full time as a consultant, but his research project meant that only part of his effort was devoted to his job, and his interviewing of others in the firm meant that he was distracting them from their proper work. In short, the nature and goals of his research deviated from, and in some cases contradicted, the nature and goals of the firm and the people with whom he was carrying out his research.

More collaboration would not resolve this, and, given the instrumental nature of consultancy work and aspects of that work that struck Stein as morally dubious, it is not clear that it should. Instead, it may be that the researcher should challenge the practices, beliefs and values of those being studied. This possibility is clearest in the study of the consultancy firms that the chapter describes, but what is in that chapter suggests that the possibility may arise in a host of other situations.

The two preceding chapters are efforts to help to explain why there is relatively little anthropological work on management. Of course there is such work, and the next three chapters illustrate it. They all revolve around the central anthropological concern with culture, though they approach it and its relationship with management in very different ways. The first of these chapters is by Greg Urban, 'Management in the Flow of Culture', which uses culture as a frame to describe and understand management activities.

Urban starts with the assumption that what people value, think, do and have, what he calls 'culture', will remain the same unless something happens that leads them to change, and this chapter considers the ways that management affects and is affected by culture and its changes. It identifies three types of force that can cause change: entropy, interest, and what he calls 'metaculture'. Urban says their influence can be transmitted in one of two ways. One is the commodified: transmission in commodity transactions, as when people buy a computer, a purchase that transmits culture and leads people to change the way that they do things. The other is non-commodified, as when people see a new hairstyle in the street and decide that they like it (e.g. Krueger 2024).

I said that one force that can cause change is entropy, an external force that impinges on culture and its continuation. That force can arise outside of the normal flow of culture, in the way that the Covid-19 epidemic arose outside of normal life, and led people to change the ways that they did things. Equally, the force can arise from ongoing activities that lead to unexpected results, in the way that curiosity about lodestones led to the development of the navigational compass, which led sailors to change the ways they did things. Another force is interest, which can lead people to change the ways they value different things, and so change the ways that they act with regard to them. Finally, metaculture differs from ordinary culture because it is not about things in the normal sense, but is about culture itself. Changes in metaculture will affect how people see and understand the world, and so affect how they do things, in the way that coming to see a firm in terms of shareholder value can change the way that those in the firm act. Metaculture is especially salient in management, for managers' statements and decisions often contain visions about what the firm is or ought to be; thus metacultural elements shape the way people see the world and act in it.

Urban is interested in the ways that a firm's managers can affect the flow of culture, and he does so by a set of examples. The first of those is of Boston Scientific, which shows how culture can be encouraged to flow between consumers and firms, a flow that usually is non-commodified when it flows from consumers to firms, and commodified when it flows in the other direction. John Abele, at the company that became Boston Scientific, was central to the development of catheters that could be steered around blood vessels. He assiduously communicated with physicians about what sorts of problems existing catheters presented and how they might be overcome, a communication that went in both directions: the physicians said what they wanted; and Abele told them of possible new catheter designs and then developed and sold catheters with these changes.

In addition, management can affect flows between firms, in this case illustrated with the development of what became the standard computer desktop. In 1981, three years before the Apple Macintosh, the Xerox corporation produced Xerox Star workstations, which had an icon-based desktop and facilities for things like a mouse and computer networking. People at Xerox said that its development was made possible by the movement of people between electronics firms and by their efforts to apply ideas that they had developed in their graduate research projects, which are non-commodified cultural flows. Confronted with such flows, a firm's management can try to encourage them, for instance by seeing what is going on at industry conferences and trade fairs. Alternatively, they can try to restrict the flow of its culture to other firms, for instance by applying for patents.

The final example of cultural flow concerns metaculture, an element of culture that affects other elements, often by presenting a new vision of what something is. In this case, that 'something' is firms, and the new vision is that their sole social purpose is to make money provided that they stay within the law. Milton Friedman promulgated this view in a newspaper article in 1970, during the Cold War, and as an element of metaculture it spread far beyond those who had read the article. This element had obvious attractions for those who wanted to make money in business, but it was also attractive because Friedman invoked Cold War imagery to indicate that worrying about the social purpose of firms was the first step down the slippery slope to Communism. This metacultural element affected the ways that firms thought about themselves and the ways they operated, and Urban illustrates this with Boeing Aircraft when it was being run by acolytes of Jack Welch, renowned for being ruthlessly concerned with cost-cutting, profit and the company's share price. Friedman was hardly the first person to say that companies are there to make a profit, but his espousal of the idea that they serve no social good beyond profit, coupled with the rhetoric of the Cold War, gave his idea a currency that it had not had since before the Depression.

In the first of the three chapters concerned with culture, we have seen that Urban used the idea of culture as a way to describe and think about what managers do, especially in their dealings with their customers and with other firms. The second of these chapters, 'Not Every Culture Has Management, but Every Management Has Culture', by Heung Wah Wong, looks at a different aspect of culture: its relationship to management.

As described in Orta's chapter and my own, for much of its history much of management has been presented as an objective and neutral tool that, correctly applied, produces the desired results. Associated with this is the idea that variation in management styles is the consequence of specific exterior factors causing deviation from management's objective and neutral core. Culture has often been invoked as such a factor, seen to impinge upon management and give it a local or national colouring. Such a view indicates that management, as that neutral and objective tool, is distinct from culture. Wong rejects that view, arguing instead that management *is* culture through and through, and that all management systems are structured and operated in their own cultural terms. He does so by investigating one element of Chinese culture, the kinship system, and the family firms that embody it.

The pertinent part of the kinship system is the *jia*, or household, and both it and the family enterprise (*gongsi*) are seen as the source of wealth. Central to the household is the relationship between fathers and their sons, which is conceived of in ways that depart from conventional European and North American understandings. The son's life comes from his father, so that they share the same life although they have different corporeal beings. They are not equal, however, for the father's life encompasses the son's and is superior to it, just as the son's life encompasses his own son's and is superior to it. The case with daughters is parallel but different, for they cannot inherit their father's life, only their husband's, and they are subordinate to and encompassed by the husband's life.

Many family firms in China are organised in terms of these household principles. The head of the firm is the founder-father, who manages the firm through a set of core members, who in turn become the centres of their own subunits. The most obvious source of core members is the founder's sons and wife. Beyond this are affines, especially sons-in-law, followed by those who have long been linked to the founder-father, such as schoolmates, neighbours and former colleagues. Lastly, core members can be drawn from those who have been in the firm for a long time and thus shown their loyalty to the founder-father.

Like the head of the household, the founder-father would expect core members to carry out his orders, and again like the household head, the founder-father would share the fruits of the firm with them. As this suggests, relationships in the firm depart from the bureaucratic model because they reflect people's relationships with each other rather than their positions in an impersonal structure. As well, those who order a core member to do something, perhaps solve a particular problem, do not specify how it is carried out. This is left to the core member, so long as it is carried out.

Just as fathers and sons in the household are different people who share being, so an important element of the relationship with subordinate core members in the firm is something like that shared being. Because of it, it is not only that subordinates have responsibilities to their superiors, but also that superiors have responsibilities to the subordinates, especially to provide them with support when they need it. As well, just as subordinates share in the glory of their superiors' honours and achievements, so superiors share in the glory of their subordinates' honours and achievements. This is because the household, the enterprise and their members are not seen as distinct in the way that they are in most Western societies. The firm and the household are parts of each other, and because of the notion of shared being, the members of the household and the core members of the firm share in the firm, and the wealth and honour that it generates.

Some Chinese family firms depart from the model that Wong provides in his chapter, and some Western firms depart from Weber's ideal-type bureaucracy. Even so, that model shows how management in many Chinese family firms rests on a logic that is very different from the logic that underlies management in Western firms. It is in this sense that management should be approached as something that is culture through and through, not an independent thing that culture affects, any more than culture is an independent thing that the firm makes use of.

The two preceding chapters have looked at management in terms of the flow of culture and as an embodiment of culture. The next chapter looks at culture as it is manifest in the everyday actions in a company's headquarters, and in the material setting in which those actions take place. It is by Emil A. Røyrvik: 'Life in the Head Office: Material Metaphors of Management'.

Much of what people think about management revolves around the decisions that managers make and the policies that shape them. Those decisions and policies are important, but attending solely to them ignores the fact that they take place in contexts that may seem to have nothing to do with them but in fact are part of the things and processes that shape and give meaning to management and its world, as they themselves are shaped and given meaning by that management world. The most obvious of these, though hardly the only one, is the physical spaces where managers work and act, and the archetype of these is company headquarters. This chapter points to some of what that ignoring leaves out, and it does so by considering the nature of the headquarters of a multinational Scandinavian company, and what goes on there.

The most concrete thing that it considers is the headquarters building, which was new when Røyrvik did his fieldwork. It was a striking modernist building, which had lots of glass walls and ceilings, stairs and doors, and by means of them projected the important notions of visibility and transparency. The expression of these notions was, however, contradicted by the physical existence of those walls, doors and the rest, which were effectively soundproof: one could see people talking, but could not hear what they were saying. It was contradicted in a different way by the limits the building imposed on where people could go. Entrance to the building required the permission of those in the reception area; many interior doors would only open if one possessed the necessary security card. Thus, the people in the building occupied a material space that was coy, offering visual access but denying physical and aural access. Moreover, that visual access had consequences, among them the fact that people were routinely on display, visible to those passing by, whether they wanted to be or not. People were, of course, aware of this and adjusted their appearance and behaviour accordingly, increasing their self-control and conformity, while occasionally showing a careful exhibitionism.

This absence of privacy reduced the likelihood that people would develop a sense of an autonomous self, and other features of the building were likely to have the same effect. Among these is the fact that the building had open-plan offices with desks that anyone could use if they needed to. This had enabled a sharp reduction in the number of offices, thus reducing the likelihood that people would develop a sense of their own space; it also reduced the number of corridors, thus lessening the number of areas where staff could meet and talk somewhat privately. Of course, the desk pooling also implied that people were only temporary, and could be replaced by others at any time.

Although the company had no formal dress code, what people wore in the headquarters was fairly uniform and contained its own meanings, and what they wore is another aspect of life in the head office that Røyrvik considers. As one might expect, what people wore reflected their position in the company: those higher up the ladder dressed more conservatively than those lower down. This was not, however, wholly uniform: pretty much regardless of their formal ranks, those in economics and finance dressed more conservatively than those in engineering, while those in projects dressed more informally than traders. Among the men, however, some sort of suit was pretty much universal. Moreover, men predominated and set the taken-for-granted norms of dress, while women's dress varied somewhat more and, especially, tended to be more individualistic and informal. Røyrvik suggests that this reflects, and reinforces, the idea that it is the men who were really there, in the sense that they defined the company's management, while women were, in some way, less significant, so that their dress made less difference.

The building and the dress that I have described, which are two of the things that the chapter considers, seem to have nothing of substance to do with company policy or executive decisions. Nonetheless, they are the context in which those policies and decisions exist, shaping them and giving them meaning, while being shaped and given meaning by those policies and decisions. Røyrvik's chapter shows that if we ignore them, our view of management, what it does and how it does it, is impoverished.

The last substantive chapter in this volume considers venture capitalists. They are different from the management considered by the other chapters, for they manage money rather than companies. In his 'Venture Capital Investors as (Asset) Managers', Johannes Lenhard shows, however, that they illustrate a concern that has recurred among those who think about company management, and that reflects a feature of the modern corporation, namely, the separation of ownership and control. The focus of the concern is what is called 'the principal–agent problem', which is a problem because the agent, the person making managerial decisions, may not want to do what the principal, the owner, wants. The principal–agent problem is the classic form of the difficulties that arise when ownership is separated from control, but as this chapter illustrates, there are other difficulties, especially when ownership and control become more complex than the simple distinction of shareholders and company managers.

Venture capitalism is easy to explain, at least in principle. Venture capitalists attract investors, who are called limited partners because they have no say in the operation of the venture-capital firm and can lose nothing more than the money that they invest. Those people give the capitalists their money, and the capitalists invest it and hope to make a profit on the investments. The capitalists make money in two ways: as an annual fee on the total amount of money that the limited partners have given them, commonly 2 per cent, and as a levy on the profits that they make when they sell the investments, commonly 20 per cent, with the rest of the profit going to the limited partners. Venture capitalists routinely invest in new companies, start-ups, for they are the ones where they can make significant gains before selling their investments after 6 to 12 years.

Following the financial crisis of 2008–10, conventional investments became less attractive than they had been, and the potential returns of venture capital led many to invest in such firms and become limited partners. This in turn meant greater competition among those firms for promising start-ups, and in the United States many of them to tried to attract those start-ups by touting themselves as what were called value-add investors, providing not only a financial investment but also useful skills and advice, which meant getting involved in the management of the start-up. The result was that there were three sets of interests: those of the venture capital firm, those of its limited partners and those of the founders of the start-up.

In theory those interests are aligned, as all want the start-up to flourish, grow and, ultimately, get sold for a lot of money or listed on a stock exchange and sell shares to the public. The venture capital firm would make a profit on its initial investment, which would benefit the limited partners, and the founders would benefit from the sale of the company, by selling their own shares at a profit or by using the money generated by the sale of company shares to strengthen the company. In practice, things did not always work out so neatly.

The most obvious source of friction is between the founders of the start-up and the venture-capital firm. Founders have their own plans for what the start-up will become and what it needs to do to get there, plans that may conflict with those of the venture-capital firm. One source of potential conflict is simply commercial judgement: the founders and the venture capitalist may have different senses of what the start-up ought to become and how to achieve it. Another source of conflict is that the venture-capital firm expects to sell its initial investment in a limited time and so produce income for the firm and its limited partners, while the start-up's founders may be thinking in terms of a much longer period.

Given the complexity of the interests involved, it is not surprising that venture-capital firms often produce disappointing results for their limited partners, and that value-added firms often put a foot wrong in the start-ups in which they have invested. In light of this, it is also not surprising that Lenhard ends his chapter by suggesting that venture capitalists behave more like ordinary investors, putting their money in a start-up that they think will flourish, leaving the founders to run things, and then taking their money out in due course. They should, that is, separate ownership and control.

The final chapter in this volume is Stefan Leins's brief 'Afterword: For an Anthropology of Management'. In it he considers some of the ways that an identifiable anthropology of management might emerge. One is to strengthen the links of the emerging subfield with anthropological work on bureaucracy, a suggestion justified by the way that many of the chapters in this volume use 'management' and 'bureaucracy' pretty much interchangeably.

Another is to consider management outside the commercial sphere. It has, after all, become an important point of reference, even if only rhetorically, in a growing number of areas, such as development aid, higher education, medicine, and the like. There is ongoing work that looks at the invocation of management in those areas, and it would be useful to see how that work can strengthen an anthropology of management, both because of the cases and processes that it describes, and because of the ways that the claims of management in them are justified.

A third is to pay closer attention to the relatively new field of critical management studies, which is attracting growing interest, especially in the UK and Scandinavia. Not only does it offer its own perspectives on management, but it is also producing a growing body of ethnographic material that can help to join the 'management, abstractly' of this Introduction's title with a corpus of 'management, concretely'.

***

I said that this volume does not pretend to be definitive, to tell us what management really is or what is the best way to study it. Rather, it is exploratory, intended to help to pry open a concept, an institution and a set of practices and beliefs that seem to characterise 'management', at least as the word is commonly used.

As such, the volume is eclectic. Contributors to it address different aspects of management as an institution, as an object of study, as related to culture and as a place where different interests can clash, and how we can help to develop an anthropology of management. There are many other aspects of management that would repay consideration, just as there are other ways that we can help to develop that anthropology.

If this volume encourages that attention and consideration, it will have achieved its goal – that is, to make management less taken for granted, natural, transparent and invisible.

Acknowledgements

My title extends the subtitle of Felix Stein's *Work, Sleep, Repeat: The Abstract Labour of German Management Consultants* (2017). I am grateful for the comments of Brian Moeran and for the thoughts of Stephan Carrier, MBA.

James G. Carrier has taught, done research and written on aspects of economy in Papua New Guinea, the United States and the United Kingdom. He has had a recurring interest in important economic institutions (e.g. *Meanings of the Market*, ed., Berg, 1997; *Ethical Consumption: Social Value and Economic Practice*, ed. with P. Luetchford, Berghahn Books, 2012) and intellectual themes (e.g. 'The Trouble with Class', *European Journal of Sociology*, 2012; 'Moral Economy: What's in a Name', *Anthropological Theory*, 2018; 'Changing Economic Experiences and Understandings', *Journal of the Royal Anthropological Institute*, 2024).

References

Bendix, Reinhard. 1962. *Max Weber: An Intellectual Portrait*. Garden City, NY: Anchor Books.

Berger, Suzanne. 1981. 'The Uses of the Traditional Sector in Italy: Why Declining Classes Survive', in Frank Bechofer and Brian Elliot (eds), *The Petite Bourgeoisie: Comparative Studies of the Uneasy Stratum*. London: Macmillan, pp. 71–89.

Berle, Adolf, and Gardiner Means. 1932. *The Modern Corporation and Private Property*. New York: Harcourt, Brace & World.

Bregman, Rutger. 2020. *Humankind: A Hopeful History*. London: Bloomsbury Publishing.

BTS. 2020. 'November 2019 U.S. Passenger Airline Employment Data'. US Department of Transportation Bureau of Transportation Statistics. Retrieved 2 August 2024 from https://www.bts.dot.gov/newsroom/november-2019-us-passenger-airline-employment-data.

Burawoy, Michael. 1982. *Manufacturing Consent: Changes in the Labor Process under Monopoly Capitalism*. Chicago: University of Chicago Press.

Census Bureau. 2022. '2019 SUSB Annual Datasets by Establishment Industry'. Retrieved 2 August 2024 from https://www.census.gov/data/datasets/2019/econ/susb/2019-susb.html.

Chandler, Alfred D. 1977. *The Visible Hand: The Managerial Revolution in American Business*. Cambridge, MA: Belknap Press.

Clark, Timothy, and Graeme Salaman. 1998. 'Telling Tales: Management Gurus' Narratives and the Construction of Managerial Identity'. *Journal of Management Studies* 35(2): 137–61.

Deloitte. 2021. Business Metrics. Retrieved 17 Dec. 2021 from https://www2.deloitte.com/content/dam/Deloitte/global/Documents/About-Deloitte/GIR2021-Business-metrics.pdf.

Djelic, Marie-Laure. 2016. 'History of Management – What Is the Future for Research on the Past?' in Barbara Czarniawska (ed.), *A Research Agenda for Management and Organization Studies*. Cheltenham: Edward Elgar, pp. 1–10.

Edwards, Richard. 1979. *Contested Terrain: The Transformation of the Workplace in the Twentieth Century*. New York: Basic Books.

EY (Ernst & Young). 2021. Global Review 2020: Facts and Figures. Retrieved 17 Dec. 2021 from https://www.ey.com/en_vn/global-review/2020/facts-and-figures.

Granovetter, Mark. 1984. 'Small is Bountiful: Labor Markets and Establishment Size'. *American Sociological Review* 49(3): 323–34.

Haan, Sarah C. 2022. 'Corporate Governance and the Feminization of Capital'. *Stanford Law Review* 74: 515–602.

Harding, Susan. 1991. 'Representing Fundamentalism: The Problem of the Repugnant Cultural Other'. *Social Research* 58(2): 373–93.

Hart, Keith. 2005. *The Hit Man's Dilemma: On Business, Personal and Impersonal*. Chicago: Prickly Paradigm Press.

Harvard Business School. 2020a. *Annual Report*. Cambridge, MA. Retrieved 15 Dec. 2021 from https://www.hbs.edu/about/annualreport/Documents/2020/HBS-Annual-2020.pdf.

———. 2020b. 'Statistics Overview'. Cambridge, MA. Retrieved 26 Dec. 2021 from https://www.hbs.edu/about/statistics/Pages/default.aspx.

Hounshell, David A. 1984. *From the American System to Mass Production, 1800–1932*. Baltimore, MD: Johns Hopkins University Press.

John, Richard R. 1997. 'Elaborations, Revisions, Dissents: Alfred D. Chandler, Jr.'s *The Visible Hand* after Twenty Years'. *Business History Review* 71(2): 151–206.

Judgemental Films. 1999. *Office Space*. [nc]: Judgemental Films.

KPMG. 2021. 'KPMG Reports Global Revenues of $32.13 Billion for FY21'. Amstelveen. Retrieved 17 Dec. 2021 from https://home.kpmg/xx/en/home/media/press-releases/2021/12/kpmg-reports-global-revenues-of-usd-32-billion-for-fy21.html.

Krueger, Alyson. 2024. 'They'll Take the Travis Kelce – Hairdo, That Is', *The New York Times*, 29 January. Retrieved 2 August 2024 from https://www.nytimes.com/2024/01/29/style/travis-kelce-haircut.html.

Leins, Stefan. 2019. 'Management', in James G. Carrier (ed.), *A Research Agenda for Economic Anthropology*. Cheltenham: Edward Elgar, pp. 80–104.

Means, Gardener C. 1931. 'The Separation of Ownership and Control in American Industry'. *Quarterly Journal of Economics* 46(1): 68–100.

Parker, Martin. 2018. *Shut Down the Business School: What's Wrong with Management Education*. London: Pluto Press.

Peters, Thomas J., and Robert H. Waterman Jr. 1982. *In Search of Excellence: Lessons from America's Best-Run Companies*. New York: Warner Books.

Pettinger, Richard, Bob Nelson and Peter Economy. 2011. *Management for Dummies*. Chichester: Wiley.

Pirone, Chiara. 2010. 'Benetton and Zara Information Systems: A Comparative Analysis'. Masters thesis, Polytechnic University of Catalonia. Retrieved 3 August 2024 from https://upcommons.upc.edu/bitstream/handle/2099.1/9456/67045.pdf?sequence=1.

Pratley, Nils. 2024. 'ExxonMobil's Attempt to Silence Activist Investors Should Be a Warning to Shareholders', *The Guardian*, 23 January. Retrieved 2 August 2024 from https://www.theguardian.com/business/nils-pratley-on-finance/2024/jan/23/exxonmobils-attempt-to-silence-activist-investors-should-be-a-warning-to-shareholders.

PwC (PricewaterhouseCoopers). 2021. 'Global Annual Review 2021'. Retrieved 17 Dec. 2021 from www.pwc.com/annualreview.

Røyrvik, Emil A. 2018. 'The Measure of Sociality: Quantification, Control and Economic Deviance', in James G. Carrier (ed.), *Economy, Crime and Wrong in a Neoliberal Era*. Oxford: Berghahn Books, pp. 66–92.

Sabel, Charles, and Jonathan Zeitlin. 1985. 'Historical Alternatives to Mass Production: Politics, Markets and Technology in Nineteenth-Century Industrialization'. *Past and Present* 108: 133–76.

Scranton, Phillip. 1983. *Proprietary Capitalism: The Textile Manufacture at Philadelphia, 1800–1885*. New York: Cambridge University Press.

Shore, Cris, and Susan Wright. 1999. 'Audit Culture and Anthropology: Neo-liberalism in British Higher Education'. *Journal of the Royal Anthropological Institute* 5(4): 557–75.

Smith, Adam. (1776) 1976. *An Inquiry into the Nature and Causes of the Wealth of Nations*. Chicago: University of Chicago Press.

Som, Ruposhree. 2021. '18 Top Business Book Publishing Companies'. Retrieved 2 August 2024 from https://writingtipsoasis.com/business-book-publishing-companies/.

Stein, Felix. 2017. *Work, Sleep, Repeat: The Abstract Labour of German Management Consultants*. London: Bloomsbury.

Strathern, Marilyn (ed.). 2000. *Audit Cultures: Anthropological Studies in Accountability, Ethics, and the Academy*. London: Routledge.

Weber, Max. 1946. *From Max Weber*, edited by Hans Gerth and C. Wright Mills. New York: Oxford University Press.

———. 1949. '"Objectivity" in Social Science and Social Policy', in Edward A. Shils and Henry A. Finch (eds), *The Methodology of the Social Sciences*. New York: The Free Press, pp. 49–112.

Welker, Marina. 2014. *Enacting the Corporation: An American Mining Firm in Post-authoritarian Indonesia*. Berkeley: University of California Press.

Chapter 1

The Production of Management and the Disappearance of the Manager in MBA Education

Andrew Orta

This chapter takes up this volume's focus on management by examining the genealogy of management training in business education. My discussion builds upon ethnographic research conducted in US MBA programmes, as well as supplementary work examining the figure of 'the MBA' and the periodically fraught status of MBA education through a set of business-focused media. That includes evergreen think-pieces about the death of the MBA, connected with recurring crises and scandals of capitalism, as well as recent marketing efforts by US MBA programmes and MBA-adjacent publications to reclaim the value of management education for the transformative times of contemporary capitalism.

I am interested in the emergence of a framing of management, along with the figure of the manager, in co-ordination with the institutionalisation of business education. At stake is the authoritative bounding of business as an object of study, yielding a continuous stream of evidence for the necessity of business management and, by extension, the necessity of university business programmes that at once document business challenges and produce the managers required to meet them.

The shifting conceptualisations of business management and the development and transformations of business education are thus entangled components of a cultural whole, itself bound up in a complex push–pull relationship with shifting framings of capitalism from the late nineteenth century through to early in the present century. This long twentieth century traces the rise of managerial capitalism (e.g. Chandler 1977, 1984) and the apotheosis of the business manager as a discretely conceived social subject. It is also marked by the unravelling over the past half century of the corporate form, which had been the justification for the MBA manager.

While the original sociotechnical rationale for the business manager has faded from view, the institutional project of managerial production has endured, with MBAs and business schools rebranding the management idea in ways that elide or mask the extractive operations of capital. This apparently disappearing manager is shaped to meet the challenges of the current moment in capitalism, managing efforts to reimagine a stakeholder capitalism, as a correction for the excesses of shareholder capitalism, for the twenty-first century (e.g. Henderson 2020).

The End of the Manager?

To judge from recent headlines, managerial capitalism, at least as embodied by its twentieth-century avatar 'the MBA', has run its course. MBA programmes have been scrambling to reinvent themselves, addressing declines in their applicant pools and the concatenated failures of financialisation and shareholder capitalism across the financial crisis of 2008 and the stresses and revelations of the Covid-19 pandemic. As *The New York Times* reports (Goldberg 2022), the anti-capitalists have set up shop in the belly of the beast, Harvard Business School, and Wharton will soon be offering MBA majors in diversity, equity and inclusion, and in environmental, social and governance factors.

Such curricular changes in management training have been a long time coming. They were evident in reassessments of MBA education in the wake of the Great Recession (Aspen Institute 2008; Datar, Garvin and Cullen 2010). They received additional encouragement from the pronunciations of the Business Roundtable (2019) and the annual shareholder letters by BlackRock CEO Larry Fink (n.d.) stressing the need for a sustainable stakeholder capitalism.

MBA programmes have nonetheless proved resilient, returning from the dead time and time again. After a precipitous decline beginning with the Great Recession, enrolments have rebounded and administrators declare that the future is bright for management education. However, while MBA programmes have reinvented themselves, it would seem that business management in the twenty-first century has little to do with business. Rather than focusing on profit and loss, and the related nuts and bolts of capitalism, business schools today market themselves as arenas for the production of 'leaders', whose talents can be focused on solving grand social challenges: inequality, political polarisation, environmental sustainability (Orta 2019a, 2022).

In a recent recruiting webinar, the dean of a top MBA programme (Byrne 2021) suggested that 'the future is bright', but it would require 'a fundamental rethinking of business education. When the MBA was first established a century ago, there was a real sense that we would be forming leaders of business and society, a focus on forming values. I see a return to that earlier concept of business education'. This, like other, similar assertions that management education is returning to these roots, is partly true: there are certainly similarities with some of the earliest framings of management at the birth of the MBA degree. However, much like the fictive capitalist originalism of shareholder value and related myths of neoliberalism, in which a remaking of capitalism is cast as a reconnection with its origins, this claimed return to the foundations of business management masks new cultural work within the project of capitalism (see, e.g., Ho 2020). This chapter is about that new work. I argue that the reimagined manager participates in a re-engineering of the extractive practices and institutions of capitalism, part of a more contemporary sleight of hand in which extractive practices are elided by the productive sociality of the talented entrepreneurial leader.

My focus is on the ways that MBA programmes have constituted and marketed themselves in coordination with the shifting idea of the (business) manager. I examine the early establishment of MBA training in conjunction with the emergence of managerial capitalism, and how business schools have serially repositioned themselves as serving the managerial needs of business while also distancing themselves from the cycle of crises and failures that are endemic to contemporary capitalism (Ho 2009; Mirowski 2014). MBA programmes are at once drivers of change and subject to corporate norms, as their recruiting relationship with firms is integral to their business model. Against this background, I examine the ways that the technically proficient MBA manager has been displaced by the MBA as leader, with a repertoire of talents and soft skills.

This is not to suggest that extractive practices are not part of the workings of contemporary capitalism. I am interested in how recent framings of the management idea divert attention from such fundamentals, locating the key to the production of value in the personal qualities of the manager-as-leader. This genealogy of the management idea as glimpsed through business schools provides a useful view of the shifting meanings of management, and of the sleights of hand entailed by discussions in and beyond MBA programmes for a kinder, gentler post–shareholder-value capitalism.

The Manager's End

The long arc of MBA education reflects a continuous struggle to legitimise and reinvent the idea of the MBA across a succession of scandals, crises and transformations of capitalism. The earliest collegiate business school was the University of Pennsylvania's Wharton Business School, established in 1881. By 1900, the University of Chicago, the University of California, New York University and the University of Wisconsin all had business programmes, with Dartmouth College introducing the first graduate school of management, offering an MS in Commerce. Harvard Business School, founded in 1908, offered the first MBA degree. By 1911 there were twenty-one business programmes at US universities; by 1917 there were thirty.

The idea that management required professional training was formalised over these decades. It was further bounded by para-educational institutions conferring credentialed legitimacy: new professional associations and business journals. The Association of Collegiate Schools of Business was founded in 1916, with accreditation standards approved in 1919. Harvard Business School launched the *Bulletin of Business Research* (1913–63) and the *Harvard Business Review* (1922– present). These publications emerged in connection with Harvard's Bureau of Business Research, which also produced early business case studies in coordination with the formalisation in 1923 of the case study method of business education (Orta 2019b).

This emergent complex of professional management training also entailed the production of authoritative representations of business, entangling the nascent business schools in defining the challenges they were ostensibly called forth to address. *System: A Magazine of Business* began publication in 1900, with reports on contemporary business practices. *System* became *Business Week* in 1929. The production of MBA managers thus developed in partnership with the conceptualisation of the field of business itself.

This business-education model advanced in the face of significant headwinds. The earliest business programmes were scholarly stepchildren, seen as lowering institutional standards with the vocational-school commonness of business education in the nineteenth century (Cruikshank 1987; Daniel 1998; O'Connor 1999). And the programmes did seem out of step with the classical training and pomp characteristic of elite universities: the MBAs awarded by Harvard Business School were the first Harvard degrees not conferred in Latin.

The programmes embedded themselves within the academy through connections to canonical disciplines of the liberal arts and sciences, especially economics and political science. Also, they sought to emulate other, established professions, such as law, engineering and medicine. For instance, the case-study method of business teaching developed in emulation of law and medicine. Alongside their efforts to situate themselves with respect to academic institutions, business schools also made the case that they were meeting an emergent societal need arising from the technical challenges of a new moment in capitalism, and from associated social needs and crises. The early alchemy of business schools was to fuse these two channels of legitimacy.

Some critics of the new business schools saw in them the invasion of the sacred spaces of classical learning by the excesses of Gilded-Age capitalism (e.g. Veblen 1918). For their part, the programmes positioned themselves as solutions to those excesses. In founding the Wharton School, for instance, Joseph Wharton was motivated by what he cast as the moral necessity of training in 'finance and economy' (Abend 2014: 234). Joseph French Johnson, dean of the recently established NYU School of Commerce, Accounts and Finance, said that proper instruction in the 'knowledge and the arts of modern finance and economy' would better prepare people for 'faithful public service in offices of trust', and encourage 'sound financial morality' in their private affairs (Johnson 1906: 30).

Early business programmes posited their own necessity with the claim that the United States was seeing a rapid expansion of the sphere of activity known as 'business', and that the growing scale of business activity as well as the compounding complexity of business operations required a new kind of technical and moral administration (i.e. management). With the expansion of business cast as a defining feature of an emerging turn-of-the-century 'Americanness' (Allen [1931] 1957), the proper management of business was fused with the proper stewarding of a dawning American modernity. Business, in this light, was a threat to the public good that management could turn into a benefit.

Managing the Modern

At the turn of the twentieth century, technical knowledge of business and finance was seen as increasingly necessary to meet the pressing need for good governance and informed civic engagement. Joseph French Johnson (1906) made the case in *The New York Times*. Business training establishes basic ethical standards in business practice: 'Nor is it only in a private, moral, and individual sense that these schools have a high function at a time when our public affairs are so largely economic'. Johnson lamented poorly informed Congressional action around matters of currency, railroads and tariffs; business schools would help to produce graduates and faculty who could provide authoritative counsel on 'business ideals' and 'commercial methods'.

The university-trained manager was cast as sitting astride and integrating a welter of diverse political interests and social forces that arose from the expansion of industrial capitalism, and this was thrown into sharper relief with the Great Depression. Indeed, the apparent precarity of capitalism was attributed to the absence of formal training in management. IBM's Thomas Watson (in Daniel 1998: 117) told *The New York Times* in 1932, 'If business, finance, and science had known the right thing to do three years ago, we would never have reached our present low economic estate. ... I believe young men should go about the study of business as never before'. Wallace Donham (1931: 154–55), dean of Harvard Business School, lamented the malaise of American business, arguing that the 'leadership of American business' carried out 'by men of the highest ability and social objectives' was 'the only hope for Western civilization'.

What exactly were these newly required managers managing? Beyond the nuts and bolts of commerce and the need to stitch together the accelerating capitalist project with the flywheels of post-Depression and interwar governance, the manager was to be a technician of a new social world enacted through the expansion of industrial operations and the dawning vertical complexities of the corporation. As we shall see, the arc of the management project traces a shift from an early focus on the coordination of a newly emergent tier of commercial activity with civic and social entailments, to a framing of managerial expertise as *sui generis*, independent of commercial applications and translatable to all realms of life (see Carrier, 'Management's Hidden Realm', this volume).

Dean Johnson (1906) explained the new business school by expanding conventional understandings of business as the commercial operations beyond the 'buying and selling of goods'. To focus on commercial operations, he writes, is to open a complex world: 'the word business covers the work of a very large proportion of the population of this country, including wholesale and retail storekeepers and their employees, bankers, salesmen, advertising men, and all those employed in the order, sales, and accounting departments of corporations'. Johnson observed that an increasing number of recent college graduates have been going directly into business. Two years later, Harvard's president Charles Eliot (in Cruikshank 1987: 35) explained the new business school in terms of 'the prodigious development of many corporate businesses in our country', and 'the fact that more than half the recent graduates of Harvard College have gone immediately into business'.

Expanding business activity entailed a complex set of business roles requiring specialised training. Johnson suggested a tripartite market segmentation matching the different enterprises teaching business skills. Vocational business colleges helped to prepare office boys, stenographers and clerks. Commercial high schools, with their more rounded curricula, produced men schooled in stenography and accounting with reasoning ability suitable to office managers and sales staff. The new 'schools of commerce' trained the ranks of 'managing officials', who owe their positions and their success to 'executive ability, sound judgement, and breadth of view, in addition to qualities of aggressiveness, originality, accuracy, etc. which other subordinates possess' (Johnson 1906). Johnson thus offers an early example of a practice at the heart of the production of the management idea: a descriptive analysis of business practices discovers and maps out the necessity of management.

President Eliot of Harvard made a similar case: '[B]usiness in its upper walks has become a highly intellectual calling, requiring knowledge of languages, economics, industrial organisation, and commercial law, and wide reading concerning the resources and habits of the different nations' (in Cruikshank 1987: 35). Similarly, Harlow Person (1920: 112), dean of Dartmouth's Tuck School, brought his engineer's eye to the production of managers. He described business as comprising three zones of activity: Zone I 'operations', Zone II 'management' and Zone III 'administration'. While those in Zone I required little more than on-the-job training and were unlikely to rise above that level, the task of business schools was to train a class of managers. They might gain experience in Zone I, but would quickly rise to higher managerial functions thanks to an ability to 'interpret [their] experience in Zone I with a grasp of the functions and problems of the next higher zone'. The administrative positions at the top of Person's schema were occupied by men with 'ripe judgement' developed from extensive business experience. However, the managers trained in business schools were expected to rise efficiently to Zone III, with the business schools serving as an incubator enabling managers to benefit from experiences more quickly and profoundly.

While early MBA programmes sought to conform to the norms of university training, they also came to ally themselves with those who complained that, whatever the needs of the growing ranks of business, classical studies did not meet those needs. As early as 1885, Joseph Medill, editor of the *Chicago Tribune*, remarked in congressional testimony: 'Our college system certainly does not train our youth in habits of useful industry'. In Medill's view, 'a knowledge of dead languages and the higher mathematics [was] ... all well enough for the wealthy and leisure classes, but is not best suited for bread-winners' (Senate 1885). Similarly, Andrew

Carnegie warned that college education was 'almost fatal to success'; and a Wall Street financier, Henry Clews, considered 'college men … spoiled for a business life' (in Daniel 1998: 26). The sentiment was more tactfully delivered by Dean Johnson: 'The broad generalizations and slowly developed conclusions, which are so highly valued in academic and scientific circles, must be avoided rather than encouraged in any really effective university course of training for business' (Johnson 1906).

A key component of the institutionalisation of management training in higher education was the substitution of the business curriculum itself for real-world business experience. MBA programmes did this in two ways. They used a curriculum that claimed to reproduce managerial experience through fast-paced, high-volume workloads, case studies and simulations of corporate life. Additionally, they fetishised an abstract notion of talent and leadership, the cultivation of which has become the primary value proposition of MBA education over the past four decades – more important, it would seem, than a focus on business fundamentals. These developments in the management idea took shape in coordination with the shifting status of MBA education as an established institution codependent on the vicissitudes, crises and contradictions of capitalism across the turn of the twenty-first century.

Corporations Are People

Business schools, then, emerged in the context of the expansion of modern capitalism in the United States, and they established their legitimacy by casting themselves as the solution to a set of related changes and challenges. At the core of these were substantial changes to the ways business was organised, as the increasing complexity and scale of some industries, as well as changes in the financing and ownership structure of large firms, shaped new types of managerial practices.

The managerial capitalism that was ascendant from late in the nineteenth century entailed a distinct set of managerial challenges (Berle and Means 1932; Chandler 1977, 1984). The vertically integrated corporation not only connected multiple business functions under a single administrative entity, it also harnessed entrepreneurial innovation and strategic decisions directly to a managerial structure (McCraw 1988). The integral role of that structure emerged as the raison d'être for the training of managers, and insofar as its reproduction was increasingly baked into corporate decisions, the strategic development of twentieth-century corporate capitalism was tightly fused to the institutional sedimentation of MBA education.

Managers emerged as technicians of the social, ameliorating the anomie of the corporate structure and blunting the traumas of assembly-line production. Psychology soon figured as a core business discipline, lending a cloak of science and introducing the social in business education. That it did so at a time when the social strife of management–labour conflicts was a primary preoccupation of government and industry helped business programmes to establish their merits in the eyes of industry leaders. Economics, long dominant in the development of business education, was gradually rivalled by social sciences (Daniel 1998; O'Connor 1999; Gabor 2000; McDonald 2017).

This turn to the management of the social entailments of the firm is exemplified by the career of Elton Mayo. A psychoanalyst in Australia, Mayo was recruited to a Rockefeller-funded appointment at Wharton in 1922, later taking a faculty position at Harvard Business School, where he remained until retirement in 1947. Mayo and his collaborators examined the effects of changing work environments on worker productivity, and concluded that changes in the physical work environment were not directly responsible for changes in productivity. Rather, the attention paid to workers, the knowledge that they were being observed, and the affect of an interested manager were key factors. Mayo's work helped to focus attention on the personal qualities of the manager, whose empathy and style were connected to the extraction of value from labour. Here is a new facet of the MBA manager, whose enlightened administration might ameliorate the afflictions of the working class and the attenuated social relations of the corporation, which were affecting industrial productivity (Hoopes 2003; Jack and Westwood 2009).

Over the 1920s and 1930s, courses like Personnel Management became staples of business curricula. The *Annals of the American Academy of Political and Social Science* devoted its entire issue of November 1923 to 'Psychology in Business'. The introduction, by former Wharton faculty member C.H. Crennan (1923: 1), noted that '[a]t the heart of every business situation is a human nature problem. ... the psychologist is in business to stay because business involves human nature'.

This turn to the social in a field that came to stand almost seamlessly with American modernity was deepened through connections with a confluence of cultural developments in the decades after the Depression. Along with the emergence of the business manager as an American cultural type, this period also saw the ascendance of the American Dream as an ideology of upward mobility and potential. The consolidation of fields such as human relations and industrial psychology in business schools intensified the engagement between business education and the emerging mid-century cultural milieu (Susman 1984; O'Connor 1999).

By the 1950s, MBA programmes were unquestioned parts of the educational and social landscape, the firm was the default exemplar of business, and business in its corporate form was increasingly seen as quintessentially American. However, the figure of the MBA manager soon became a victim of its own success. From experts brokering the operational and sociopolitical complexities of the modern corporation, the MBA had *become* the organisation man (Whyte 1956), a cog in the machinery of business and an exemplar of a new kind of capitalist malaise, not on the factory floor but in the expanding offices of middle managers. And so, much as capitalism has been an ongoing project, the cultural work of bounding and legitimating management has also been ongoing, and tightly linked to shifting accountings of the changing world of business.

Much of this moment is condensed in the work of Peter Drucker, 'the man who invented management' (Lewis 1998; Byrne and Gerdes 2005). Drucker held faculty positions at Sarah Lawrence in economics and Bennington College in political philosophy before joining the business school at New York University in 1950 (Gabor 2000; Hoopes 2003; Gilman 2006). That CV frames his work well, as his focus was on the corporation and the mass-production plant as the emblematic social institutions of contemporary Western society. Crises such as the rise of Fascism and the Depression could only be averted, in his view, if such institutions were in harmony both internally and with the values of society.

In his 1946 book *Concept of the Corporation*, based on a quasi-ethnographic study of corporate management at General Motors, Drucker argued that the collective power of the corporation marked a new capacity for coordinating human productive power and economic activity, but risked violating the strong social ideals of individualism, which Drucker understood to be the core value of American society and therefore the source of any legitimacy for the corporation as a social institution. Drucker's interest in the role of institutions in harmonising individual and collective interests is sometimes contrasted with the more singular profit motive often ascribed to neoliberalism. Nonetheless, the managerial ideal that Drucker helped to establish would facilitate the implementation of neoliberal capitalism in the United States through the generalised recognition that a primary site for value creation was managerial action and expertise (as opposed to, say, labour) (Gilman 2006; Hanlon 2016).

By 1950, a few years after *The Concept* was published, business education was a well-established part of higher education in the United States. The number of business bachelor's degrees awarded increased from 1,576 in 1919 to 72,137 in 1949, a rate of increase greater than for all bachelor's degrees over that time. The stability of business education was further indexed by the adoption in 1949 by the Association to Advance Collegiate Schools of Business, the successor to the Association of Collegiate Schools of Business, of a resolution on the core fields of business education: 'economics, accounting, statistics, business law, finance, marketing, and production or industrial management'. Unlike undergraduate business degrees, MBA degrees had increased from 110 in 1919 to 4,335 in 1949, gaining popularity much more slowly (all data in this paragraph are from Daniel 1998: 149–51). That was about to change.

Crisis Management

In a 1950 essay in *Fortune*, Peter Drucker noted the postwar arrival of graduate business education, with large corporations increasingly looking to business programmes for new managerial talent. Drucker signalled the increasing influence of MBA programmes by recounting a 'Wall Street joke ... that the center of financial decisions has not, as it is commonly believed, shifted to the Federal Reserve Bank, but rather to [NYU] Professor [Marcus] Nadler's money-market seminar' (Drucker 1950: 92–93). At the same time, Drucker pointed to the shortcomings of professional management training. 'The MBA' was taught to consider himself a 'crown prince', trained to view things from the top. Even worse, these entitled MBAs, placed in positions of responsibility, were essentially 'young men without adult experience'. All too often, he lamented, the MBA princelings became administrators of a routine status quo. This is the dystopic organisation man; without his antithesis (the entrepreneur), Drucker warned, 'the large corporation turns arteriosclerotic' (ibid.: 94).

Drucker was articulating a wider ambivalence about the MBA that intensified into a mid-century crisis for business education. In response, business programmes rebranded the management idea. Following a pattern that would recur in subsequent crises, a series of reflections from those in business education yielded a set of reforms to MBA education presented as at once a response to the transforming demands of business, and continuous with the longer arc of the management idea. The MBA project is thus always cast as responding to the challenges of the time, rather than being one of their causes.

A pair of landmark reports commissioned by the Carnegie and Ford foundations critically reviewed the state of business education, recommending changes to address the challenges of the day (Gordon and Howell 1959; Pierson 1959). The reports focus on business administration, praising the integrated knowledge of the MBA model over specialised functional training in accounting, finance and the like. Both reports position their aims as analogous to the consolidation of professional standards for medicine or law, yet the case they make is that the goals of business education are qualitatively different: the rapid changes in postwar business practices require the production of managers prepared for the unprecedented.

The studies recommend an expansion of business education, proposing what became the standard two-year MBA curriculum in US business schools. The stress is on preparing managers to solve problems connected to the expanding role of science and technology in business, the increasing complexity of firms,

> the increasing attention to human aspects of internal company operations, to relations between a firm and its external environment, and to a firm's social responsibilities ... [and] the need for maintaining the growth rate of the American economy through the development of new products, cheaper methods of production, new materials, improved quality, and wider distribution – in essence the continual search for the new and the untried. (Pierson 1959: 14)

Robert Gordon and James Howell argue that the accelerating pace of technological change requires 'enterprising and competent leaders of industry and society, capable of facing up to the demands of the increasingly complex and science-based economy', and also that there is an increasing role for social science and statistics in management, and a need for 'human relations engineers' to help to balance the needs of individuals alongside their integration within organisational environments (Gordon and Howell 1959: 14). They continue:

> The increasing complexity of the firm's external environment has steadily added to the difficulties of the businessman's task. This is by now a familiar story: the increase in the power of organized labor and the steady upward pressure on wages; the expanding role of government; the Cold War and the precarious state of international relations; changes in the distribution of political and economic power and in the climate of public opinion; and so on. (ibid.: 15)

The Talented Manager

These reports signal the alignment of two elements of the management idea in the middle of the twentieth century that have taken on new implications in the twenty-first. One is the civic function of management, as business administration is increasingly seen as engaging directly with the social challenges of the changing times. This civic function has broadened in recent decades in the context of the entrenchment of neoliberalism and the suffusion of economic rhetoric (market-speak) as a grammar of social analysis and policy. The second element is the framing of management training around a standardised two-year MBA curriculum offering a compressed presentation of a register of business fundamentals (accounting, marketing, finance, etc.). This condensed curriculum has in fact served to make the technical operations of business less relevant to the role of management. Instead, and as detailed further below, the intensive assimilation of a welter of skills has become an index of additional personal qualities, forged in a simulation of the real world of business, where rapid decision-making based on always-imperfect information is the stock-in-trade. Business management at the dawn of the twenty-first century thus appears as a consolidation of talent and leadership, capacities that can be tapped and cultivated through MBA training but cannot be taught (Orta 2019a). For the select few who have it, this management talent increasingly entails applications beyond 'just business'.

Even over the latter half of the twentieth century, the MBA became a repository of promise and the answer to every question: synthesising the gamut of hard and soft knowledge; charting a successful course in the postwar economy; ameliorating tensions between labour and management, between individualism, human fulfilment and conformity, between free enterprise and government; and developing brand 'USA' within an unstable and shrinking world. It is little wonder, then, that honorifics such as 'management guru' and 'business guru' were introduced in the 1960s and 1970s to refer to leading management theorists.

The 'guru' label, invoking the idea of a spiritual master, has become a routine way of thinking about management expertise: there is a subsidiary branch of business journalism focused on profiles and lists of the 'top management gurus'. This also indexes the tight connection in the United States between business management and personal fulfilment, with roots in the industrial psychology of Mayo and mid-century concerns about corporate anomie. But the staying power of the term discloses the ways that business management has become a site for the generation of a new and prized kind of sociality.

The institutional consolidation of the 1950s precipitated the dramatic expansion of MBA education. The number of MBA programmes increased by an average of 20 per year between 1950 and 1975; more MBAs were awarded during the 1970s (over 387,000) than in the previous seven decades combined (Daniel 1998: 196ff.). The introduction of rankings in the 1970s intersected with corporate recruiting to solidify a spiral of top programmes placing MBAs in lucrative positions in top firms, who came to compete with other firms to hire the MBAs from the top programmes.

Against the economic malaise of the late 1970s, the MBA degree increasingly seemed like a golden passport (Van Maanen 1983; McDonald 2017).

Post-corporate Capitalism

The apotheosis of the MBA coincided with the systematic dismantling of the corporate form that was the founding rationale for management education. By the turn of the twenty-first century, more than 55 per cent of the highest paid CEOs in large US firms had MBAs, compared with less than 20 per cent in the 1980s (Frydman 2019: 4957). This cohort of managers oversaw a dramatic remaking of the management idea under the ascendant frame of neoliberalism, which included a reframing of the purposes of a corporation, increasingly understood as having its principal obligation to its shareholders (Jensen and Meckling 1976).

The resulting unwinding of the firm as a social unit with enduring commitments to employees, communities and customers was explained as a natural function of market logic, which increasingly meant financial markets for corporate equity and debt (Davis 2009; Carbone and Levit 2017; Ho 2020). And this ethos of capitalist management was tightly bound to a philosophy of governance that sought to create an environment for the unfettered operation of markets and that increasingly suffused discussions of governance and social policy with terms and concepts borrowed from capitalist business practices.

The core sensibilities of neoliberal thought were integrated in and reproduced by the management curriculum of MBA programmes, which also rode the ascendance of neoliberalism, as the seductive images of corporate raiders and rich investment bankers further fuelled the enrolment boom in business schools. Finance emerged as a dominant specialisation for budding MBAs, and the young MBA princelings of financialisation emerged with evermore esoteric schemes for generating value through trades in financial markets with things like credit default obligations and other forms of securitisation that became infamous in the wake of 2008.

Management curricula helped to instil the sensibilities of neoliberal capitalism in multiple ways. Although a common view is that MBA programmes are merely credentialing exercises and that MBAs learn nothing of substance, they do get more than they bargained for. As I have detailed elsewhere, course content may be simplified and compressed, but it takes on compelling depth through the reinforcement of material across the curriculum. Claims that the firm is 'a bundle of cash flows' and 'an entity that bears risk' for the benefit of its investors, for instance, are cast as immutable truths and instilled as compulsions of a managerial habitus (Orta 2019a: 43). Programmatic simulation of professional life inculcates a norm of fast-paced decision-making based upon imperfect information, and MBAs learn to frame this as an index of hard work, for which they should be highly compensated. There is less reflection on how the focus on speed and execution participates in an extractive project of financialisation screened from view by the managerial flair for accelerated competence (Orta 2022).

MBA programmes have also developed a connected value proposition: alongside technical skills are a set of other qualities and talents required by an effective 'leader'. The programmes sell themselves as spaces for the cultivation of talent, helping students to become better versions of themselves in order to be more effective versions of 'the MBA'. The X factor of talent is cast as the necessary supplement to the shortcomings of technical business teaching when faced with the real world, and the connections of the MBA to the technical operations of capitalism as a systemic form of profit extraction are increasingly masked by the rhetoric of talent.

We can track the development of this framing through a series of influential statements about the management idea from the 1970s to the present day that have appeared in the *Harvard Business Review* (*HBR*). I offer brief summaries of each piece here as data points for the emerging (talented) management idea alongside the unwinding of the corporate form since late in the twentieth century. In a concluding section I will connect these developments to current efforts, detailed at the outset of this chapter, to rebranding the MBA in light of its civic applications.

In 1975 in the *HBR*, Henry Mintzberg argued against a growing sense that the task of the capitalist manager was quickly becoming a function of scientific or technical skills. Rather, he insisted that business management was not reducible to 'planning, organizing, coordinating or controlling', and that the real work of managers always exceeds their technical job description (Mintzberg 1975: 49). Against the backdrop of the unmaking of the firm, it is not surprising to find the claim that managerial work is other than we thought. Mintzberg called for programmes to better prepare MBAs for the unseen social work of management. By presupposing the necessity of managers, he makes the MBA project of producing more perfect ones inevitable.

In his account there is a whiff of the poor overworked manager constantly interrupted and working well beyond his official role, and a celebratory sense that, in this excess social labour, managers effect productive connections between 'an organization and its environment' (Mintzberg 1975: 51). Mintzberg refers to other 'managers', from US presidents (Roosevelt, Truman, Eisenhower) to 'street gang leaders', to evoke the necessity of soft skills, along the way framing a sense of business leadership that is partible from and always exceeds the business context.

Mintzberg's questions about the role of social intuition and soft skills in business management crystallised into a focus on 'emotional intelligence', cast by Daniel Goleman as comprising a bundle of five skills: self-awareness, self-regulation, motivation, empathy, and social skills (Goleman 1998). This is the second of the three *HBR* articles I am highlighting here. Goleman (ibid.: 94–95) cites other research documenting that 'when senior managers had a "critical mass" of emotional intelligence capabilities, their divisions outperformed yearly earnings goals by 20%'. The 20 per cent payoff and the concrete metaphor of 'critical mass' surely help to sell the fuzzier themes of emotions and soft skills to the calculating managers, who are inculcated with the adage 'If you can measure it, you can manage it'. During my field research among MBAs stretching from 2006 to 2017, programmes used Myers-Briggs personality tests and related tools to produce commensurable forms of self-knowledge, which were considered an indispensable instrument of management. By then, however, the role of soft skills, 'gut' instincts and states of creative 'flow' were widely accepted as ineffable qualities of 'the art' of management that distinguished the most successful business leaders (Orta 2019a: 55–57; Orta 2019b: 52, 57).

The routinisation of this characterisation of managers is apparent in a third and more recent article in the *Harvard Business Review*, 'What Makes a Great Leader?' by Linda Hill and her colleagues (Hill et al. 2022). They introduce their own shorthand for the key soft skills of leaders: 'the ABCs of innovation' (i.e. Architect, Bridger, Catalyst). Like others before them, they point to an urgent need for a new kind of manager – one who is able to deal with the contemporary transformations of capitalism that are making business leadership harder than ever.

The imperative of innovation today includes the contemporary challenges of inclusive capitalism, and Hill and her colleagues return repeatedly to a leader's accountability beyond the organisation. A 2014 study by many of the same authors focused on leadership for innovation within organisations; today, they argue, successful leadership requires innovation that expands to engage stakeholders beyond the organisation. This is where the 'ABCs' come in. In particular, the 'bridger' and 'catalyst' functions reflect the necessity for leaders to connect their firms within a wider 'ecosystem', generating a 'web of interdependencies' involving 'unusual suspects': 'companies, governments, or individuals outside the industry or sector' (Hill et al. 2022).

Conclusion

Taking this set of *Harvard Business Review* articles as an index of the ongoing reframing of the management idea, and against the backdrop of the history of that idea in coordination with the institutionalisation of the MBA degree, I offer three concluding observations.

First, the increasingly ineffable qualities of leadership establish the manager as a locus of value creation of almost inscrutable complexity. In this regard, the expansive potential of the talented leader, able to guide a business venture to success with a blend of talent and intuition, stands as a magical analogue to the celebrated capitalist wonder of the market, mysteriously able to synthesise a vast set of variables and contextual complexities, and generate profitable choices (Orta 2019a; Skovgaard-Smith and Hirst 2023).

Second, the work of the manager-leader is explicitly about empowering and enabling the work of others. The added value of the leader is the orchestration and application of other managerial talent. This is the payoff of Goleman's emotional intelligence, and is exemplified by Hill and her colleagues' vision of a leader as a catalyst of 'collective genius': 'inviting others to co-create the future with them – a process driven by teams composed of individuals with diverse expertise and experience who were willing and able to collaborate, experiment, and learn together' (Hill et al. 2022: 4–5).

Managers hoping to achieve this 'must be prepared to transform themselves' (Hill et al. 2022: 13). It is this instrumentalised managerial self, rather than technical knowledge of cutting costs and increasing profits, that contemporary MBA programmes described at the outset of this chapter are selling. Seen in terms of managerial leadership, capitalism is a collaborative 'ecosystem' of talent (rather than an extractive organisation of labour) in which managers generate value from 'organisations' – not 'firms' or 'corporations' or 'businesses' – that Hill and her colleagues characterise as assemblages of 'slice[s] of genius' (ibid.: 5).

Finally, the urgency of current calls for managerial innovation (and for innovations in the management idea) directly reflects the malaise of capitalism in the wake of 2008 and the multiple disruptions connected to Covid-19, climate change and intensifying inequalities. MBA programmes have been at pains in recent years to rebrand the management idea as one that is consonant with calls for stakeholder capitalism, a reimagined sense of sustainability, and a recognition that the post-pandemic economy will likely entail a new sort of social contract between capital and government. In the wake of the Great Recession, MBA programmes were already shifting away from a focus on finance and offering elective tracks in sustainability and social entrepreneurship, a trend that has only intensified. Of particular note currently is the ways manager-leaders are increasingly cast as applying their talents to the work of governance. For their part, Hill and her colleagues repeatedly list government among the 'unusual suspects' in the collaborative ecosystems of their ABC leaders.

The point is made even more starkly by MBA administrators, who are marketing their programmes as sites preparing MBAs to solve grand sociopolitical challenges: diversity, sustainability, equity, increasing political polarisation and uncertainty. In this framing of the management idea, MBA training enables aspiring leaders to develop their 'moral compass', to 'look beyond prosperity' and to reflect 'a broader understanding of business that includes politics, legal, and economic frameworks' (Mullins 2023; see also Ethier 2023).

From the vantage of MBA programmes, the leadership talent they cultivate can help to address a broader political crisis: a loss of trust in governmental and non-governmental institutions. At the same time, MBA administrators argue that 'the level of trust has gone up dramatically in the business community'. According to my notes, one dean put it this way in a webinar on 'The Future of Business Education' (Byrne 2021):

> This is a great time for the business platform. An opportunity that goes well beyond anything that has been there before. … We can now tackle issues that go beyond traditional profit and loss. We can have a bigger impact on society. … [T]he expectation is there that business will step in.

As James Carrier points out in his Introduction to this volume, 'management' is neither new nor limited to the rubric of 'business'. My goal has been to trace the arc of the management idea as it has been institutionalised through MBA programmes over the long twentieth century. MBA programmes did not invent the idea of management, but they did articulate an influential framing of the idea in coordination with their institutionalisation in the landscape of higher education. Current efforts to rebrand management for an emergent post–shareholder-value capitalism stress continuities with the framing of business management as a civic good early in the twentieth century. However, as with other claims of capitalist originalism, such as the assertion that shareholder value and other attributes of neoliberalism mark a return to business fundamentals, appeals to the continuity and stability of management mask significant transformations in capitalism. Approaching the management idea genealogically helps to illuminate the ceaseless reframing of management in coordination with the ongoing project of capitalism.

Acknowledgements

The arguments in this chapter build in part upon ethnographic research in US MBA programmes supported by funding from The Wenner Gren Foundation for Anthropological Research and the University of Illinois Research Board.

Andrew Orta is professor of anthropology at the University of Illinois at Urbana-Champaign. He has conducted field research with Aymara communities in Bolivia and in MBA programmes in the United States. His publications include *Making Global MBAs: The Culture of Business and the Business of Culture* (University of California, 2019), and *Catechizing Culture: Missionaries, Aymara, and the 'New Evangelization'* (Columbia University, 2004). His current work is focused on the production and circulation of statistical representations of Andean societies.

References

Abend, Gabriel. 2014. *The Moral Background: An Inquiry into the History of Business Ethics*. Princeton, NJ: Princeton University Press.

Allen, Frederick Lewis. (1931) 1957. *Only Yesterday: An Informal History of the 1920s*. New York: Harper & Row.

Aspen Institute. 2008. *A Closer Look at Business Education: Finance Faculty Reflect on the Financial Crisis*. Washington, DC: Center for Business Education, Aspen Institute.

Berle, Adolf, and Gardiner Means. 1932. *The Modern Corporation and Private Property*. New York: Harcourt, Brace & World.

Business Roundtable. 2019. 'Statement on the Purpose of a Corporation'. Washington, DC: Business Roundtable. Retrieved 7 August 2024 from https://s3.amazonaws.com/brt.org/BRT-StatementonthePurposeofaCorporationwithSignaturesJanuary2023.pdf.

Byrne, John A. (moderator). 2021. 'Webinar: The Future of Business Education'. *Poets & Quants*. Petaluma, 27 July.

Byrne, John A., and Lindsey Gerdes. 2005. 'The Man Who Invented Management: Why Peter Drucker's Ideas Still Matter'. *Businessweek* 3961: 96–103.

Carbone, June, and Nancy Levit. 2017. 'The Death of the Firm'. *Minnesota Law Review* 101: 963–1029.

Chandler, Alfred. 1977. *The Visible Hand: The Managerial Revolution in American Business*. Cambridge, MA: Harvard University Press.

______. 1984. 'The Emergence of Managerial Capitalism'. *Business History Review* 58(4): 473–503.

Crennan, C.H. 1923. 'Human Nature in Business'. *The Annals of the American Academy of Political and Social Science* 110(1: special issue, *Psychology in Business*): 1.

Cruikshank, Jeffrey L. 1987. *A Delicate Experiment: The Harvard Business School 1908–1945*. Boston, MA: Harvard Business Review Press.

Daniel, Carter A. 1998. *MBA: The First Century*. Lewisburg, PA: Bucknell University Press.

Datar, Srikant, David A. Garvin and Patrick Cullen. 2010. *Rethinking the MBA: Business Education at a Crossroads*. Cambridge, MA: Harvard Business School Press.

Davis, Gerald. 2009. 'The Rise and Fall of Finance and the End of the Society of Organizations'. *Academy of Management Perspectives* 23(3): 27–44.

Donham, Wallace Brett. 1931. *Business Adrift*. New York: Whittlesey House / McGraw-Hill.

Drucker, Peter F. 1946. *Concept of the Corporation*. New York: John Day Company.

———. 1950. 'The Graduate Business School'. *Fortune* 42: 92–116.

Ethier, Marc. 2023. 'The Crystal Ball: B-school Leaders Offer Predictions – and More Than a Dash of Hope – for 2023'. *Poets & Quants*. Petaluma, 3 Jan. Retrieved 7 August 2024 from https://poetsandquants.com/2023/01/03/the-crystal-ball-b-school-leaders-offer-predictions-and-more-than-a-dash-of-hope-for-2023/.

Fink, Larry. n.d. 'Annual Letter to CEOs'. Retrieved 7 August 2024 from https://www.blackrock.com/corporate/investor-relations/larry-fink-ceo-letter.

Frydman, Carola. 2019. 'Rising Through the Ranks: The Evolution of the Market for Corporate Executives, 1936–2003'. *Management Science* 65(11): 4951–79.

Gabor, Andrea. 2000. *The Capitalist Philosophers*. New York: Times Books.

Gilman, Nils. 2006. 'The Prophet of post-Fordism: Peter Drucker and the Legitimation of the Corporation', in Nelson Lichtenstein (ed.), *American Capitalism: Social Thought and Political Economy in the Twentieth Century*. Philadelphia: University of Pennsylvania Press, pp. 109–32.

Goldberg, Emma. 2022. 'Have the Anticapitalists Reached Harvard Business School?' *New York Times* (28 Nov). Retrieved 7 August 2024 from https://www.nytimes.com/2022/11/28/business/business-school-social-justice.html.

Goleman, Daniel. 1998. 'What Makes a Leader'. *Harvard Business Review* 76: 93–102.

Gordon, Robert Aaron, and James Edwin Howell. 1959. *Higher Education for Business*. New York: Columbia University Press.

Hanlon, Gerard. 2016. *The Dark Side of Management: A Secret History of Management Theory*. New York: Routledge.

Henderson, Rebecca. 2020. 'Reimagining Capitalism in the Shadow of the Pandemic'. *Harvard Business Review* (28 July). Retrieved 7 August 2024 from https://hbr.org/2020/07/reimagining-capitalism-in-the-shadow-of-the-pandemic.

Hill, Linda A., Emily Tedards, Jason Wild and Karl Weber. 2022. 'What Makes a Great Leader? Mastering the ABCs of Innovation at Scale'. *Harvard Business Review* (19 Sep.). Retrieved 7 August 2024 from https://hbr.org/2022/09/what-makes-a-great-leader.

Ho, Karen. 2009. *Liquidated: An Ethnography of Wall Street*. Durham, NC: Duke University Press.

———. 2020. 'In the Name of Shareholder Value'. *Seattle University Law Review* 43: 609–30.

Hoopes, James. 2003. *False Prophets: The Gurus Who Created Modern Management and Why Their Ideas Are Bad for Business Today*. New York: Basic Books.

Jack, Gavin, and Robert Westwood. 2009. *International and Cross-Cultural Management Studies: A Postcolonial Reader*. Basingstoke: Palgrave Macmillan.

Jensen, Michael C., and William H. Meckling. 1976. 'Theory of the Firm: Managerial Behavior, Agency Costs and Ownership Structure'. *Journal of Financial Economics* 3(4): 305–60.

Johnson, Joseph French. 1906. 'The Business School and What it Should Do'. *The New York Times* (15 Sep.): 9.

Lewis, Michael. 1998. 'The Man Who Invented Management'. *The New York Times* (11 Jan.): sect. 7, p. 5.

McCraw, Thomas K. (ed.). 1988. *The Essential Alfred Chandler: Essays Toward a Historical Theory of Big Business*. Boston, MA: Harvard Business School Press.

McDonald, Duff. 2017. *The Golden Passport: Harvard Business School, the Limits of Capitalism, and the Moral Failure of the MBA Elite*. New York: HarperCollins.

Mintzberg, Henry. 1975. 'The Manager's Job: Folklore and Fact'. *Harvard Business Review* 53(4): 49–61.

Mirowski, Philip. 2014. *Never Let a Serious Crisis Go to Waste*. London: Verso.

Mullins, Stephanie. 2023. 'What Are Business Schools Doing to Meet the Challenges of 2023 and Beyond?' *EFMD Global* (9 Jan.). Retrieved 7 August 2024 from https://blog.efmdglobal.org/2023/01/09/what-are-business-schools-doing-to-meet-the-challenges-of-2023-and-beyond/.

O'Connor, Ellen S. 1999. 'The Politics of Management Thought: A Case Study of the Harvard Business School and the Human Relations School'. *The Academy of Management Review* 24(1): 117–31.

Orta, Andrew. 2019a. *Making Global MBAs: The Culture of Business and the Business of Culture*. Berkeley: University of California Press.

______. 2019b. 'Imagining the Unmanageable: MBAs at the Limits of Neoliberalism'. *Culture, Theory and Critique* 60(1): 50–65. Special Issue, *Instruction and Improvisation Under Neoliberalism: Essays in Honor of Bonnie Urciuoli*, edited by Ilana Gershon and Chaise LaDousa.

______. 2022. 'The MBA Won't Die. But It Is Trying to Disappear'. *FocaalBlog* (30 Mar.). Retrieved 7 August 2024 from https://www.focaalblog.com/2022/03/30/andrew-orta-the-mba-wont-die-but-it-is-trying-to-disappear/.

Person, Harlow. 1920. 'The Basic Elements and their Proper Balance in the Curriculum of a Collegiate Business School: Discussion'. *Journal of Political Economy* 28(2): 109–12.

Pierson, Frank Cook. 1959. *The Education of American Businessmen: A Study of University-College Programs in Business Administration*. New York: McGraw-Hill.

Senate (United States Senate, Committee on Education and Labor). 1885. *Report of the Committee of the Senate upon the Relations between Labor and Capital*, Vol. 2. Washington, DC: Government Printing Office.

Skovgaard-Smith, Irene, and Alison Hirst. 2023. 'Marcel Mauss and the Magical Agents of Our Time'. *Journal of Classical Sociology* 24(2): 171–85.

Susman, Warren. 1984. *Culture as History: The Transformation of American Society in the Twentieth Century*. Madison: University of Wisconsin Press.

Van Maanen, John. 1983. 'Golden Passports: Managerial Socialization and Graduate Education'. *The Review of Higher Education* 6(4): 435–55.
Veblen, Thorstein. 1918. *The Higher Learning in America: A Memorandum on the Conduct of Universities by Business Men*. New York: B.W. Huebsch.
Whyte, William H. 1956. *The Organization Man*. New York: Simon & Schuster.

Chapter 2

Management's Hidden Realm

James G. Carrier

In the Introduction to this volume I said that the two functions of management are conventionally taken to be direction and coordination, and that they can be served in a variety of ways. This raises the question of how that serving takes on particular institutional forms.

Alfred Chandler (1977) explained the form that he calls modern management in terms of technological changes in the United States in the second half of the nineteenth century that led to the emergence of large modern corporations. Those changes were real, but focusing on them ignores the social and political-economic factors that shape the development of complex institutions like modern management and large corporations (see, e.g., Marglin 1974). Here I want to consider one of those factors: the ways that the hierarchical structure of management is justified, both individually in terms of the relation of managers to their subordinates and collectively as an institution.

In Weber's ideal type, management and managers' positions are justified by the fact that they are appointed according to the rules, just as the acquiescence of their subordinates is justified by their own acceptance of employment in their positions. However, managers as individuals and management as an institution seek a legitimacy beyond the impersonal rules. As well, subordinates are unlikely to want to follow directions simply because they are paid to do so; as Keith Hart (2005) argues, some sort of justification seems necessary to convert impersonal obligation into willing acceptance.

There are many ways that management can be justified. Some are concerned with its presumed effects, for instance the idea that good management leads to efficient firms and so to a healthy economy. Reflecting the point that '[e]conomic efficiency has been the greatest source of social legitimacy in the United States for the past century' (Nelson 2001: xv), a stress on efficiency and its virtues recurs in justifications of management. Here, however, I focus on the skills and knowledge that management is said to represent and that individual managers are said to possess.

Justifying Management

Direction and coordination in much of the English economic history that I know best were located in an owner who runs the enterprise. Through the eighteenth century, a key form of these enterprises was the artisan's workshop. That artisan owned the premises and much of the equipment and raw materials in it, and engaged and supervised assistants, who would have been apprentices or journeymen and who would have carried out much of the work.

Artisans' control of their enterprise usually rested on two factors: one was that they owned the enterprise and hired their subordinates; the other was that they knew the craft and were recognised for it. When apprentices and journeymen were told what to do, then, it was by someone who knew what they were supposed to do and was probably able to do it better than them (see also Yanagisako 2002: 90–92).

That knowledge was acquired by working one's way up the ranks, and in areas that had craft guilds, as was the case with most trades in English towns of any size, it was recognised formally when one became a craft master, having served as an apprentice and then a journeyman. In that service, one learnt the technical aspects of the craft, perhaps making shoes and other leather goods. One also learnt what was a sound piece of work and what was not, as well as what customers should pay for it, which is to say craft custom. In addition, one learnt the more social side of the craft. This included the craft's saints and their holidays and processions, as well as one's fellows in the craft, their suppliers and customers, and how one ought to deal with them and be dealt with by them.

A journeyman who aspired to be a master could produce a piece of work in order to demonstrate their skill, called a masterpiece; if accepted, the journeyman would become a guild master. Masters had a number of rights and duties related to the guild and enforced by it, including engaging and overseeing journeymen and apprentices of their own. A significant part of the justification of the position of the head of the enterprise, then, was mastery of the skills, practices and relations of the trade (in 2019, Germany reintroduced a craft-master system in certain trades; Oltermann 2019).

With the spread of factory production in England in the late eighteenth century, enterprises grew larger and the boss was less likely to be a craft master (Veblen 1923). This was especially so after 1813, when the repeal of parts of the Elizabethan Statute of Artificers undercut the guilds. The boss, then, was no longer a guild master, but continued to have the authority that came from being the owner and employer, and perhaps the authority that came from knowledge of the work.

Over the last half of the nineteenth century this was decreasingly the case, as joint-stock companies became more and more common, and it was during this period that schools of commerce and management began to appear. By the end of the First World War it had become obvious that large businesses were likely to be owned by shareholders and run by managers who were paid for their services (Berle and Means 1932). Because those managers were not clearly capitalist or proletariat, they presented Marxian analysts with a problem (Parkin 1979: chap. 1). Debates about class were important, but they did little to address a question raised by what Berle and Means described (I will return to the question of class later on). If ownership, mastery of the work and control no longer marched together in the way that they had previously, how was that control justified?

For lower-level managers, control is justified formally by their position in the organisation. If they achieve it by working their way up the organisational chart, it can also be justified substantively by the knowledge and skills that they acquired. The growing number of people who enter management after graduating from those schools of commerce and business, or after getting their undergraduate degree, likely have no such justification. Those near the top of the organisational chart, senior management, face the problem in more acute form. They are extremely unlikely to have learnt by working their way up through the organisation, and because of their greater discretion and control their need for justification is more pressing than it is for those lower down. The result is what Felix Stein (2017: 9), drawing on the work of Gerd Spittler (2016), calls 'a management legitimation deficit'.

In the paragraphs that follow I point to some of the institutions and beliefs that are associated with management that help to reduce that deficit by justifying management both as a set of positions and as the particular individuals who occupy those positions, and that help to make it appear to be what Marie-Laure Djelic (2016: 1) described: taken for granted and natural.

Management's Hidden Realm

> Banks were admittedly old-fashioned, but Thatcher had been reared in the belief that the way to become a banker was to train as a banker. The prevailing philosophy these days seemed to be that a management elite existed. A cadre of men trained in principles so broad that they could leap with the merriest abandon from the communications industry to the automobile industry to the steel industry. (Lathen 1964: 141)

Classic professions like law and medicine rest on a distinct body of knowledge and skills, defined and monitored by some combination of professional associations and state licensing boards, which thereby regulate 'entry to key positions in the division of labour' (Parkin 1979: 61). Formal certification testifies to an individual's possession of them and right to exercise them (Freidson 1989). That knowledge and those skills have three attributes that are important here. Firstly, they are seen to be esoteric, in the sense that they cannot be acquired in the normal course of events but require special training. Secondly, they are seen to be universal, as in principle they apply to all situations that come within their ambit. Thirdly, in the hands of those with the right skills, that knowledge is efficacious and can produce the desired results. I will illustrate this with conventional medicine.

The human body, its parts, operations and afflictions are complex, and knowledge of it is esoteric because mastering it is seen to require special training – this much is fairly straightforward. Medical knowledge also is universal, as it for it is taken to apply to all human bodies. So, the skill of diagnosing someone with an irregular heartbeat and preparing a plan of treatment requires both the pertinent knowledge and the ability to translate that particular patient and heartbeat into its terms, which means seeing the heartbeat as a symptom of a medical condition, and hence being able to prescribe a particular course of treatment.

Taken together, the 'esoteric' and 'universal' nature of a body of efficacious knowledge and skill mark the existence of a hidden realm – hidden because it is an abstract entity separated from mundane reality. Hence, it cannot be apprehended directly, any more than gravity can be apprehended, no matter how many apples one sees falling from trees: it required the genius of Newton to postulate its existence and nature.

The claim that there is such a hidden realm and that one has access to it and the skill to apply it is important for justifying the authority of specialists (Freidson 1989). I have illustrated this with medical knowledge, but the same sort of thing applies to all professions, quasi-professions and skilled trades. Car mechanics may not have the same status or length of training as, say, cardiologists, but their job as mechanics is justified by their ability to see the pinging noise or uneven acceleration of a car in terms of its internal structure and operation, and so identify and fix the problem. Similarly, the position of lawyers is justified by their ability to see the client's property, family and wishes, and apply the law to draw up a valid will.

Many see management also as resting on a hidden realm, and the foundations for that were laid early on. One of the first influential books on management is Frederick Winslow Taylor's *Principles of Scientific Management*, and in it he said that his principles apply universally, to 'all social activities: to the management of our homes; the management of our farms; the management of the business of our tradesmen, large and small; of our churches, our philanthropic institutions, our universities, and our governmental departments' (Taylor [1911] 1919: 8).

His assertion of the universalism of management fell on fertile ground. The two leading American business schools after the Second World War were at Columbia and Harvard, and Susan Aaronson said that they taught their students that 'if one knows how to manage, one can manage anything and anyone at any time' (Aaronson 1992: 173). This view is apparent in the words of a man who graduated from the Harvard Business School in 1949: 'when most of us went to the Business School, we had no idea *what* we wanted to manage, all we knew was *that* we wanted to manage. And that seemed fine, because the way it was presented to us was that managing was a skill unto itself' (in Shames 1986: 103).

A recent illustration of this universalism is Siobhan McArdle, who resigned as chief executive of the South Tees Hospitals Foundation Trust in the UK in 2019 (Campbell 2019). So far as I can tell, McArdle, who was in charge of a number of National Health Service (NHS) hospitals, had no significant background in medicine or hospitals. She did, however, have a background in management. According to the trust's web site (South Tees nd) the woman 'worked as a Management Consultant working nationally and internationally on strategy development, performance improvement, turnaround and transformational change in partnership with large global corporate organisations, high growth SMEs and public sector organisations, including the NHS'. Her background looks problematic if you think that someone running hospitals ought to know about medicine and hospitals. However, given the idea that management is universal, the woman's background is unexceptionable.

I have argued that management often claims one aspect of hidden realms, universalism. That speaks of the way organisations of all sorts work, just as medicine speaks of the way all human bodies work, and it promises that the knowledge in that hidden realm can make organisations work better. In this, as Djelic (2016: 8) observes, management commonly 'presents itself as preoccupied only with efficiency questions, not power issues'. Stein (2017: 7–11) points to the importance of those power issues, and they are apparent in what Barbara and John Ehrenreich (2013) say of the decline of what they and others (e.g. Gouldner 1979) were calling the professional–managerial class (PMC) late in the twentieth century. That decline was marked in the United States by the elimination of about two million positions in middle management between 1985 and 1991, where many in the PMC lived (Business Week 1992; Fefer 1994), so that 'managers went from one of the most secure organizational occupations to one of the least' (Kunda and Ailson-Souday 2006: 210).

From what the Ehrenreichs say, it was a decline foretold, as the PMC sought what Frank Parkin (1979: chap. 5) calls 'usurpationary closure': an attempt to challenge the power of its superiors (usurpation) by securing control (closure) of an important resource. The resource that the PMC sought to secure was its own hidden realm: '[S]ince what was truly "rational" in the productive process was not always identical to what was most immediately profitable, the PMC often sought autonomy and freedom from their own bosses … proposing that theirs was the only social group capable of impartial leadership, based on science' (Ehrenreich and Ehrenreich 2013: 4; see also Blim 2020: chap. 7). Their conflict with their superiors in the companies that employed them, as well as their eventual defeat, seemed inevitable.

I said that another aspect of those realms is efficacy – the idea that knowing and applying the hidden realm to concrete cases is likely to produce desired outcomes. In medicine, treatments are tested to see if they are beneficial. The same cannot be said for lawyers or car mechanics, but wills do or do not make it through probate, and cars do or do not run smoothly.

Management's Efficacy

The case with management is not so simple. I address this first in terms of management consultancies. I treat them as a distilled and portable form of management that often seems to serve as a vehicle for the spread of the idea that there is a management hidden realm, commonly expressed in terms of the idea of best practice (e.g. Beaverstock 2017: 235–38; Chong 2018). As Felix Stein puts it:

> Consultants try to analyse entire companies or business divisions, yet they do not know most of the people in them, they have hardly any understanding of their social relations, and often they only superficially grasp the material

> set-ups under which people in a client company operate. This problem reflects the wider managerial condition of contemporary capitalism. (Stein 2017: 94)

Beyond reports such as Stein's, studies of the effects of hiring management consultants are almost non-existent. A number of things can help to account for this, including that firms are reluctant to describe their engagement with consultants (see, e.g., Chong 2018: Intro.). There is one study, however, that seems to have dealt with these problems in a reasonable way. It is by Ian Kirkpatrick and his colleagues (Kirkpatrick et al. 2019), and it investigated the use of consultants by NHS acute hospital trusts in England. Taking into account a number of pertinent variables, it investigated the relationship between the amount of money that each trust spent on consultancy between 2010 and 2013, and the trust's economic efficiency. The focus on efficiency is reasonable because consultancies are routinely touted as a way to make organisations more efficient economically, so that they will end up saving more than the cost of the consultancy. Their study concluded, however, that the more that a trust spent on consultants the less efficient it became, while there was no material change in the quality of their medical care (see also Guardian 2023).

For regular management, a casual search shows a number of studies of and arguments about its efficacy. Many of them are concerned with what is often called performance management, which is focused on employee commitment to the work and to the firm, motivation, engagement and the like; advocates hold that treating employees the right way will encourage them to be conscientious and productive so that the firm will be more profitable. This seems unexceptionable, but is related only tenuously to the direction and coordination at the core of management. Having workers who are motivated does not, after all, address what they ought to be motivated to do or how their different doings ought to relate to each other.

Performance management includes a variety of specific techniques, such as ways of assessing workers, training them, setting goals for them and rewarding them. These techniques are plausible, which doubtless helps to account for the popularity of performance management. Indicating the uncertain efficacy of the knowledge in management's hidden realm, however, it is not clear that performance management works or that there is agreement about what 'works' might mean. That, at least, is the concern that Deidra Schleicher and her colleagues (Schleicher et al. 2019: 851–52) raise in their review of published work on the theory and practice of performance management (PM). They point to a 'lack of clear and compelling evidence for the effectiveness of PM', which has led to 'debates about whether or not formal PM is even necessary', brought about in part by the existence of 'multiple types of PM evaluative criteria'.

The literature on and for management is vast, and in referring to performance management I have touched on only one small bit of one corner of it. I have done so only to indicate that the idea of a body of efficacious management knowledge of general applicability is problematic. This does not mean that management makes no difference or that management theories have no impact – they do. The difference and impact, however, are likely to be much more uncertain than advocates seem to think, and may well come about for no obvious reason, or at least probably not the reason that advocates assume.

A classic example of this is the study of the Hawthorne Western Electric factory in the United States in the 1920s under the direction of Elton Mayo, which among other things experimented on workers to see if productivity would be improved with better lighting. Experimenters increased the lighting and productivity went up; they increased it again and so did productivity. Then they lowered the lighting, and productivity increased again; and a further lowering led to a further increase. This became known as the Hawthorne Effect, and it generated substantial debate. Jim McCambridge and his colleagues published a review of studies of the effect of this sort of management intervention on workers, as well as the results of their own experiments. Illustrating the state of the knowledge in management's hidden realm, they concluded that such intervention appears to have effects, 'although little can be securely known about the conditions under which they operate, their mechanism of effects, or the magnitude', and almost a century after the original experiments, they called for further research (McCambridge, Witton and Elbourne 2014: 276).

In addition to literature on practical matters like performance management and the effects of lighting, there is also the highly visible output of what Greg Bamber and others call management gurus. Bamber distinguishes between management fashions and fads. By the former he means 'the body of knowledge and practice which is currently seen as constituting good management' which he says changes only gradually. Fads, on the other hand, 'tend to emerge quickly, have a brief life, and may not leave much of a lasting legacy' (Bamber 1999: 2; see also, e.g., Barley and Kunda 1992). Management gurus are the ones who propound the ideas that become fads.

Because such work is presented as how to run a successful business, it appears to be aimed at senior management. However, the sales of the books and the size of the audiences indicate that the appeal is much broader. For instance, *In Search of Excellence*, by Tom Peters and

Robert H. Waterman, was published in 1982. It sold 122,000 copies in the first two months and more than five million copies by 1998 (Clark and Salaman 1998: 140). Bamber (1999: 4) says that Taylor is arguably the first management guru of the twentieth century, and that he once attracted an audience of almost seventy thousand to a lecture on scientific management in New York.

Management has seemed particularly prone to gurus and fads, especially since the 1980s (Clark and Salaman 1998: 1). Factors that might contribute to this include more and more people coming to think that there is increasing competition among firms that are innovating all the time and doing so in unpredictable ways (see Wilf 2019). This may be, but it is likely that fads would have less appeal if there were a secure body of knowledge and theory about what firms are and what management is – which is to say, a management hidden realm.

Social Aspects of Management Thought

Gurus and fads are different from reasoned talk about performance management. From what I have described, however, it seems likely that the fads are only an exaggerated form of what occurs in the reasoned talk: the propounding of ideas in the absence of secure facts and theories. This raises the question of why gurus and fads are attractive, and if those attractions exist for the reasoned talk as well.

Timothy Clark and Graeme Salaman review a number of attractions, but two are especially pertinent here. One is that gurus and their theories help to buttress the authority of management: 'They tell managers why they are important, why they matter, why their skills are critical' (Clark and Salaman 1998: 153). The other is that gurus and their ideas give managers a sense of order in a world that they see as chaotic (ibid.: 142). Both of these reasons would seem to apply to management thought generally, both the fads and the reasoned talk.

In an earlier work, Paul DiMaggio and Walter Powell (1983) suggested a different sort of reason. They were not concerned with management fads but with why firms in a commercial sector tend to resemble each other; why, that is, banks all tend to have the same structure and practices, just as airlines resemble each other. They said that the structures and practices are justified in terms of efficiency and other rational economic factors, but that there is no real evidence to support that. Instead, they said, firms need to deal with other firms, for instance as suppliers and customers or as fellow members of a sector, and are better able to do so if those other firms take them seriously. This means being a firm that looks like a proper bank, airline, or whatever. Translated into terms of management thought, DiMaggio and Powell's argument suggests that if managers, or firms, want to be taken seriously, they have to know and espouse the current thought, management's claimed hidden realm, which is the one that serious managers and firms know and espouse, whether it is Bamber's fad or fashion.

This desire to be seen to be *au courant* with current thinking takes different forms. One of the more noticeable is what I call 'management-speak'. A recent example is how a firm explained what it would be doing to carry out a contract with the British government to produce a new system of operation for the government's test and trace (T&T) system for the Covid-19 virus. The company said it would be working

> 'on an agile basis' with 'dedicated layer leads from NHS T&T and [Public Health England]', the consultants will be 'defining the customer segments and support articulating volumes; articulating an improved and simplified customer journey ... developing a channel approach and map to services/products/journey ... compiling an as-is organisational baseline and "factpack"'. (Private Eye 2021; ellipses and insertion in original)

While not always this opaque, the fact that management-speak is pervasive indicates how widespread is the desire to be *au courant*, to know the hidden realm and to be seen to know it.

A different example is what David Evans, the general secretary of the Labour Party in the UK, said about what the party administration should become. According to Sienna Rodgers (2021), he said that 'Labour will work "collaboratively" in "multidisciplinary teams", which will "adopt a product-mindset using agile ceremonies, be empowered to make decisions and encouraged to focus on rapid prototyping, deployment and iteration"'. Such talk not only marks Evans, and through him the party, as *au courant*, it is also likely to mark his difference from ordinary party administrative staff, assumed not to be *au courant*, as well as his authority over them. This indicates that management-speak can address a number of different audiences directly and indirectly, have a number of different effects, and serve a number of different purposes (such as advancing one's position in the organisation: Watson 1994: 899).

What I have said of management-speak can be said as well of a range of management activities, like decisions to outsource a set of company activities, or to adopt what is seen as best practice in accounting, or to hire consultants to make the firm more innovative. These will have a range of consequences, significant and minor, intended and unintended. Following what I said of DiMaggio and Powell, for instance, managers who are adept at management-speak may make their position in the firm more secure, while firms that hire consultants to teach innovation may shore up their commercial reputation. These relate primarily to the indicative nature of those things, by which I mean what they indicate about the people and organisations that produce them. Equally, though, there are likely to be effects related to the content of those things, by which I mean what the talk says about the world, and how the policies and actions affect the world. For instance, the decision to adopt best practice in accounting may mean that the firm will be seen to be up to date, but equally it is likely to mean changes in how the firm's accountants work and the sort of accounts they produce.

In different ways, both sorts of effect can be a form of virtualism (Carrier and Miller 1998). This begins with a virtual reality, a view of the world that is based on abstract ideas about what the world really is, underneath surface appearances. That virtual reality produces virtualism when it motivates people who see a disjunction between the world and the ideas to act in ways that bring the world into line with the ideas rather than bring the ideas into line with the world.

Consider, for instance, the abstract idea that fundamentally a company is an economic entity that generates a return for those who invest in it, what Karen Ho (2009: chaps 3, 4) describes as shareholder capitalism. This idea can be the basis for changes in accounting procedures that result in accounts, which are pictures of the company, that focus attention on things related to the cost and income of different aspects of it, return on capital and the like. This in turn is likely to encourage people to act, intentionally or not, in ways that bring the company into line with that abstract concept, perhaps by selling off parts of it that have a low return on investment, or by assessing proposed company activities in terms of their projected return on capital (e.g. Røyrvik 2011: chap. 4). If this occurs, what was a complex entity that operates in terms of a variety of dimensions and relationships gets rendered as, and to a degree turned into, a purely financial being, in accord with the abstract idea that started it all.

Virtualism of a less material sort can occur as well. As I described, Clark and Salaman (1998: 153) said that one common aspect of management gurus and fads is their portrayal of the manager as a potent figure, which buttresses managers' status claims. To the degree that those gurus and their ideas are popular, they influence many more people than senior management, and so spread a particular vision of management more broadly, one that indicates that there is a hidden realm and that trained and skilled managers have access to it and its potency (for some of the complexities of this, see Orta this volume).

Management as a Class

I now wish to return to a matter I mentioned earlier, class. From a conventional Marxian perspective, I said, managers are awkward because they straddle the boundary between capital and labour. However, they resemble a distinct class if we approach them from a Weberian perspective, which bases class on market power, on the ability to influence the price of whatever it is that people transact, including their labour and services (Weber 1946: 180–86).

This resemblance arises in part from the ways that management has attributes that mark the professions, or at least claims to have them. One pertinent attribute that management claims is access to an efficacious hidden realm. I have shown that there is good reason to doubt that claim, but the fact that it has been around since Taylor's advocacy of scientific management over a century ago suggests that it has persistent attraction.

As indicated by the words of that graduate of the Harvard Business School, business schools are an important way of perpetuating the idea of a hidden realm, and they are important in shaping management (see Orta this volume). Business schools have attracted criticism, with books having titles like *Shut Down the Business School* (Parker 2018). There are some who present cogent arguments about why business schools are flawed. Martin Parker (2016: 149), the author who wants to shut them down, wrote: 'In order to stand a better chance of getting the cash, it is a good idea to teach things that flatter the wealthy and powerful'. Applying this to universities and their business schools, he says: 'So, in marketing terms, it seems sensible that when business people have the money, universities should teach courses that place them at the centre of history'.

Such criticism, however, often seems to be more a rejection of the values that the schools inculcate and the behaviour of their graduates than considerations of the validity of the idea that there is a management hidden realm. Thus, a long and often critical history of the Harvard Business School (McDonald 2017) is concerned mostly with what the book's subtitle says is the moral failure of the school and the people it trains. Similarly, the field of critical management studies is based on 'deep scepticism regarding the moral defensibility and the social and ecological sustainability of the prevailing forms of management and organization' (Adler, Forbes and Willmott 2007: 2). Such criticisms merit attention, but they raise questions about the suitability of the presumed hidden realm and the uses to which it is put in management practice, rather than about its existence.

The claim that there is a hidden realm and that managers know it and can use it is important for justifying what, Clark and Salaman said, gurus and their fads do: indicate why managers are important, especially those in the upper ranks and those who aspire to join them. In its turn, this justifies setting management apart as something like the established professions, one whose experienced members can, like the woman at the South Tees Hospitals Foundation Trust, manage anything.

There are other, more institutional aspects of professions that are important for considering management. One, according to Eliot Freidson (1989: 425–26), is that in professions 'members control recruitment, training and the work that they do' and that 'only members of the profession may supervise and evaluate the work' (see Brint 1993). Here Freidson points to the market power of professions, which is increased by their influence on the supply, control and evaluation of professional labour. Management is not a full profession in Freidson's terms, but it echoes some aspects of the professions.

Management lacks the license to practice sanctioned by the state and professional associations found in the full professions. However, late in the 1940s the British Institute of Management was founded, and in 2002 it received a royal charter, becoming the Chartered Management Institute. The charter is granted by the monarch on the advice of the Privy Council, which says that new charters 'are normally reserved for bodies that work in the public interest (such as professional institutions and charities) and which can demonstrate pre-eminence, stability and permanence in their particular field' (Privy Council nd). Thus it seems that, in the UK at least, the state sees management as something like a profession.

As I noted above, Freidson said that only professionals evaluate their fellows' work. Managers are employees, and thus are subject to the evaluation of their superiors. Except at the very highest levels, those superiors are, of course, other managers. For large companies in the United States, the closer we get to the highest level the more likely it is that a separate body will produce an evaluation of managers' work and a recommendation about their pay, and present them to the board of directors for consideration. Those bodies are called compensation committees, the members of which are entirely or predominantly what is called independent directors – roughly those who hold no management position in the company employing those being evaluated (Segal et al. 2015: 4, 73). Although the members of such committees may be independent directors and hence formally independent of the management of the company, it is not clear how independent they are substantively, either from the managers they are evaluating or from a belief in a management hidden realm.

In this system, which is supposed to operate at arm's length, the pay of company heads has increased smartly. As Lawrence Mishel and Jessica Schleder put it: 'Over the last several decades, CEO pay has grown much faster than profits, the pay of the top 0.1 per cent of wage earners, and the wages of college graduates. CEOs are getting more because of their power to set pay, not because they are more productive or have special talents or more education' (Mishel and Schleder 2018: 2). And this is not just the pay of CEOs: '[O]utsized CEO pay growth has had spillover effects, pulling up the pay of other executives and managers' (ibid.: 3).

This increase in management pay does not exist on its own, for in the past forty years or so in the United States it has been accompanied by shifting a growing proportion of the worth of workers' output from those workers to the companies that employ them. Between 1979 and 2020, productivity in the US economy increased by 65 per cent, while the pay of non-supervisory workers in the private sector increased by only 17 per cent (Economic Policy Institute 2022). This may well have made the increase in CEO pay more acceptable to companies, and the increase was substantial. During that period the compensation granted to CEOs increased by 1,614 per cent, just over three times the increase in the price of stocks in the Standard & Poors 500 (Bivens and Kandra 2022: 8).

Charles Elson and Craig Ferrere (2013) have analysed common features of the process of evaluating senior managers and setting their pay, and what they say supports some of the points that I have made about the profession- and class-like nature of management. They say that there are two common arguments used to account for the rapid acceleration of executive pay since late in the twentieth century, and one less common one.

The first common one holds that 'personal and professional connections with the management inhibit the board from engaging in effective and autonomous oversight [of senior management], and the board lacks a meaningful incentive to do so' (Elson and Ferrere 2013: 102). This suggests that there is something like class solidary at work at the professional and personal levels. The other common argument explains the rising pay in terms of 'the operation of a competitive market – the market for scarce and valuable managerial talent' (ibid.: 103). They say that this argument fails because it wrongly assumes that there is a competitive market for executives and, particularly related to my argument here, because it wrongly assumes that executive talent is transferable, that doing a good job in one company means that the executive is competent to do a good job in another, which would be the case if management knowledge were efficacious and universal (ibid.: 105).

The less common argument, which is more recent, echoes what I said about the argument that DiMaggio and Powell made. It sees 'overwhelming ambiguity as essential to the nature of any appraisal of executive worth', so that pay is 'determined through reference to the normative practices within a topography of local networks – in a large part as a response to the need to provide legitimacy to external constituents – and pay is therefore in fact largely unrelated to traditional economic marginal value' (Elson and Ferrere 2013: 104). In other words, pay is determined in large part by the desire of the firm to be taken seriously.

From what I have said, it seems that competent management has come to be defined by managers themselves. In Freidson's terms, the result looks like professionals evaluating their fellow professionals; in Weber's terms, it looks like members of a class securing their market power.

Challenges to the Hidden Realm

Elson and Ferrere are not the only ones who challenge aspects of the idea that there is a management hidden realm. Notable among the challengers is Henry Mintzberg (1996, 2004, 2013). He says that management cannot be taught in the classroom, that it is not the basis of a profession like medicine or law. Instead, he holds (Anon. nd: 1:05) that it is obvious, at least to those who are willing to look at managers and what they do, that management is a practice carried out in a particular context.

Such challenges exist, but they are likely to face strong, if often unspoken, resistance, which arises from a number of forces. One of these is the search for something that makes the power of management legitimate; another is the related pressures and practices that help to secure the position of management as a class. It is not clear that critics who, like Mintzberg, deny the existence of a management hidden realm will be able to overcome those forces. Indeed, rather than being challenges to the existence of such a realm, it seems likely that the ideas of critics will turn into the basis of alternative hidden realms.

In challenging conventional teaching and elevating practice, Mintzberg and those like him challenge the prevailing structure of management knowledge and its construction of what is in the world that managers confront. In denying an underlying order in the pertinent part of the world and instead stressing the contingencies of managers' immediate context, Mintzberg is advocating what looks like anti-structure. That is an element of what Victor Turner (1969) called 'communitas', and as Turner noted, communitas is difficult to maintain. For one thing, it denies what systems of conceptual order supply, a way to make sense of an inherently untidy existence (Douglas 1966: 4). Also, communitas takes a lot of collective work to maintain. In other words, it is socially costly, in the way that the anti-structure of Occupy Wall Street was costly: participants spent a lot of time and effort figuring out ways to eliminate collective structure in their meetings. Taken together, these pressures indicate that while movements that deny the existence of a management hidden realm may appear from time to time, they are unlikely to last long. A new structure will likely emerge. One reason for this is that different views of management will end up being institutionalised and expressed in common structural forms, which, because they are not innocent, constrain and shape those views.

This appears to be the case with Mintzberg's ideas. With titles like *Managers, not MBAs* (2004; see also Anon. nd), they carry a distinct air of anti-structure, but they perform the conventional task of marking the importance of managers, albeit managers who do not appear to have the conventional business-school orientation. Also, as is the case with that conventional orientation, they conform to the common structure in that they are taught in business schools and in special programmes, with students being awarded degrees and diplomas at the end of their courses to testify that they have been through the requisite training and learnt the important lessons. To recall what I said of DiMaggio and Powell's arguments, we would expect this to happen. That is because people would want to show that they should be taken seriously as adherents of Mintzberg, or whoever has presented a popular dissident approach to management, just as they would want that approach to be taken seriously, the sort of thing taught in serious business schools and published in places like the *Harvard Business Review* (e.g. Mintzberg 1996).

For good social and cultural reasons, then, it seems likely that dissident approaches, including those that start out challenging the idea of a management hidden realm, will confront forces that encourage them to promulgate a hidden realm of their own. That hidden realm may not be the sort of universalist insights associated with people like Peter Drucker, who advocated management by objectives and the outsourcing of back-office operations so that firms can focus on front-office work. Instead, they may be the sort of thing that Mintzberg espouses: a set of techniques to bring people together and have them talk about their problems and how they are dealing with them, as well as the accumulated and systematised knowledge of those problems and possible solutions. A different hidden realm, but a hidden realm even so.

Acknowledgements

I thank Michael Blim, Emil Røyrvik and Felix Stein for their thoughts on an earlier version of this chapter.

James G. Carrier has taught, done research and written on aspects of economy in Papua New Guinea, the United States and the United Kingdom. He has had a recurring interest in important economic institutions (e.g. *Meanings of the Market*, ed., Berg, 1997; *Ethical Consumption: Social Value and Economic Practice*, ed. with P. Luetchford, Berghahn Books, 2012) and intellectual themes (e.g. 'The Trouble with Class', *European Journal of Sociology*, 2012; 'Moral Economy: What's in a Name', *Anthropological Theory*, 2018; 'Changing Economic Experiences and Understandings', *Journal of the Royal Anthropological Institute*, 2024).

References

NB: Articles in *The Guardian* can be found by searching their website: www.theguardian.com/uk.

Aaronson, Susan Ariel. 1992. 'Serving America's Business? Graduate Business Schools and American Business, 1945–60'. *Business History* 34(1): 160–82.

Adler, Paul S., Linda C. Forbes and Hugh Willmott. 2007. 'Critical Management Studies.' *The Academy of Management Annals* 1: 119–79.

Anon. nd. 'Mintzberg On Managing'. Retrieved 2 August 2024 from www.youtube.com/watch?v=K7My9mZUUVs.

Bamber, Greg. 1999. 'Fads, Fashions and Fantasies: Reflections on Management Trends and on University Business Schools'. Professorial lecture, Griffith University. Retrieved 2 August 2024 from https://research-repository.griffith.edu.au/bitstream/handle/10072/368706/bamber99.pdf?sequence=1&isAllowed=y.

Barley, Stephen R., and Gideon Kunda. 1992. 'Design and Devotion: Surges of Rational and Normative Ideologies of Control in Managerial Discourse.' *Administrative Science Quarterly* 47(3): 363–99.

Beaverstock, Jonathan V. 2017. 'The Spatial Mobility of Corporate Knowledge: Expatriation, Global Talent, and the World City', in Heike Jons, Peter Meusburger and Michael Heffernan (eds), *Mobilities of Knowledge*. Berlin: Springer-Verlag, pp. 227–46.

Berle, Adolf, and Gardiner Means. 1932. *The Modern Corporation and Private Property*. New York: Harcourt, Brace & World.

Bivens, Josh, and Jori Kandra. 2022. 'CEO Pay has Skyrocketed 1,460% since 1978'. Washington, DC: Economic Policy Institute. Retrieved 2 August 2024 from www.epi.org/publication/ceo-pay-in-2021/.

Blim, Michael. 2020. *The Rise of the American Ruling Class, 1865–1920*. MS.

Brint, Steven. 1993. 'Eliot Freidson's Contribution to the Sociology of Professions'. *Work and Occupations* 20(3): 259–78.

Business Week. 1992. 'Downward Mobility'. *Business Week* (23 March): 56–63.
Campbell, Denis. 2019. '"Life's too short": NHS Trust Boss's Excoriating Resignation Letter'. *The Guardian* (2 Sept.).
Carrier, James G., and Daniel Miller (eds). 1998. *Virtualism: A New Political Economy*. Oxford: Berg.
Chandler, Alfred D. 1977. *The Visible Hand: The Managerial Revolution in American Business*. Cambridge, MA: Belknap Press.
Chong, Kimberly. 2018. *Best Practice: Management Consulting and the Ethics of Financialization in China*. Durham, NC: Duke University Press.
Clark, Timothy, and Graeme Salaman. 1998. 'Telling Tales: Management Gurus' Narratives and the Construction of Managerial Identity'. *Journal of Management Studies* 35(2): 137–61.
DiMaggio, Paul, and Walter Powell. 1983. 'The Iron Cage Revisited: Institutional Isomorphism and Collective Rationality in Organizational Fields'. *American Sociological Review* 48(2): 147–60.
Djelic, Marie-Laure. 2016. 'History of Management – What is the Future for Research on the Past?' in Barbara Czarniawska (ed.), *A Research Agenda for Management and Organization Studies*. Cheltenham: Edward Elgar, pp. 1–10.
Douglas, Mary. 1966. *Purity and Danger*. London: Routledge & Kegan Paul.
Economic Policy Institute. 2022. 'The Productive–Pay Gap'. Washington, DC. Retrieved 2 August 2024 from https://www.epi.org/productivity-pay-gap/.
Ehrenreich, Barbara, and John Ehrenreich. 2013. *Death of a Yuppie Dream: The Rise and Fall of the Professional–Managerial Class*. New York: Rosa Luxemburg Stiftung.
Elson, Charles M., and Craig K. Ferrere. 2013. 'Executive Superstars, Peer Groups and Over-Compensation — Cause, Effect and Solution'. New York: Investor Responsibility Research Center. Retrieved 2 August 2024 from https://cpb-us-w2.wpmucdn.com/sites.udel.edu/dist/f/506/files/2012/10/Executive-Superstars-Peer-Groups-and-Over-Compensation-10-10.pdf.
Fefer, Mark D. 1994. 'Wall Street Loves Layoffs'. *Fortune* (24 January): 12.
Freidson, Eliot. 1989. 'Theory and the Professions'. *Indiana Law Journal* 64(3): 423–32.
Gouldner, Alvin. 1979. *The Future of Intellectuals and the Rise of the New Class*. New York: Seabury Press.
Guardian. 2023. 'The Guardian View on Management Consultants: Overused, Underperforming'. *The Guardian* (17 Apr.).
Hart, Keith. 2005. *The Hit Man's Dilemma: On Business, Personal and Impersonal*. Chicago: Prickly Paradigm Press.
Ho, Karen. 2009. *Liquidated: An Ethnography of Wall Street*. Durham, NC: Duke University Press.
Kirkpatrick, Ian, Andrew J. Sturdy, Nuria Reguera Alvarado, Antonio Blanco-Oliver and Gianluca Veronesi. 2019. 'The Impact of Management Consultants on Public Service Efficiency'. *Policy & Politics* 47(1): 77–96.
Kunda, Gideon, and Galit Ailson-Souday. 2006. 'Managers, Markets, and Ideologies: Design and Devotion Revisited', in Stephen Ackroyd, Rosemary Batt, Paul Thompson and Pamela S. Tolbert (eds), *The Oxford Handbook of Work and Organization*. Oxford: Oxford University Press, pp. 200–19.

Lathen, Emma. 1964. *Accounting for Murder*. New York: Avon Books.

Marglin, Stephen A. 1974. 'What Do Bosses Do? The Origins and Functions of Hierarchy in Capitalist Production'. *Review of Radical Political Economics* 6: 60–112.

McCambridge, Jim, John Witton and Diana R. Elbourne. 2014. 'Systematic Review of the Hawthorne Effect: New Concepts Are Needed to Study Research Participation Effects'. *Journal of Clinical Epidemiology* 67(3): 267–77.

McDonald, Duff. 2017. *The Golden Passport: Harvard Business School, the Limits of Capitalism, and the Moral Failure of the MBA Elite*. New York: Harper Business.

Mintzberg, Henry. 1996. 'Managing People: Musings on Management'. *Harvard Business Review Magazine* (July–August). Retrieved 2 August 2024 from https://hbr.org/1996/07/musings-on-management.

______. 2004. *Managers, not MBAs: A Hard Look at the Soft Practice of Managing and Management Development*. San Francisco: Berrett-Koehler.

______. 2013. *Simply Managing: What Managers Do – and Can Do Better*. San Francisco: Berrett-Koehler.

Mishel, Lawrence, and Jessica Schleder. 2018. 'CEO Compensation Surged in 2017'. Washington, DC: Economic Policy Institute.

Nelson, Robert H. 2001. *Economics as Religion: From Samuelson to Chicago and Beyond*. University Park: Pennsylvania State University Press.

Oltermann, Philip. 2019. 'Germany Reintroduces "Meister" Qualification for Craftspeople'. *The Guardian* (13 Dec.).

Parker, Martin. 2016. 'Towards an Alternative Business School: A School of Organizing', in Barbara Czarniawska (ed.), *A Research Agenda for Management and Organization Studies*. Cheltenham: Edward Elgar, pp. 147–54.

______. 2018. *Shut Down the Business School: What's Wrong with Management Education*. London: Pluto Press.

Parkin, Frank. 1979. *Marxism and Class Theory: A Bourgeois Critique*. London: Tavistock.

Peters, Thomas J., and Robert H. Waterman Jr. 1982. *In Search of Excellence: Lessons from America's Best-Run Companies*. New York: Warner Books.

Private Eye. 2021. 'Argot Noughts'. *Private Eye* 1556: 10.

Privy Council. nd. 'Royal Charters'. London: The Privy Council Office. Retrieved 2 August 2024 from https://privycouncil.independent.gov.uk/royal-charters/.

Rodgers, Sienna. 2021. 'Exclusive: Labour General Secretary Unveils New Party Structure to Staff'. *Labour List* (17 August). Retrieved 2 August 2024 from https://labourlist.org/2021/08/exclusive-labour-general-secretary-unveils-new-party-structure-to-staff/.

Røyrvik, Emil A. 2011. *The Allure of Capitalism*. New York: Berghahn Books.

Schleicher, Deidra J., Heidi M. Baumann, David W. Sullivan and Junhyok Yim. 2019. 'Evaluating the Effectiveness of Performance Management: A 30-Year Integrative Conceptual Review'. *Journal of Applied Psychology* 104(7): 851–87.

Segal, Michael J., David E. Karp, Jeannemarie O'Brien, Andrea K. Wahlquist, Adam J. Shapiro and David E. Kahan. 2015. 'Compensation Committee Guide'. New York: Wachtell, Lipton, Rosen & Katz. Retrieved 2 August 2024 from https://www2.deloitte.com/content/dam/Deloitte/za/Documents/governance-risk-compliance/ZA_Compensation_Committee_Guide_02062015.pdf.

Shames, Lawrence. 1986. *The Big Time: Harvard Business School's Most Successful Class – and How it Shaped America*. New York: HarperCollins.

South Tees. nd. 'Chief Executive and Accountable Officer'. Middlesbrough: South Tees Hospitals NHS Foundation Trust. Retrieved 10 Sep. 2019 from www.southtees.nhs.uk/about/board/.

Spittler, Gerd. 2016. *Anthropologie der Arbeit: Ein Ethnographischer Vergleich*. Wiesbaden: Springer.

Stein, Felix. 2017. *Work, Sleep, Repeat: The Abstract Labour of German Management Consultants*. London: Bloomsbury.

Taylor, Frederick Winslow. (1911) 1919. *The Principles of Scientific Management*. New York: Harper & Brothers.

Turner, Victor W. 1969. *The Ritual Process: Structure and Anti-structure*. Chicago: Aldine.

Veblen, Thorstein. 1923. *Absentee Ownership and Business Enterprise in Recent Times*. New York: B.W. Huebsch.

Watson, Tony J. 1994. 'Management "Flavours of the Month": Their Role in Managers' Lives'. *The International Journal of Human Resource Management* 5(4): 893–909.

Weber, Max. 1946. *From Max Weber*, edited by Hans Gerth and C. Wright Mills. New York: Oxford University Press.

Wilf, Eitan Y. 2019. *Creativity on Demand: The Dilemmas of Innovating in an Accelerated Age*. Chicago: University of Chicago Press.

Yanagisako, Sylvia. 2002. *Producing Culture and Capital: Family Firms in Italy*. Princeton, NJ: Princeton University Press.

Chapter 3

Writing Managers and Management

Anthropology's Last Repugnant Other?

Michael M. Prentice

It would not be controversial to say that an anthropology of management has not emerged within Europe or North America, a topic this volume seeks to address. While not every topic needs its own 'anthropology of', management is a notable absence on a disciplinary landscape that has taken a number of Western institutional categories as its core objects of enquiry, such as science, bureaucracy, law, medicine and even advertising. There are many plausible reasons for this absence. Most notable might be management's role as the practical arm of capitalism, arguably anthropology's main target of critique since the 1970s. Similarly, conducting embedded, long-term fieldwork, a staple of anthropological ethnography, has proved increasingly difficult for exploring core management functions or actors, as they remain shielded by physical spaces and protected by normative groups.

Managers as figures and management as a function have not, however, been entirely absent from ethnographic portrayals; indeed, managerial figures and criticisms of management are frequently represented in ethnographic literature. Given that representation, the question this chapter then asks is: What is it about managers and management that makes them taboo as a recognised anthropological topic? Focusing in particular on American anthropology, which has engaged with managers, management and corporations extensively, I suggest that managers and management represent cultural Others in a particular American imaginary that informs both the study of them and their reception in the discipline.

As Others, managers are not just actors within capitalism, for they also symbolise or embody undesired aspects of it, representing its core ideas, extremities and contradictions. In this sense, managers occupy a role akin to what Susan Harding (1991) called the repugnant Other, a status that prevents them from receiving consideration as proper ethnographic subjects and, by extension, a role in contributing to broader anthropological theory. Understanding management as a cultural category, then, can help to explain what narratives around management are told, how anthropologists position themselves vis-à-vis managers, and what moves of association and disassociation are made to sort some individuals into the manager slot and others out of it. The broader picture I will paint is of a field that has difficulty representing certain subjects within capitalism, particularly compared to other kinds of anthropological subjects – this in spite of the fact that scholars in related disciplines have made significant headway in developing approaches that historicise, provincialise and situate management, both in the West and elsewhere.

This chapter is motivated by my own experience situating my research among South Korean white-collar corporate managers. To be a manager in South Korea is to be many things: to have prestige in the middle class; to exist within complex and stratified corporate bureaucracies; to have relatively limited power over administrative tasks; and to have a moral responsibility to care for, train and evaluate those being managed. White-collar middle management has never replaced an artisanal, pre-capitalist economy in South Korea (Koo 2001), and has often had a combative relationship with capitalist owners (Janelli and Yim 1993). To argue that managers in South Korea are not hegemons, or even that the idea of management itself is not necessarily a Western import imposed on South Koreans, necessitates narrative scaffolding to assure that some ethnographic subjects might be on the good side because they resist or deflect aspects of capitalism (the young, the laid-off, those dreaming of escape), and others on the bad side because they reinforce aspects of capitalism. Identifying this as an American cultural category has come into relief by my being based in the UK, where discussions of management are associated with the toil of bureaucracy (for instance, Brown, Reed and Yarrow 2017; see also Watson 1994) and not with the phenomenon of managerialism, which has its roots in particular American ideas about powerful strangers, technology and hidden forces. I discuss these at length later in the chapter.

It is worth considering another possible reason why there is presently no anthropology of management: management itself no longer exists. There is some truth to the argument that Alfred Chandler's (1977) classic image of a hierarchical management profession embedded in organisational structures has eroded in the second half of the twentieth century, as has been argued by sociologists and organisational studies scholars

(Davis 2009; O'Doherty and Ratner 2017). This is true with reference to the rise of financial capitalism and ideas of the flexible new economy (Fisher and Downey 2006) amidst a new spirit of capitalism (Boltanski and Chiapello [1999] 2018) that promotes freedom and flexibility over organisation and hierarchy. In this light, anthropology of management might seem a dated concern, amidst shifts to finance, technology, new currencies and various offshore projects in a more fractured institutional landscape without a defined class of managers who preserve their positions. To study the classic white-collar, grey-suited manager would indeed seem an anachronism in the twenty-first century (but see Røyrvik this volume).

There are two reasons management is not dead. First, formal managerial hierarchies are still important and evolving in regions like East Asia, where even under conditions as diverse as state-sponsored capitalist China and neoliberal Japan, professional positions in large corporations (often with formal attire) are still normative sites of educational fulfilment and middle-class desire for men and women alike (see Gagné 2021; Peng 2022; Prentice 2022). Assuming that we do not see such contexts as temporally lagged versions of Western capitalism, they should continue to garner attention as sites where management interacts with culture and society in interesting ways, and where an anthropology of management, in the organisational sense, can continue to be studied.

Second, even accepting that middle-management hierarchies have withered, particularly in North America and Europe, the discourse of management has continued to expand. Management is still arguably the dominant form of governance for public and private institutions in industrialised economies around the world. This is evident in the proliferation of management terms even in a field like finance, which is understood to have eroded the traditional role of the managers. We have concepts like asset management, risk management, portfolio management and the like, in which management operates on things beyond personnel and decision-making, the classical loci of management. As Andrew Orta's (2019; and this volume) work on American MBA schools attests, the classic image of enlightened managers leading corporate organisations is anachronistic, but it continues to provide mystique within MBA programmes.

There is considerable room to explore the diffusion of the management concept from an anthropological perspective. Indeed, as the continued expansion of areas like new public management or cyber-securitisation of data suggest, new objects are continuously being understood within a management framework or logic, alongside new people, things and entities that can be said to manage. Anthropologists should be well positioned to handle these shifting discursive phenomena and the new vectors of local agency that they engender when they become unmoored from their traditional sociological or institutional bases. Given that, a question arises: What, to the anthropologist, is so bad about being a manager that it resists conceptualisation, let alone thick(er) description?

One might argue that the anthropology of neoliberalism can or should serve as the effective stand-in for an anthropology of management. There is already a robust literature by anthropologists working on and with neoliberalism as a concept. There are some benefits to this: taking a critical approach to neoliberalism does not naturalise or universalise management, and foregrounds the ulterior motives behind more milquetoast views of management as simply white-collar professional work or a technique of organisational governance, as well as helping us to trace the logics of power that have been imposed on various domains of life in work and elsewhere. While there has been ample debate about whether neoliberalism does in fact exist or is the same everywhere, the term is still the most common starting point for situating and understanding global economic change and, within that, the role of management.

One problem with an approach that foregrounds neoliberalism, at least from the point of view of understanding management, is that the concept has never clarified a stance with regard to management. In some readings, neoliberalism can appear to be anti-management, from the perspective of destroying salaried labour in favour of flat, individualised or unmanaged work structures. In others, neoliberalism can be demonstrably pro-management, if one considers that elites impose management forces on everyone else or if one holds that neoliberalism itself is an ideology of the global managerial elite. Work on neoliberalism in anthropology has not necessarily provided more insight into theorising management as a profession, as an economic-governance function or as a cultural discourse, so it is difficult to make use of it when it comes to actual instances of management in situated times and places (cf. Kipnis 2007). I will suggest that many ethnographic accounts of neoliberalism follow broader trends in treating managers and management as repugnant Others, one result of which is narratives that explain complex political, economic and cultural dynamics within simpler dimensions.

This chapter proceeds first by arguing that management represents one of anthropology's last repugnant Others, the figure about whom it is okay to not think anthropologically. I draw a parallel with the figure of Harding's original object of study, fundamentalist Christians, and look at the impact her work had on subsequent work in the anthropology of Christianity. My main focus is depictions of managers and management in contemporary ethnographies, which show that management is not neglected per se, but exists within certain genre tendencies that have come to shape the production and reception of studies of global capitalism. Drawing on recent works that have contributed significantly to anthropological studies of capitalism, I highlight three different narrative tropes by which the Otherness of managers and management gets portrayed, and ways that implicitly American ideas about management as an undesired embodiment of capitalist development are embedded. The narrow framing of this figure has meant that it is other disciplines that have developed perspectives on management using postcolonial, critical-historical and other approaches. The chapter suggests that, ultimately, greater nuance in how we represent managers and management in our writing can help to rid the field of its last Othered figure.

Anthropology's Last Repugnant Other?

It is helpful to approach representations of managers and management in light of how different Others have been discussed, critiqued and revisited. Alongside various 1980s reckonings on the writing of non-Western anthropological subjects as exotic Others (e.g. Fabian 1983), there were also reckonings closer to home. Susan Harding's (1991) 'Representing Fundamentalism', for instance, took fundamentalist Christians as Others within modernist American discourse.

Harding's article discussed historical depictions in the media of opposing parties in the Scopes evolution trial of 1925, particularly the depiction of fundamentalists as backward, irrational and rural because of their lack of acceptance of the theory of evolution. Her article also directs attention to anthropology at the time she was writing, in which her ethnographic study of fundamentalism was seen as peculiar given fundamentalism's strong anti-modern position in secular US society. She describes this assertion of peculiarity not as a judgement for being non-modern, but for being *repugnantly* non-modern. That is, there are those who should be modern, liberal and rational, but who are not, or appear to choose not to be. Harding clarifies that she is not necessarily referring to an observable sociological phenomenon of being non-modern, but rather 'a modern discursive production' about fundamentalism, 'for neither [their] numbers nor [their] actions had meaning, much less power, apart from how they figured in the modern imaginary' (Harding 1991: 392). The framing of fundamentalists as non-modern by news writers of the 1920s and by academics contemporary to Harding revealed a cultural framework in American society in which fundamentalists slotted in as cultural Others.

Harding's article has been credited with helping anthropology to overcome its biases about 'disappointing subalterns' (Maxwell 2006: 10, in Bialecki, Haynes and Robbins 2008: 1140) and to develop a more robust anthropology of Christianity not predisposed to privilege certain kinds of Christianity over others (e.g. Robbins 2003; Howell 2007; King 2014). Harding's approach has continued to find relevance. Eduardo Dullo (2016: 134) notes that certain native subjects who have 'a different political or moral stance from the anthropologist' are 'subjected to denunciation or suspicion' and continue to be seen as repugnant, despite anthropology's claims to speak for everyone. Where Harding and others have grappled with religious Others in secular society, I suggest that treatments of management in general, as well as of specific managers, cast them as anthropology's last repugnant Other.

By a 'repugnant Other', I refer to a figure that is not given the gift of ethnographic description in the round; these are figures seen to deserve contempt because of their imbrication with broader economic, state, imperial or oppressive forces, or their refusal to accept plain facts as they pursue other goals, like wealth or power. Normative or hegemonic forces can reinforce who these figures are, but the manager seems an unlikely repugnant Other, for it is a standard middle-class identity in most capitalist societies. Further, in comparison to fundamentalists, managers do not reject modernity; in fact they may be very modernist, secular and rational in their thinking. I suggest there is a different reason they are repugnant within the same American milieu that Harding described. Managers, in ethnographic descriptions, embody not just modernity, but hypermodernity, standing outside culture in the pursuit of capitalist rationality and efficiency. Managers and management typically come to stand for greed, contractual relations and cold calculation, the figurative opposite of what is often seen as the good anthropological subject, which is the person or community embedded in a complex of social relations and motivated by ends that are cultural rather than just economic.

Unlike exoticised Others, who drew attention because of their stark differences from the West, repugnant cultural Others are denigrated precisely because they are familiar. Joel Robbins (2003: 193) notes that it 'is the closeness of Christianity that makes its otherness so potent'. Annelise Riles (2006: 6) similarly notes that what prevented studies of bureaucracy from emerging was plausibly the fact that bureaucrats used inscriptional techniques similar to anthropologists, limiting their use as 'different' anthropological subjects. One could draw perhaps an even closer parallel between managerial techniques and the modern professoriate.

Like managers, professors are in competitive hierarchical organisations where their individual expertise is ranked according to their outputs (on the professorial hierarchy in Germany, see Peacock 2015). Those engaged in laboratory research manage teams of subordinates and large budgets, and thus resemble managerial figures. If fundamentalists were once particularly jarring to American anthropologists because they were middle-class White Americans who chose otherwise, it may be that managers are repugnant to anthropologists because they represent a fear of what academic anthropologists might become, or maybe already are (indeed, many have discussed how the field has become shaped by neoliberalism; see Carrier 2016).

Looking beyond the fear induced by professional likeness, there is an older American concern about managers as unwelcome bearers of change. Narratives of technology and its opposition to culture have informed certain threads of twentieth-century elite discourse, which in turn relate to older American narratives of fears of modernity as a cold, ruthless and rational form of technology that is separated from and antagonistic to human concerns. Managers are today stand-ins for what Leo Marx ([1964] 2000) identified long ago as the 'machine in the garden'. This was his analysis of literary images of modern technology that disrupt or destroy the American pastoral ideal. Where the steam engine or out-of-state corporation might have once occupied this slot, we can see how related figures of modern institutions, such as capitalism, bureaucracy, finance and management, can also be slotted into a narrative as agents of mechanical disruption and the source of alienation as times have changed.

This categorical discomfort seems markedly American. Harold Perkin (2003), a historian of twentieth-century Britain, reflects on how the advent of 'professionalism' affected the British middle classes in the twentieth century, abolishing the old ideas of feudal or aristocratic relations. The notion of being a professional affected jobs across both public and private sectors, doctors, bureaucrats and academics. Perkin's *The Rise of Professional Society* argues against the narrative of 'managerialism' expounded by the American philosopher James Burnham (1941) in his *The Managerial Revolution*. In Burnham's account, managerialism represented control by a new, shadow class of managers who would take over from the capitalist class in American society. In Tony Watson's (1994) sociological ethnography of British managers, he makes it clear that many newly minted British managers are not afraid of managers or management, but rather are uncomfortable narrating themselves as part of the upper-middle class.

In this light, American treatments of being a manager exist within a cultural narrative of capitalism's gradual takeover of traditional life. It is not too difficult to see how this has marked much of American anthropological concern with modern capitalism in the rest of the world, from postwar anthropology concerned with development of the underdeveloped to a view in the 1970s and 1980s that development was leading to 'assault[s] on paradise' (Kottak [1984] 2006). The motif of the assault on paradise places the anthropologist between American multinational corporations and local populations, coming to a head in the figurative gardens being invaded and destroyed by an imperialising capitalism. One can see this theme run from Michael Taussig's *The Devil and Commodity Fetishism* (1980), where local conceptions of the devil come to mediate new capitalist modes of production, to Julia Elyachar's *Markets of Dispossession* (2005), where an array of forces converge to impose market values on a local economic system that is closely entwined with culture. My point is not to criticise these works, but to note how a repugnant Other becomes situated within narrative schema or rhetorical moves that are mediated by norms in anthropological writing (Clifford and Marcus 1986). There is of course much at stake in this when it comes to claiming that anthropological knowledge has a special and valuable view of any and all kinds of topics.

Within ethnographic writing, a repugnant Other is not baldly disparaged as an immoral actor, but emerges from within complex ethnographic contexts, and conveys a range of assumptions and associations about what management is for the anthropologist, and how it contrasts with other figures. Let me give an example. Susanne Cohen has described American expatriate managers in charge of implementing an egalitarian communication ethos at a Russian plant with Russian workers. Cohen presents the workplace plans of the American managers as a combination of the latest trends in capitalism mixed with American cultural ideologies that produce a phoney conception of self-development. Describing the key terms of an American management manual, Cohen sceptically observes: '"Self-esteem", "responsibility", and "involvement" are all highly valued in contemporary US culture. "Growth" and "development" are as well, and we are meant to see the inherent goodness of an approach that has traded Fordist domination for self-actualization and valuing the whole person' (Cohen 2015: 329).

The company's management here is presented as a direct reflection of the latest stage of American capitalism, which is understood to have become adaptive to the times, cleverly integrating new language of therapy and communication into its evolving models of control. The reader can thus readily judge the managers as trying to justify themselves morally through double-voiced management-speak, which is one way to situate them for the readers as repugnant. On the other hand, Cohen's Russian managers are presented as more complex ethnographic subjects: they realise the farce of the American managerial imposition on their factory, they demonstrate sincere (not phoney) care for each other, they joke of Russian corruption, and they are aware of the kinds of complex relationships with others that cannot be determined by formal rules alone – they even exchange gifts. As a result, they are counterposed to the expat American managerial figures who misunderstand the Russians and attempt to impose a variety of American management projects that readers are primed to view sceptically.

Many anthropologists studying contemporary capitalism encounter managerial figures who espouse virtuous or moral stances to management, capitalism or even making money, and there are a variety of ways that the ethnography comes to situate those characters as repugnant in the narrative unfolding of ethnographic description. In what follows, I identify three tropes that surround how managers are described: that managerial subjects totter between culture and capitalism; that the anthropologist can act as the voice of reason; and that management itself exists offstage and carries certain inherent logics. I identify these tropes in terms of specific ethnographies: Marina Welker's *Enacting the Corporation*, Karen Ho's *Liquidated* and Noelle Molé's *Labor Disorders in Neoliberal Italy*. I focus on the details of writing tropes because it is in ethnographic writing that norms can be unconsciously shared and reproduced; similarly, it is there where the field has often worked through its dilemmas to find ways of thinking otherwise.

Writing Management I: Tottering between Culture and Capitalism

The first trope that I present is the depiction of managers as tottering between culture and capitalism. By this, I refer to ways of representing 'culture' and 'capitalism' as heuristics in ethnographies of political economy that mark two moral poles in terms of which actors can be situated. Managers typically fall on the 'capitalism' side, and many locals, natives or conscientious resisters fall on the 'culture' side. One form of this trope is to show how managers begin on the side of culture but end up choosing or falling into capitalism. As well, some managers who appear to be on the side of culture are revealed to have duplicitous motives in the service of capitalism. This narrative construction does not just demonstrate a static figure of the repugnant Other, but also shows a process of moral loss, as individuals move from one position to another or reveal their true intentions. The broader impact of this construction is that it juxtaposes pro-capitalist and anti-capitalist positions, with positive social values such as care, ethics and non-monetary values being contrasted with a capitalist lack of values.

I discuss this trope in the context of Marina Welker's (2014) ethnography of the multinational mining firm Newmont. Her *Enacting the*

Corporation is a multi-sited ethnography of company headquarters in the United States, and its mine in Indonesia. Welker's broader argument is that corporations are unstable entities, and the idea that they are unified with clear motivations or intentions is purely post hoc reasoning. In the book's language, corporations come to be enacted in different encounters, following a relational model or partible personhood. Newmont and its mining activities shape-shift in different enactments in the Denver community where it is based, in the halls of the company offices, and in the village in Indonesia where one of its mines operates.

This is a rather radical approach to thinking about business corporations and an excellent fit for multi-sited research on multinational corporations. Profiteering, Welker suggests, is not an inherent drive of corporate entities, but often one that is only identified after the fact. Indeed, in the opening pages of her ethnography she depicts managerial figures much different from what we might expect: one executive has a background in anthropology and another in applied philosophy. These figures, called Macdonald and Anderson, were in charge of corporate social responsibility (CSR) functions at Newmont's headquarters in Denver. They are sympathetic, not least because they were marginalised within Newmont because of their attempts to elevate environmentalist projects to the level of company-wide prominence. Such managers are seen within the company as hippies and liberals, reflecting that they are the good kind of Other to the anthropologist: those who appear to work against dominant corporate interests, which at the time were largely opposed to environmental and CSR measures. Anderson, Welker (2014: 74) suggests, 'strove ... to highlight the human dimensions of the company rather than allow it to be faceless'. They are clearly on the 'culture' side.

Welker's depictions of other managers and executives paints an opposed image of corporate dynamics. In contrast to the sympathetic CSR executives are others who uphold 'basic corporate production and profit-making functions' (Welker 2014: 70) in a context in which 'financial resources signify and constitute power' (ibid.: 72). In the face of a serious environmental incident caused by a mine by-product leaking, Newmont's CEO represents a familiar image of the evil manager on the 'capitalism' side:

> Cutting short his trip to Indonesia and flying immediately to Peru, ... [the CEO] had visited the hospital room of the victim worst afflicted. He displaced Newmont's responsibility for her [the victim's] dire condition – she was unlikely to recover and regain a normal life – by noting it might have been caused by a severe allergic reaction to the medicine administered to treat her. (Welker 2014: 82)

While Welker is revealing the extraordinary lengths a company executive would go in the face of a company accident, the juxtaposition of conflicting actions (care and non-care) enables the reader to situate the CEO's ultimate motivations on the side of corporate preservation. He is capitalism masking as culture, a process that the anthropologist can reveal to the reader.

It is interesting that the sympathetic CSR executives eventually shift their allegiances. They become company creatures because of the need to 'strengthen the position of CSR within the corporate hierarchy' (Welker 2014: 90). Macdonald and Anderson ultimately develop an Integrated Management System that relies on objective standards, clear metrics and documentation, and follow conventional management-speak as they seek to generate 'buy-in' and get their system 'rolled out', with the help of the CEO. The former academics who want success in their new careers gradually find ways of fitting into the organisational culture, including adopting dual strategies for both charisma and rationalism.

What is surprising is the degree to which the process confirms much of what we might already assume about the force of the corporation as a machine of capitalism that gradually absorbs resistant actors and turns them into its mouthpieces. While Newmont may not be a bounded entity with its own agency or will, it becomes clear that there is a corporate position that individual managers are drawn to enact in similar ways. The pro-corporate position protects the organisation against various threats while promoting it as morally good. Ultimately, the different enactments of the corporation appear to serve a singular purpose: the corporate objective of extracting ore for sale on global markets in the most efficient and socially acceptable way possible. The diverse enactments, in other words, appear to be different obstacles in the way of an a priori goal.

Newmont seems particularly adept at adapting itself to local conditions. In Indonesia it was active in building up the infrastructure of the local village, such as water irrigation channels and schools. This is what Welker (2014: 138) describes as the 'patronage model', in which Newmont's local managers might 'open the faucet of development'. Newmont also had to battle protests and extortionists in a political climate that changed significantly after the fall of President Suharto. At times, Newmont officials appear to make strategic choices to ingratiate themselves at the political level through their dealings with local officials. These entanglements appear ultimately to be instrumental choices, given that Newmont rarely sought to fulfil its long-term responsibilities to the local area.

Interestingly, even local managers hired by Newmont, such as Welker's informant Ibu Comdev, come to follow this implicit script. At first Comdev appears 'to enact Newmont as a company that cared about local women, albeit indirectly (through NGO labour rather than development of in-house expertise) and in domains conventionally coded as feminine (education and health)' (Welker 2014: 146). However, she eventually turns these projects into vehicles for supporting the corporation's extractive purposes, which were being impeded by the locals' anti-capitalist attitudes. Comdev eventually reveals herself to be a 'bad' manager as she adopts a neocolonial view of her compatriots' work ethic. She 'readily grasped the implicit telos of Newmont's economic development efforts, but her formulation also cut to the core of a perception widespread among Newmont officials, including some Sumbawans, that the latter were frustratingly "difficult" to develop because they lacked a strong work ethic and were often stubborn, irrational, emotional, lazy, and undisciplined' (ibid.: 151).

The broader argument of *Enacting the Corporation* is that the boundaries of corporations are not fixed, which is evident in the complex of relations Newmont undertakes to make its Indonesian mine successful. At the same time, Welker's ethnography contains recognisable notions of corporations (and managers as their agents) that have recognisable styles of working, ultimate goals and beliefs about non-corporate types. This comes into relief when the ethnography shows how certain characters occupy different sides of the capitalism–culture divide, and interestingly come to switch sides at key moments. While it is evocative to see that actors can adopt either position (such as the hippie CSR executives, or the local Indonesian manager), it is their binary opposition that makes the radical story of a distributed corporation feel all the more familiar as a story of global capitalist conquest. If economic anthropology seeks to challenge the neoclassical image of the universal, rational economic actor driven by a profit motive, we might want to think about how we can use ethnography not only to mark this opposition, but also to muddy it more thoroughly.

Writing Management II: Anthropologist as the Voice of Reason

The second trope I focus on is that of the anthropologist as the voice of reason. Anthropology as a discipline, more than the other social sciences, is reluctant to provide an objective account of the state of the world, and most anthropologists take their informants seriously when discussing spirits, cosmologies, causality, or norms that go against Western reason or conventional wisdom. There are certain kinds of encounters, however, that engender a different stance, in which the anthropologist acts as the voice of reason against the claims of informants, such as those who harm, exploit or dominate others. In these instances, anthropologists can go against their informants in order to make claims about the inner workings, ideological mechanisms or linguistic codes of the people and institutions that they study (see Marcus 1986).

This means that when the anthropologist encounters managers or experts whose views appear to align with or reaffirm capitalist claims, the analysis, and by extension the anthropologist, can serve as a voice of reason to intercede between subject matter and analysis. This is evident in Karen Ho's *Liquidated* (2009). Her ethnography of Wall Street in the early 2000s showed how much Wall Street thrives on risk and destruction as positive economic forces, echoing anthropological work that was beginning to look at how risk was being deployed in the American economy as a fundamentally good, not destructive, thing.

Ho's work paints a picture in which Wall Street traders, consultants and bankers see themselves as standing against and superior to the classic corporate manager, reflecting their belief that traders, with their 'lean and mean' Wall Street orientation, are in fact better managers than managers themselves. What emerges is an account of whole swaths of traditional corporate managers who were laid off and superseded by managers and firms who used new tools and tactics, like leveraged buyouts. Ho documents the new economic stories that were being told in neoclassical economics that justified the belief that efficient management lay in the hands of shareholders, not corruptible managers. She describes the thrust of those stories: 'Managers were the new and unknown consequences of the modern corporation; their control threatened the foundations of business common sense, and so they came to be the key targets of shareholder value advocates' (Ho 2009: 189). It is interesting in this telling that traditional managers come to appear sympathetic: different from shareholders, they have long-term visions and non-economic allegiance to their firms and employees, and so act in the interest of organisation, community and society. In this view, the investment bankers, with their disdain for society, fit into the 'repugnant Other' slot.

In making the distinction in this way, Ho's ethnography uses narrative scaffolding to make the actors whom she describes appear detached from positive sociality. One technique she uses is to frame herself as the audience to seemingly outlandish Wall Street truths. For instance, Ho begins her book with an account of her confusion about why the share price of AT&T went up after the company had announced massive layoffs:

> I first became interested in studying Wall Street on 21 September 1995. AT&T had just announced that it would split into three different companies, engendering one of the largest dismantlings of a corporation in US history: 77,800

> managers received 'buy-out offers' and 48,500 workers were downsized. Living in New Jersey at the time, I was dismayed by the extent of downsizing-induced worker trauma, and even more troubled to hear that, on the first day of the announcement, AT&T stock leaped 6.125 points to 63.75, or 10.6 percent of its total value, 'growing' another $9.7 billion. But what shocked me the most, upon further investigation, was that the stock prices of Wall Street investment banks also rose. (Ho 2009: 1)

Ho describes a similar sentiment in a footnote: 'Shockingly, when I later discussed this revelation with a friend in business school, he said quite matter-of-factly, "Well, that's the first thing you learn in business school!" … that corporate health is a high stock price, that corporations = shareholders' (ibid.: 337 n5).

These kinds of accounts leave two points unsaid: that such statements are believed to be true by those who make them; and that they are self-evidently abhorrent to the reader as they juxtapose human life with the pursuit of money. This technique allows the reader to align with Ho's own stance on the issue and conclude that these logics are ultimately false (surely corporations cannot be reduced to their shareholders alone).

Ho's informants have their own explanations of the stock market and its impact on their jobs, but her analysis disregards their statements, on the grounds that they misunderstand the culture within which they work or that they have become so enculturated that they come to believe it without question. As Ho notes, 'This assumption [that Wall Street is in a riskier industry than others], I argue, resorts to market externalizations … instead of recognizing that Wall Street's corporate culture constructs investment bankers' experiences of and approaches to job insecurity, and localizes their very understanding of "market"' (Ho 2009: 230). And she reports of an interview with a manager, 'When I asked Bennett what reasons the senior managers gave to justify their job loss, she uttered one word: "Market"' (ibid.: 233). Ho's view is that the market is fetishised, seen as a potent external force rather than as something created or narrated by Wall Street culture itself, and this belief is then internalised as a reason why job security should fluctuate alongside it.

Ho focuses on the job security of middle-level managers as a sign of investment-bank managers' lack of empathy, both for others and themselves. In this sense, Ho's view that a proper managerial career should mean long tenure with one firm sets her apart from those in the industry, whose view seemingly reflects the fact that they benefit from frequent job changes and boom-and-bust pay. Similar to Welker's case, in which demonstrations of care towards others are treated as better kinds of social relations, Ho (2009: 217) marks out one manager as an exception to the prevailing norms:

> Our boss and managing director Kevin Ferguson had often talked about how he was construed as 'odd' on Wall Street because he cared about managing a group of people, about building a business, and his leveraging of his senior position so that employees could use the resources of the workplace to find another job while still getting paid demonstrated this commitment.

Kevin appears as a sympathetic figure because of his demonstration of care towards his employees. From an 'objective' perspective, however, he is also a managing director in a Wall Street firm involved in reproducing the very destructiveness that Ho describes by allowing his employees to seek out other employment while still being employed. The idea of the manager as a 'repugnant cultural Other' means that there is a tendency to apply it to whoever appears captured by capitalism's latest logics, but not to those who, like Kevin, appear more resistant to them.

In any ethnographic encounter there are some characters who espouse the narratives or buzzwords of the workplace more than others. Some of these do enact a kind of political double speak of 'corporate oxymorons' (Benson and Kirsch 2010), particularly within harm industries. Anthropologists are necessarily embedded in ethnographic descriptions and can rhetorically use their own interior narratives to question or call out these forms of speech. However, deploying the voice of reason is a double-edged sword: sympathetic displays witnessed ethnographically (from close informants, from situated victims, etc.) might cause us to overlook other kinds of claims to power that such actors reasonably make; surely they should garner critique as beneficiaries of such a system too. If one of the bases we use to judge managers morally, and by extension to understand the everyday workings of capitalism, is simply the degree of closeness or affinity shown towards the researcher, this is potentially a problem, especially when it appears alongside appeals to reason. In short, the voice of reason can be a strong narrative tool in seeing through the fog of competing claims, of which there are no shortage in a complex organisation or industry; but as Ho's book illustrates, it can lead to downgrading the claims of some simply because of the pole that they occupy. Likewise, simply because traditional corporate managers have experienced harm from Wall Street finance should not mean that we overly sympathise with them as victims or heroes in a broader presentation of capitalism.

Writing Management III: Management, Management Everywhere

In my consideration of the two preceding narrative tropes I focused on the portrayal of managers, and I have treated them as fairly indistinguishable from management, for as ethnographic figures both play similar roles as identifiable actors in broader narratives of capitalist forces. My focus in this section is how the concept of management can serve the function of an outside force with inherent logics that are imposed on local actors. It is thus an object that can be invoked as a negative actor that can be used to explain the hidden motives or outside decision-making within capitalism. One way to do this is to pair management with something that is valued positively, so that it appears contradictory and hence fit for moral criticism. An example is the idea of management of the self, which becomes a self-evidently negative concept precisely because management should not operate on the self. I consider how aspects of this trope operate in Noelle Molé's *Labor Disorders in Neoliberal Italy* (2012).

Molé's ethnography is a discussion of mobbing in Italy in the early 2000s, 'mobbing' being the name for the psychological harassment of individual workers. Mobbing emerged in the context of strict Italian labour laws that made it difficult to fire workers, leading co-workers or managers to harass problematic workers until they quit. The ethnography identifies a particular public discourse that emerged late in the 1990s in the context of the neoliberalisation of the labour market and the precaritisation of work. It links these to the way many people began to positively identify themselves as 'mobbees' or 'mobbers'. Molé's ethnography thus deals with how the culture of mobbing infuses daily work life and becomes a discourse through which people understand work conflicts and shifting contractual regimes.

One case the ethnography describes is a worker named Cris, who was under significant pressure at his company, particularly from his supervisor Gianni, whose own contract was as a freelance worker. We are told that Gianni ended up firing Cris because of his supposed inability to adapt. Molé (2012: 49) says that Cris and Gianni are both 'examples of neoliberal political subjects who define themselves by how they view their economic and social self-management, even as the precarious labour market fuels and shapes the ways in which they relate to one another'. Molé is arguing that under new neoliberal conditions workers put the responsibility for their work on themselves, not on the new market and regulatory conditions. In interviews with other male workers, it is revealed that men in particular make a virtue of this necessity, claiming they do not want to be full-time salaried employees because that would reduce their relative independence. By claiming that workers now engage in self-management, Molé suggests that they have unwittingly taken on additional labour. Self-management is thus crueller than traditional organisational management, which is seen as a more desirable form that workers would want if economic and political conditions were different.

At the same time, mobbing appears as an aspect of management strategy rather than something that appears in the absence of management. Citing a report about mobbing behaviours, Molé notes that '"[n]o perspective" and "submerged actions" are part of the generalized unknowing and left-in-the-dark *style of management* where most workers are not allowed to know about the next steps for closures, layoffs, or off-shore investments' (Molé 2012: 114, emphasis added). In this view, the management is a set of unknown superiors who use mobbing to their advantage, in this case through the absence of information, which leads workers to feel stress and anxiety so that they quit without any management intervention. Here, then, management returns in a more familiar guise as a clever actor that has invented self-management to control surplus or problematic labour.

Interestingly, management also appears inadvertently as a general governance concept, yet it garners little mention. For instance, Molé describes 'how a heightened somatic uncertainty and precariousness are precisely the cultural forces that propel medical *management* of the workplace' and 'citizens' desires for work and for more robust state *management*' (Molé 2012: 159, 166, emphasis added). These uses of 'management' illustrate how expansive the potential for management can become, and how, when applied to things outside capitalism like medicine or government bureaucracy, its use can pass almost unnoticed. Italy's neoliberal conditions led to a reorganisation of managerial powers and capacities, including new medical specialities to deal with mobbing, as well as legal structures to manage mobbing cases. (This points to one of the apparent contradictions in the argument that neoliberalism encourages the abandonment of care and its replacement with self-management, for it begets other forms of management as well.)

What is worth pointing out here is how individuals in this new labour regime, made to 'manage risk', become a sign of a breakdown in the broader society and of the potential for alienation from both the self and the society at large. Here the repugnant Other is more abstract and acts on individuals, or induces individuals to mob each other. Yet at times this abstract force becomes concretised in a set of offstage actors who exercise some instrumental intent.

Molé's book reveals how difficult it is to deal with management both ethnographically and empirically, because of the variety of its forms and locations, and because of the strong moral valences it has in some places and not in others. Were there to be an anthropology of management, then, one of its features must be to account for the ways that the very discourse of management has become a frame of reference for many different functions: it is how individuals manage themselves free of any institutions, but it is also how non-business institutions come to understand new responsibilities. It may be too demanding to focus on all kinds of management in the same ethnography, but even so it is worth considering how our own heightened awareness of certain kinds of management as negative signs of capitalism's reach can exist alongside seemingly unremarked forms of management. Being aware of these blind spots might lead to new insights into how we can reframe narratives of management.

Provincialising Management

Before concluding, I invoke one last work, Andrew Orta's ethnography of MBA programmes, to make a claim about the unmarked status of America in stories of global capitalism. His *Making Global MBAs* is an exploration of the production of future business subjectivities in an American context that is largely post- or anti-management (but still very much pro-business). Orta's broad concern is how American business schools have adapted, as stable corporate managerial hierarchies have given way to new flexibilities in a seemingly flattening world (see Orta this volume).

Orta argues that business schools collectively have cast themselves as new agents of globalisation, not management knowledge per se, and do so by harking back to an imagined past, when managers were globe-trotting quasi-neocolonial masters. For Orta (2019: 43, 47), business schools shape people who are in the process of becoming 'theoretical representation[s] of contemporary capitalism'; their students are taught how to reproduce 'capitalist authority', which is the 'reproduction of dispositions to the world thought to be essential to successful contemporary business management'. He invokes the unmarked notions of 'contemporary business management' and 'contemporary capitalism', but one is tempted to ground his claims in aspects of American culture and society, rather than in universal aspects of capitalism or business management, particularly when the MBA is a unique rite of passage for many of the American business class and those who seek to join it. Framing business management and contemporary capitalism as universal rather than situated in a local context allows the ethnography to make claims about American capitalism *as* contemporary capitalism.

While there is truth to the claim that American management trends and knowledge influence other sites, it would be a stretch to say that they determine, let alone speak for, other forms of business management. German, British, Italian, Japanese and Chinese business managements, to give each a national label, have their own trajectories, institutional dynamics and cultural discourses, and understanding those trajectories makes broad claims to a single 'contemporary capitalism' seem overreaching. If there is one truth that one can glean from studies of American corporate managers abroad, it is that often they are less knowledgeable than their counterparts about wider aspects of management theory and cultural diversity (Cheung 2008; see also Cohen 2015, discussed earlier). Yet we might ask why we often see American managers as the primary actors of global capitalism.

Part of the answer might be that seeing them that way supports the productiveness of the 'repugnant Other' as a recognisable actor within American anthropology as a discipline. By making the American manager a bearer of universal capitalism, not just national capitalism, anthropological critiques can in turn claim a much wider scale of impact, and justify the manager's Otherness. Yet it is the very oddity of para-capitalist institutions in America, like the MBA, that have a symbiotic relationship to American business organisations and knowledge production, that marks them as interesting in the first place to many outside observers. In other words, by asking what is American about the mystique of the MBA, we might generate answers that can help to explain the tensions and contradictions present in contemporary American capitalism. We might also move away from giving managers more credit than they deserve in orchestrating capitalism.

Conclusion

This chapter has highlighted rhetorical habits and narrative frames in anthropological writing on managers and management, and offered one explanation of why the figure of the manager remains recognisably familiar across depictions: it is shaped by the American cultural figure of the manager as a repugnant Other. I traced this figure back to ideas of technology as an intrusion on traditional life. It is perhaps possible that managers do fit such an image, shaped by a shared and universal drive associated with modern capitalism, but it is more likely that they exist within a particular American imaginary, prominent among anthropologists, as a repugnant cultural Other, which in turn shapes their ethnographic representation and reception. It undoubtedly shapes the kinds of stories we tell and the kinds of research that we pursue. As is apparent at various points in this chapter, however, cases of global capitalism do not always generate clear heroes and villains in the same vein as older narratives about traditional economies and their subsequent forced development or proletarianisation. The relationship between individuals, management as a profession, management as a function, and other professions and functions within global capitalism (such as finance) is complex, and does not always generate a clear narrative.

Unlike a subordinate cultural Other, such as Harding's fundamentalists, I have suggested that managers are repugnant for their perceived embrace of capitalism and consequent rejection of positive sociality, qualities that are meant to be evidently undesirable. This might help to explain why, to repeat a point made earlier, an anthropology of management has never got off the ground, unlike other strands of modernist institutional analysis that are now active sites of cross-cultural theorising, such as bureaucracy, medicine, science and law. It also helps to explain why it can be difficult to challenge this framing, given the apparent self-evidence of capitalist critique and management's role within capitalism. Cases that do not fit the narrative might face scepticism from those seeking ulterior motives behind managerial actions.

It is not difficult to imagine what a possible alternative might look like. Critical scholars in organisation studies have already brought postcolonial perspectives to areas of organisations and management thinking in an effort to go beyond Eurocentric tropes when it comes to international management literature (e.g. Prasad 2003; Banerjee and Prasad 2008; Jack and Westwood 2009). Similarly, scholars in China have adopted approaches to indigenise management theory without recourse to Western economic or managerial concepts (Li et al. 2012). But one need not rely solely on those from adjacent disciplines to go beyond the binary. Even academic management scholarship can be useful precisely because it is not weighed down by the conventional narrative schema that has shaped anthropological work, and is itself, perhaps to the surprise of some, very sceptical of trends, ideologies and power imbalances in the management field (see, e.g., Cummings et al. 2017).

Alongside such work, the broader question remains: What of a possible anthropology of management? The present volume offers many possible directions, but gaining legitimacy or analytical value in the broader discipline may not require a specific subtopic and body of knowledge. What would seem just as fruitful would be to reframe our concerns at the level of ethnographic writing itself, where repugnant Others still appear in somewhat familiar guises. What would happen if we turned the common figures of the manager and 'the management' that continue to structure ethnographic writing and anthropological thinking into proper anthropological subjects, in all their messy complexity?

Acknowledgements

This work was supported by the Core University Program for Korean Studies of the Ministry of Education of the Republic of Korea and the Korean Studies Promotion Service at the Academy of Korean Studies. AKS-2023-OLU-2250003.

Michael M. Prentice is a lecturer in Korean Studies at the University of Sheffield. Trained as a linguistic anthropologist at the University of Michigan, he has conducted ethnographic research at the intersection of communication, management and large organisations in South Korea since 2011. His monograph *Supercorporate: Distinction and Participation in Post-Hierarchy South Korea* (Stanford, 2022) addresses the tensions among competing ideals of what office work should be in twenty-first-century South Korea.

References

Banerjee, Subhabrata Bobby, and Anshuman Prasad. 2008. 'Introduction to the Special Issue on "Critical Reflections on Management and Organizations: A Postcolonial Perspective"'. *Critical Perspectives on International Business* 4(2/3): 90–98.

Benson, Peter, and Stuart Kirsch. 2010. 'Corporate Oxymorons'. *Dialectical Anthropology* 34(1): 45–48.

Bialecki, Jon, Naomi Haynes and Joel Robbins. 2008. 'The Anthropology of Christianity'. *Religion Compass* 2(6): 1139–58.

Boltanski, Luc, and Eve Chiapello. (1999) 2018. *The New Spirit of Capitalism* (trans. G. Elliott). London: Verso.

Brown, Hannah, Adam Reed and Thomas Yarrow. 2017. 'Introduction: Towards an Ethnography of Meeting'. *Journal of the Royal Anthropological Institute* 23(S1): 10–26.

Burnham, James. 1941. *The Managerial Revolution: What Is Happening in the World.* Bloomington: Indiana University Press.

Carrier, James G. (ed.). 2016. *After the Crisis: Anthropological Thought, Neoliberalism and the Aftermath.* London: Routledge.

Chandler, Alfred D. 1977. *The Visible Hand: The Managerial Revolution in American Business.* Cambridge, MA: Belknap Press.

Cheung, Lenis Lai-Wan. 2008. 'Let the "Other" Speak for Itself: Understanding Chinese Employees from their Own Perspectives'. *Critical Perspectives on International Business* 4(2/3): 277–306.

Clifford, James, and George E. Marcus (eds). 1986. *Writing Culture: The Poetics and Politics of Ethnography.* Berkeley: University of California Press.

Cohen, Susanne. 2015. 'The New Communication Order: Management, Language, and Morality in a Multinational Corporation'. *American Ethnologist* 42(2): 324–39.

Cummings, Stephen, Todd Brigman, John Hassard and Michael Rowlinson. 2017. *A New History of Management*. Cambridge: Cambridge University Press.

Davis, Gerald F. 2009. *Managed by the Markets: How Finance Reshaped America*. New York: Oxford University Press.

Dullo, Eduardo. 2016. 'Seriously Enough? Describing or Analysing the Native(s)'s Point of View', in James G. Carrier (ed.), *After the Crisis: Anthropological Thought, Neoliberalism and the Aftermath*. London: Routledge, pp. 133–53.

Elyachar, Julia. 2005. *Markets of Dispossession: NGOs, Economic Development, and the State in Cairo*. Durham, NC: Duke University Press.

Fabian, Johannes. 1983. *Time and the Other: How Anthropology Makes Its Object*. New York: Columbia University Press.

Fisher, Melissa A., and Greg Downey. 2006. *Frontiers of Capital: Ethnographic Reflections on the New Economy*. Durham, NC: Duke University Press.

Gagné, Nana Okura. 2021. *Reworking Japan: Changing Men at Work and Play under Neoliberalism*. Ithaca, NY: Cornell University Press.

Harding, Susan. 1991. 'Representing Fundamentalism: The Problem of the Repugnant Cultural Other'. *Social Research* 58(2): 373–93.

Ho, Karen Z. 2009. *Liquidated: An Ethnography of Wall Street*. Durham, NC: Duke University Press.

Howell, Brian M. 2007. 'The Repugnant Cultural Other Speaks Back: Christian Identity as Ethnographic Standpoint'. *Anthropological Theory* 7(4): 371–91.

Jack, Gavin, and Robert Westwood. 2009. *International and Cross-Cultural Management Studies: A Postcolonial Reading*. New York: Palgrave Macmillan.

Janelli, Roger L., and Dawnhee Yim. 1993. *Making Capitalism: The Social and Cultural Construction of a South Korean Conglomerate*. Stanford, CA: Stanford University Press.

King, Rebekka. 2014. 'The Anthropology of Christianity Goes to Seminary'. *Religion & Society* 5(1): 255–60.

Kipnis, Andrew. 2007. 'Neoliberalism Reified: *Suzhi* Discourse and Tropes of Neoliberalism in the People's Republic of China'. *Journal of the Royal Anthropological Institute* 13(2): 383–400.

Koo, Hagen. 2001. *Korean Workers: The Culture and Politics of Class Formation*. Ithaca, NY: Cornell University Press.

Kottak, Conrad. (1984) 2006. *Assault on Paradise: Social Change in a Brazilian Village*. Long Grove, IL: Waveland Press.

Li, Peter Ping, Kwok Leung, Chao C. Chen and Jar-Der Luo. 2012. 'Indigenous Research on Chinese Management: What and How'. *Management and Organization Review* 8(1): 7–24.

Marcus, George E. 1986. 'Contemporary Problems of Ethnography in the Modern World System', in James Clifford and G.E. Marcus (eds), *Writing Culture: The Poetics and Politics of Ethnography*. Berkeley: University of California Press, pp. 165–93.

Marx, Leo. (1964) 2000. *The Machine in the Garden: Technology and the Pastoral Ideal in America*. New York: Oxford University Press.

Maxwell, David. 2006. *African Gifts of the Spirit: Pentecostalism and the Rise of a Zimbabwean Transnational Religious Movement*. Oxford: Oxford University Press.
Molé, Noelle J. 2012. *Labor Disorders in Neoliberal Italy: Mobbing, Well-being, and the Workplace*. Bloomington: Indiana University Press.
O'Doherty, Damian, and Helene Ratner. 2017. 'The Break-up of Management: Critique Inside-Out'. *Journal of Cultural Economy* 10(3): 231–36.
Orta, Andrew. 2019. *Making Global MBAs: The Culture of Business and the Business of Culture*. Berkeley: University of California Press.
Peacock, Vita. 2015. 'The Negation of Hierarchy and its Consequences'. *Anthropological Theory* 15(1): 3–21.
Peng, Xinyan. 2022. *Corporate Women in Contemporary China: 'We've Always Worked'*. London: Routledge.
Perkin, Harold. 2003. *The Rise of Professional Society: England since 1880*. London: Routledge.
Prasad, Anshuman (ed.). 2003. *Postcolonial Theory and Organizational Analysis: A Critical Engagement*. New York: Palgrave Macmillan.
Prentice, Michael M. 2022. *Supercorporate: Distinction and Participation in Post-Hierarchy South Korea*. Stanford, CA: Stanford University Press.
Riles, Annelise. 2006. *Documents: Artifacts of Modern Knowledge*. Ann Arbor: University of Michigan Press.
Robbins, Joel. 2003. 'What is a Christian? Notes toward an Anthropology of Christianity'. *Religion* 33(3): 191–99.
Taussig, Michael T. 1980. *The Devil and Commodity Fetishism in South America*. Chapel Hill: University of North Carolina Press.
Watson, Tony J. 1994. *In Search of Management: Culture, Chaos and Control in Managerial Work*. London: Routledge.
Welker, Marina. 2014. *Enacting the Corporation: An American Mining Firm in Post-Authoritarian Indonesia*. Berkeley: University of California Press.

Chapter 4

Against Collaboration

The Ethics of Studying Corporate Management

Felix Stein

Collaboration has become a firmly established virtue in anthropological thought and practice. As anthropologists we are regularly encouraged to collaborate with researchers from other disciplines and subdisciplines, with the organisations that finance and assess our work, with staff and students at our research institutions, and with partner institutions in project-based research. Most importantly, anthropologists are meant to collaborate with the people and communities they study by conducting 'collaborative ethnography' – that is, 'the collaboration of researchers and subjects in the production of ethnographic texts, both [in] fieldwork and writing' (Lassiter 2005a: 83; see also Boyer and Marcus 2020).

Research participants in these instances are no longer considered 'informants' or 'research subjects' but 'collaborators', people who, whilst being studied, 'participate in the research design, execution, publication and outcomes potentially related to community or individual improvement of well-being' (Fluehr-Lobban 2008: 175). Collaborative research is so popular that it has become equated with 'ethically conscious' research, preferable on epistemic, political and moral grounds to 'the older, more hierarchical model of research planned, executed, and published by the anthropologist alone' (ibid.). Indeed, researchers who do not show enough enthusiasm for collaborative work stand accused of overly celebrating their individual achievements, possibly according to gendered or culturally inflected norms (Gottlieb 1995).

Contemporary calls for more and deeper collaboration with research participants draw on several long-standing debates in anthropology

(Lassiter 2005a). They build on challenges to academic authority by the *Writing Culture* school (Clifford and Marcus 1986), which argued that ethnographic knowledge is inherently partial, and has always been produced in a collaborative fashion. As a result, anthropology is held to require 'an alternate textual strategy, a utopia of plural authorship that accords to collaborators not merely the status of independent enunciators, but that of writers' (Clifford 1983: 140; see also Marcus and Fischer 1996).

Current calls to collaborate also draw on feminist insights that research inevitably includes frequently exploitative power hierarchies, that researcher positionality matters, that particularly in ethnographic research our private and professional lives are enmeshed, and that it is difficult to write for multiple audiences at the same time (Haraway 1988; Stacey 1988; Abu-Lughod 1990). Attempts at valorising and adequately representing research participants led to demands for 'much greater respect for and power to one's research "subjects" who, some feminists propose, can and should become full collaborators in feminist research' (Stacey 1988: 22).

As well, calls for collaboration draw on long-standing attempts to decolonise research, to foreground anthropology's past and present role in imperial and colonial dominance and exploitation along ethnic, cultural and national lines (Asad 1973; D'Amico-Samuels 1997; Harrison 1997; Smith 1999). Collaboration, notably with activist groups and community organisations, has been suggested as one of the means to improve research and make it reflect and be relevant to the concerns of colonised and marginalised groups (D'Amico-Samuels 1997; Cervone 2015). This suggestion is increasingly taken on by Euro-American research councils, which now tend to make collaboration with policymakers and partner organisations a prerogative for obtaining research funding.

Most recently, calls for collaboration also have been made to deal with the major ecological challenges of our time (Mathews 2020). In the face of climate change, mass species extinction and planetary pollution, some scholars advocate greater collaboration with non-human beings. This can take the form of trying to mimic their sociality to define research strategies or thinking about knowledge production in new and unforeseen ways (Inoue 2009).

Interestingly, the growth of collaboration as a guiding virtue for anthropological research echoes its rise in the corporate world. In recent years, a whole 'collaboration economy' has been celebrating collective work that transcends traditional institutional structures and economic relationships (Rajak 2011; Riles 2015). Collaboration is now a ubiquitous virtue in business, legal and policy circles, where it has accompanied advances in communication and audit technology, the rise of the platform economy, and a loss of faith in the power of public- and private-sector institutions to work separately (Riles 2015; Petropoulos 2017). It may thus be unsurprising to learn that anthropologists in and of management also have called for greater collaboration between managers and scholars (Stewart and Aldrich 2015; Tett 2021; Maurer and Mainwaring 2022).

In order to investigate this idea of collaborative ethnography in management contexts, this chapter will draw on my attempts in 2012 to obtain permission to do research in the Berlin-based global strategy consultancy company where I was employed at the time. My attempts at gaining research permission took place in a corporate context, where I had two main managerial tasks: I was a consultant for managers of other companies and I helped senior consultants to manage our own projects. The ethnographic material I present will indicate a series of complications that are not satisfactorily addressed, and often are even worsened, by insisting on ever closer collaboration. The epistemic, political and moral incompatibilities that arose as part of my ethnographic work stem from management's specific way of exerting power and from operating in a corporate context.

I argue that anthropologists should not try to paper over the shortcomings of collaboration when studying managers or studying corporate forms. Rather than pretending that a full harmony of means and ends between our research and the work of corporate management is possible or desirable, we should be much more open about the political, epistemic and moral dimensions that distinguish anthropological research from the work of corporate management. By implication, we should be honest as well about persisting differences between our research, in which we describe and theorise people's lives, and the activities of most of the people and non-human agents we study. Once we know and state what these differences are, they open up a panoply of possible relations with our research subjects. Importantly, they show that the decision to collaborate with other people depends to a large degree on the nature of the activities in which they engage, as collaboration is not a virtue in and of itself.

Why Collaborate?

Collaboration can broadly be defined as working together (Lassiter 2005b: 15). More precisely, we can understand it as a set of activities that are structured, outcome-oriented and productive (the 'working' part) (Harris 2007; Spittler 2016), in which several different entities purposefully pursue broadly similar goals and means (the 'together' part). Consequently, the statement that 'ethnography is, by definition, collaborative' (Lassiter 2005b: 16) applies in at least three ways.

Firstly, all participant observation requires some degree of consent by research participants as to the goals and means of our research. While the degree of consent is variable and contested, to the extent that it may constitute little more than acquiescence, fully covert ethnographic research is not permitted. The American Anthropological Association (2012), for example, holds that 'clandestine or secretive research that manipulates or deceives research participants about the sponsorship, purpose, goals or implications of the research, do[es] not satisfy ethical requirements for openness, honesty, transparency and fully informed consent'. In a weak sense, then, people who let anthropologists study them could be seen to collaborate with them to at least a minimal degree.

Secondly, participant observation often relies on creating personal relationships with research participants (e.g. Howell 2018). This inevitably entails many moments of working together, for example when sharing domestic chores, engaging in care, preparing ritual festivities, or attending and contributing to community or neighbourhood meetings. Such moments of practical collaboration are unavoidable in long-term fieldwork, and they often provide us with the detailed kind of knowledge that sets ethnography apart from other qualitative research methods.

Third, participant observation tends to require at least a minimum of theoretical collaboration, in that anthropologists base their work on the epistemic help of others. In defining a research site and making initial sense of it, anthropologists tend to rely on the assessments and opinions of first contacts, teachers and gatekeepers, including translators, language experts, informed individuals and other researchers. Their knowledge and views necessarily guide our inquiry, especially in the early stages of research, when almost everything we do is marked by a lot of ignorance.

While a minimal degree of collaboration is thus present in all ethnographic fieldwork, the kinds of work involved in it tend to be unequally distributed. Research participants may focus more on the tasks that govern their daily lives, while researchers and translators tend to be more heavily involved in following an additional set of ethnographic purposes, linked to description and theory building.

All that said, anthropologists in favour of collaboration as a research virtue want to go beyond this bare collaborative minimum that enables and conditions our research (e.g. Holmes and Marcus 2008). They want instead to deliberately and explicitly emphasise collaboration at every point in the ethnographic process (Lassiter 2005a, 2005b). Collaboration in this strong sense is meant to attenuate an assumed power differential between authoritative researchers and largely powerless research subjects. This power differential must be nuanced, as anthropologists are often quite powerless during fieldwork, and anthropological writing is rarely the most direct or effective tool for political engagement (Carrier 2019). However, broadly speaking, power differentials between professional researchers and most research participants still hold, given the researchers' general access to education, academic jobs, research funds, passports, international networks and at times even social elites who wield power in much more tangible and observable ways. Whenever such power differentials prevail, making an effort to co-produce reports, articles or maybe even entire monographs with research participants, and to participate in their political efforts 'beyond the text', reflects anthropologists' deep involvement in other people's lives (Hale 2006; Kirsch 2018).

Politics aside, collaboration can be a useful epistemic technique as well. The people we study do not just provide us with factual information, they also enable us to learn about the blind spots, incoherencies and unspoken assumptions of our own analyses. Acknowledging their expertise and points of view enriches social analysis, to the extent that collaboration can include co-theorisation, the collective production of concepts, theories and research approaches, grounded not only in anthropological theory but also in the modes and systems of thought of our interlocutors (Rappaport 2008). This provides an alternative to being focused exclusively on existing academic debates and methods. It also foregrounds the sophistication of the people we study, and makes the heterogeneity, ambivalences and dynamism of their lives and thought visible to us (ibid.). In these instances, collaboration serves as an intellectual stimulus and as an antidote to essentialising others. Moreover, in a context where researchers represent not only themselves but also their discipline or maybe even the social sciences at large, collaboration may facilitate field access for future researchers, serving as a research technique that stretches beyond individual projects.

Lastly, collaboration is seen by many of its proponents as a moral prerogative. The inequality, exploitation and dehumanisation that mark the lives of many of our research participants, whether compared to outside researchers or compared to other, more privileged members of their own social groups, push many of the anthropologists who learn about these issues to act on them. They are 'a function of our primary intersubjectivity as live beings' (Pina-Cabral 2020: 51). Thus, in a strong sense, collaboration features in moral appeals for 'public anthropology' (Osterweil 2013), 'engaged anthropology' (Kirsch 2018) and 'activist research' (Hale 2006).

A second, and I believe more complicated, form of moral reasoning equally makes the case for collaboration. It is the conviction of some anthropologists that their ethics should correspond, at least to a degree, to the moral convictions of the people they study. Social groups that are themselves egalitarian may thus exert moral pressure on the researcher to use egalitarian methods, simply because the latter feels compelled to establish not just conceptual correspondence with them, but also a minimal degree of moral correspondence (Walker 2020).

When it comes to studying corporate management, arguments for collaboration are mostly made on epistemic grounds. The corporate form is by now such an important social institution that it must take a central place in anthropological scholarship (Nader 1972; Welker, Partridge and Hardin 2011). At the same time, public and private corporations often enable their members, particularly their managers, to lead sheltered lives, hidden away behind the turnstiles, receptionists and badge-locked doors that protect office towers, airport lounges, hotels, bars, restaurants and gated neighbourhoods (Stein 2017). Accessing these powerful but hidden groups may not just require 'institutional kinship', such as links with elite universities (Ho 2009) or personal ties (Zaloom 2006; Holmes 2013), but may also require agreeing to collaborate with them, via formal employment, for example as a back-office worker (Chong 2018).

Beyond issues of research access, some hold that collaborating with corporate managers brings additional epistemic advantages. Given that managerial work is carried out in increasingly abstract social settings, it can be considered hard to study based on experience alone (Holmes and Marcus 2006; Stein 2017). As managers have become knowledge workers in 'soft-capitalism' and 'surveillance capitalism', where information is increasingly important (Thrift 1997; Zuboff 2019), they tend to be academically trained and have a great amount of factual knowledge. They also increasingly engage in para-ethnography, relying on narratives, intuition and anecdotes to make sense of their jobs and of the economy in a self-reflexive manner (Holmes and Marcus 2006). Collaborating with managers and other people in corporate settings is thus no longer based on the idea that any way of thinking that is radically different from that of anthropologists can be intellectually stimulating (Lévi-Strauss 2021). Instead, we are meant to harness the *specific* intellectual prowess, factual knowledge and critical capabilities of our managerial interlocutors.

An ethnographic example may help us to critically assess these arguments for collaboration with corporate management, and point us towards an alternative.

Research Permission in a Management Consultancy

In September 2011, I began working as a management consultant in Berlin. I had been in a PhD programme in social anthropology at the University of Cambridge, but a major scholarship fell through. I was facing a five-digit student debt and could no longer afford to conduct PhD research. Instead, I applied for various jobs, mostly with non-profit development organisations but also in the for-profit sector, seizing the first opportunity I got. This was a job in management consulting, for which I moved to Berlin right after the first year of my PhD. There I bought suits and a carry-on suitcase, and I soon learned that my new colleagues and I would specialise in 'strategic' managerial advice, meaning that we would mostly provide middle and upper management with market and organisational analyses (Stein 2017). At times, we drew up blueprints for organisational change and oversaw how it was carried out; at others, we simply supported upper management in an ad hoc way with whatever tasks they needed to get done.

The term 'strategic' had several connotations in this setting, linked to the term's original military use (Freedman 2013). Firstly, it referred to the rationalistic aspirations and assumed medium- and long-term timescales of our work. Secondly, it was an indicator of hierarchy, pointing out the fact that we desired to work with company chief executive officers (CEOs) and upper layers of management. In an influential article on strategy that we learned about as part of our consulting training, strategic work was held to be concerned with the entirety of a firm's activities (Porter 1996). The article's author, Michael Porter, also made his conviction clear that 'managers at lower levels lack the perspective and the confidence to maintain a strategy' (ibid.: 53), so the term denoted topics that concerned the higher echelons of managerial rule.

As well, the term 'strategy' had the important feature that it did not refer to any specific kind of work. This was one of the aspects of our job that surprised my colleagues and me the most: one day we would write plans about how to render the staff of an insurance company healthier and happier, yet on another we would contribute to the management of a struggling energy company in laying off tens of thousands of employees. Our employer would sometimes support hospitals in their attempts to improve healthcare provision, but would also enable weapons and tobacco manufacturers to sell more of their products in whatever ways they could. We would back German ministries, trying to improve their work of day-to-day governance, as much as clients explicitly trying to undercut national legislation in the pursuit of profit. Generally speaking, therefore, the term 'strategy' revealed a nihilistic functionalism in our work, according to which anything would get done, as long as it was legal, paid our salaries, and made some sense from the client's business perspective.

Mirroring this process-oriented disposition of management consulting, our work ethics were, broadly speaking, not so much concerned with what we did but with how skilled we were at doing it. In this context, important markers of professionalism were linked to knowing and supporting intra-corporate hierarchies, keeping up with the intense temporal rhythms of work, and emulating an outcome-focused rhetoric that marked our daily lives (Stein 2018b). A final important marker for ethical behaviour was whether we respected corporate desires for secrecy, expressed as 'client confidentiality'. Because the business model of consultancy firms is based on obtaining access to detailed information regarding their clients' current activities and plans for the future, consultancy companies fear that if this information were to be made public it would compromise the trust that clients have in them, thereby risking a loss of potential contracts. Newly hired management consultants everywhere are taught this lesson, usually through speeches, training sessions, obligatory online courses, technological barriers to information exchange, on-the-job reminders from colleagues, and threatening texts at the bottom of corporate emails.

In my case, guidelines concerning confidentiality were communicated through all of these channels. In lectures and online courses, I was taught that buying and selling stock in the companies for whom we were consulting was illegal. On the job, colleagues reminded me to password-lock my computer and pack away my notes whenever I left my desk. When talking about work in taxis or restaurants, colleagues and I would lower our voices and refer to clients with names such as 'the red ones' or 'the green ones', depending on the colour of their brand logo. We thereby ensured confidentiality, but we also turned ostensibly public spaces into 'spaces of discretion', creating a sense of complicity that tied us together (Mahmud 2014). Much of this behaviour was based on threatening rumours of people who had been speaking badly about their clients in a public space, only to learn the next day that they were now without a job as the CEO of the client company had overheard them.

Apart from personal conduct, technology was crucial for defining and ensuring secrecy and information control. Shredders and locked bins for confidential documents were as much part of our daily surroundings as posters above photocopying machines warning us never to talk about work with friends or family. Special USB sticks allowed us to transfer information between certified computers only, and calls with IT support revealed on a regular basis that our laptops were not private, as remote IT staff could take control of the cursor on our machines in a matter of minutes. Furthermore, rumours circulated among friends of mine working for other consultancy companies of how people who had downloaded too many internal documents from their company intranet had been approached by IT staff, asking them why they had done so.

In this environment of totalitarian corporate information control, about a year into my job I asked for permission to study my employer. There were many reasons for this, but three are worth mentioning. Firstly, I was not aware of any anthropologist having had research access to management consultants before, so I thought that this study could be interesting in and of itself. Secondly, the abstract nature of the kind of work that we carried out (Stein 2017), its internal contradictions and the vast amounts that were being paid for it had an alienating effect on me, and studying this work environment was one way of dealing with this. Lastly, I felt that I could not continue working as a consultant, because the nihilistic ethics outlined above, which were primarily based on following client desires within the limits of managerial business sense, appeared morally dubious to me.

I came to this conclusion during my first year of work when carrying out a short-term 'diagnostic' for the management of a Polish paper mill (Stein 2018b). I realised then that my participation in this project as a young, extremely well-paid German who knew very little about paper production and who flew business class could potentially lead to the layoff of Polish factory workers, who were much older than me, who knew quite a lot about their work and who were, in my eyes, poorly paid. While these layoffs may have been inevitable from a managerial perspective, I did not have clarity on this matter myself, and decided there and then that I desired a job that was a little less militaristic and in which ethical decision-making would not be so fully subordinated to market logics. I therefore resolved either to quit my job or to turn it into a research project.

As a result, I sent a draft of a PhD proposal to the senior consultant who led the office to which I was affiliated, whom I shall call 'the Office Director'. My proposal was entitled 'Conceptions of value among business consultants'. The Office Director told me via email that it was not up to him to decide upon this matter, as my project concerned the entire company rather than just our office. Therefore, it had to be dealt with by the Head of Communications (HoC) for all of Germany. The latter responded to my request a few days later, stating briefly via email that he had seen my proposal and that unfortunately he could not support it as it threatened 'client confidentiality'.

Frustrated, I approached another senior consultant, who served as my career advisor within our firm. He found my research proposal interesting but he also saw it with a critical eye. He advised me to find a respected member of our firm who would be willing to support me and to talk to both the Office Director and the HoC once more. Notably, he himself did not offer to provide the kind of support that I would have needed. At a loss about who to approach for assistance, I decided to send my research proposal to the global CEO of our company, whom I had heard speak only a few days earlier. He had struck me as a charismatic and liberal man, whose international upbringing and frequent travel promised some open-mindedness. His secretary kindly agreed to print my message and research proposal, and to put them on his desk. He responded several days later via email, saying that he thought my research was a 'great idea' as long as I 'stuck to confidentiality rules', and he was 'looking forward to seeing the results'.

With this email in hand, I returned to the Office Director. Unfortunately, he had already heard about my exchange with the CEO, and felt both betrayed and infuriated. After all, I had not copied him into the exchange with the CEO and I had not mentioned the HoC's prior refusal in it. After a sincere apology from my side, the Office Director explained in a much more supportive manner that such decisions really lay with the HoC and with the managers of our projects, known as 'Partners', who would be involved in my research. He illustrated this by means of an anecdote about how he had once wanted to start a new kind of charitable consulting project, which had been met with significant scepticism by many of his colleagues. However, by sticking to his idea and by convincing a Partner to support him, he had eventually carried it out successfully.

Motivated by this meeting, I scheduled a phone call with the HoC. I asked him whether research permission had to be obtained from him or from many different Partners. He told me that contacting other Partners was certainly my right, but that his view was that the company had 'absolutely no institutional interest' in seeing my research realised, and that he would consider it his duty to work against it 'with all his might'. He considered our consultants to be operating in a 'Habermasian discursive situation', where 'whenever the topic of value came up in public discussion' he had to 'fight with all his power to push it back down again'. Regardless of whether I would argue that consultants create a lot of economic value or whether I would develop a critical perspective, the mere fact that this issue would become a topic of public conversation was a big enough threat for him to veto my project. I understood his concern only later in my research, when I realised how polarised public opinion was regarding the work and social position of management consultants in Germany (Stein 2017).

This was the moment when my frustration peaked: I had angered the Office Director, the HoC had overtly threatened to become my enemy, and the thought of having to ask further Partners for permission only promised to lead to additional conflict. Therefore, I assured the HoC that I had no intention of causing power struggles between him and his senior colleagues, and that as an anthropologist I could not carry out the research without official company permission. In a corporation as large and heterogeneous as a global consultancy company, ethical approval relied to a significant extent on the willingness of powerful individuals to speak for the company as a whole. I made clear to the HoC that I needed the company to speak with one voice on this matter, and that in this case it seemed that the voice had to be his.

He agreed on the last point, and told me that his main concern lay with the topic of my research proposal. Regarding my question of what could be done to make *any* kind of research project possible, he replied that if I was to write about a matter other than value creation, he would reconsider the idea. Here, I must confess that I had remembered and consciously applied a clunky rhetorical technique that I had been taught in one of several consulting training camps. It was called 'putting the monkey on someone else's back', and it consisted of asking interlocutors in a moment of conflict to provide a solution for you. Knowing that ethnographic research tends to evolve over time, I reluctantly agreed, and two weeks later sent him a second proposal on the subject of 'The nature of advice in the new economy'. He replied via email that he 'much prefer[ed] this proposal and that he [did] … not want to stand in its way', upon which my career advisor congratulated me over the phone, adding that 'persistence had eventually paid off'. He thereby framed my attempts at corporate ethnography as exhibiting the company values of entrepreneurialism and perseverance.

From there onwards, I started taking notes while at work, mentioning my ongoing ethnographic research to all my colleagues and clients whenever possible. My email exchange with the company CEO inspired awe among some of my peers, and was soon turned into a reference for jokes of all sorts. After ending my job, I interviewed consultants from comparable companies in Berlin, so as to write more about the industry and less about an individual company. In my written work I anonymised all research subjects and corporate entities, to the point that I changed the gender of some of the people I describe, as well as the nature of some of the firms that I wrote about. To reduce the risk of misrepresenting my colleagues, I asked several of them to comment on drafts of my work. I was relieved to see over the course of my research that I was not able to gather much data on the topic of value creation after all.

The Limits of Collaboration

My tiring and confused quest for research access could easily be framed as supporting collaboration as a virtue of anthropological research. After being initially confused about how to ask for research permission, I eventually came to identify the right people, and pushed them to speak with one voice. I tapped into corporate values of entrepreneurialism, perseverance and senior support, and thereby managed to turn a research project that was initially not in line with company interests into one that the HoC accepted and that the company CEO himself was actually looking forward to. Maybe both of them would eventually read my analysis and think about their work in a new way, turning this research project into another successful example of collaborating with corporate managers.

Unfortunately, this is not at all the whole story. My quest for research access also highlights some of the fundamental epistemic, political and moral problems, which seem characteristic of ethnographic research with corporate managers, and which clash with the virtue of collaboration. On an epistemic level, the above-mentioned potential benefits of working with management were outweighed by the fact that anthropological modes of thought were mostly useless at work. Ethnographic writing requires more-than-utilitarian thinking, a liking for serendipity, paradoxes and inconsistencies, slow temporalities, embodied knowledge and largely unconstrained intellectual exchange (Eriksen 2016; Howell 2018; Stein 2018a). This stood in stark contrast to the epistemic demands of my colleagues and clients, who wanted me to think about how they could fulfil their short-term goals, generally aiming at increasing corporate profit and in turn making work processes more effective or efficient. My research did not do that; it did not improve my clients' day-to-day work, or ameliorate our consulting activities in any obvious way. Neither did it promise new project acquisitions. On the contrary, carrying out ethnographic research meant that my mind was sometimes only half engaged in my consulting work, as I was also trying to analyse what was happening from a social science perspective. This is not what I had been hired for. Indeed, my work contract had stipulated, with only some hyperbole, that I was expected to 'dedicate all of my labour power [*Arbeitskraft*] and capabilities to my employer'.

The short-term uselessness of social science research was also a problem for those colleagues who found my research interesting and would have liked to contribute to it but could not. Often, they simply did not have the time or energy to give me an interview, because our work was physically and mentally too demanding and time-consuming, and because many more pressing tasks needed to be prioritised (see, e.g.,

Boyer and Hannerz 2006; Stein 2018b). Several interviewees ended up giving me largely distracted and hard-to-understand interviews whilst driving, or when moving from one meeting to another. Moreover, in the strongly hierarchical environment of a corporate partnership, the fact that I was a junior consultant meant that my project was of a low institutional priority, simply because it did not come from or directly benefit the people at the top.

On a political level, my research was also not in the institutional interest of the corporations that I studied. Some of this tension stemmed from the political nature of management itself. Managers have been shown to be in a somewhat fragile social position in so far as they are meant to exert detailed control over the work of others, without necessarily being able to master the work themselves (Spittler 2016; see Carrier, 'Management's Hidden Realm' this volume). This is all the truer for top corporate managers, who oversee the work of thousands or tens of thousands of employees, and it is paramount for management consultants who occupy a liminal position as they analyse and interact with several industries at once (Stein 2017: 80). Unrestricted research about managers risked undermining this fragile managerial authority, especially if the research were to uncover that managerial behaviour was poorly justified or did not conform to its professed values.

The greatest political risks, however, were linked to the *public* discourse about management consultants. The fact that my career advisor and the Office Director ultimately referred me to the HoC, despite overall support from our company's CEO, makes this clear. The HoC's trepidation about my research topic reflected an institutional fear of public critical thinking, which might compromise future project acquisition and recruiting. He considered this to be so dangerous that even individual concepts such as 'value' were simply taboo. I thus had to agree to censor my initial research topic in the light of corporate aspirations to determine the public discourse. In addition, the HoC and other colleagues anxiously monitored press releases, immediately judging them as to whether they were 'for' or 'against' my employer. This is why I eventually decided not to approach Germany's popular press to diffuse my research findings.

The frequently expressed and legally enforced value of corporate secrecy or confidentiality reflected and enshrined this fear of public critical thinking further, as most training sessions about confidentiality taught us not to bring knowledge from the inside of our company or our client companies to the outside. Most confidentiality technologies also aimed to prevent such information leakage. Even legal measures were in place, and in theory my research made many of my interviewees or interlocutors, as well as myself, liable for breach of contract. It therefore strikes me as an unfortunate coincidence of our time that calls for evermore collaboration in corporate settings coincide with the rise of confidentiality as general corporate policy.

Lastly, some moral friction also limited collaboration between the consultants, client managers and myself. As mentioned above, the values that dominated consultancy work were rationalism, respect for hierarchy, profit-oriented nihilism and the importance of form over content (see also Bogdanich and Forsythe 2022; Mazzucato and Collington 2023). Our knowledge work was also engaged in forms of market-based abstraction that ultimately facilitated decisions in which individual and public concerns were more easily subordinated to corporate ones (Stein 2017: 129).

These values of consulting stood in some contrast with those developed as part of anthropological research, as the latter tends to focus on the truthful description and appropriate theorisation of sociocultural life, as well as care for our research subjects and the public. Anthropology's descriptive and intellectual goals are thereby more abstract than those of corporate managers. When anthropologists feel compelled to take a more specific moral stance, they often try to err on the side of the powerless and the marginalised (e.g. Hale 2006; Dullo 2016). Changing roles from consultant to anthropological researcher made this moral difference obvious. It enabled me, partially, to remove myself morally from consulting as I now got to follow an alternative set of goals and values that could more easily be aligned with my personal convictions.

The importance of these epistemic, political and moral difficulties of studying corporate management is made evident by the fact that I had established myself as a company insider long before I asked for research permission. Even so, senior colleagues hesitated to allow my research to go ahead. Similarly, interview partners from different consultancy firms were eager to ensure that they be anonymised during interviews, and sometimes repeatedly asked how exactly I was going to use their answers. One, who had just started a family, eventually decided halfway through a particularly careful interview that he was in fact too busy to participate in my study. Research participants thus often feared for the good of their own company and of client companies, as well as for their own careers and the financial well-being of their families (see Mosse 2006).

Calls for more collaboration do not sufficiently address these epistemic, political and moral differences between researcher and corporate manager. My research participants were surely highly educated, reflexive and critical, to the point of teaching me how to gain research permission and mentioning Habermas in the process. However, their para-ethnographic critical faculties did not go so far as to supersede their more immediate institutional obligations. Anthropological modes of thought were often unwanted as they did not subordinate critique to business activity but dared to subject the fundamentals of business activity to critique (Stein 2017: 177).

For all those reasons, less collaboration was called for. I had been collaborating as fully as possible with my employer when I had been working for them, behaving in accordance with their key concepts, values and objectives. Establishing a research project was a means to epistemically, politically and morally distance myself from the institution. My research project reduced collaboration as it ended the near-perfect harmony of means and ends between my employer and myself. It was an act of concretely actualised alienation or partial detachment (Candea et al. 2015), which allowed me to add objectives, values, methods and concepts to my daily round beyond those of my colleagues. Ethnographic research thus came with extra-managerial and extra-corporate epistemic, political and moral goals. The fact that anthropologists frequently find themselves accused of being spies (Verdery 2018), and their history of actually being so on numerous occasions (Price and Kilman 2022), indicate that the ends of fieldwork systematically exceed those of the people we study. These differences of means and ends between the work of anthropologists and many of their research subjects are particularly stark when studying corporate management, so much so that reference to mere 'frictions' that arise in all collaborative work does not do justice to them.

Alternative Relations

What this example demonstrates is that collaboration is not a virtue in and of itself. This is especially relevant when studying corporate managers, whose job is often to engage in work that is so abstract and formalistic that it can have all kinds of content. Corporate management can be socially useful or pointless (Graeber 2018), life enhancing or a force of necro-economics (e.g. Bogdanich and Forsythe 2022), helping the natural environment or destroying it. So it is hard to justify an inherent ethical or political imperative to collaborate with corporate managers (or to stigmatise them; see Prentice this volume).

Instead, the pursuit of knowledge, and for many anthropologists the pursuit of social justice, engenders a great diversity of research relations beyond collaboration, which may be favoured on epistemic, political and moral grounds. While it may at times be desirable to collaborate with managers, it is often preferable to keep our relations with them somewhat detached, living and working alongside them without getting too involved. Such detachment can be marked by respect or mere tolerance. It may also become outright provocative in nature if anthropologists decide to make epistemic, political or moral alternatives explicit. Building lasting research relations may sometimes even be downright impossible, particularly if managers ask for too much control over our research results or if they are engaged in politically or morally questionable activity.

One way to create appropriate epistemic, political and moral relations with corporate managers beyond collaboration is to remember that anthropologists need to balance their ethical obligations to research participants with those towards colleagues and wider society (Gough 1968). In Europe, where much of my consulting activity took place, people from various backgrounds and walks of life continue to be affected every day by the work of management consultants. Consultancy projects were involved in job creation, in laying off thousands of people and in substantially changing their work routines. In all of these situations, the lives of their family members, friends and business partners may equally be transformed. Moreover, management consultants in Germany have long been shaping public policy, thereby affecting the lives of millions of citizens in yet other ways.

Given such widespread influence of managers, ethnographic work may require us to make our stance towards our research subjects less collaborative, working more with benefits for the public in mind. In these instances, anthropological research ethics may approach those of journalists, who are less driven by long-term ties with or care for their informants, and more by the pursuit of factually accurate and enlightening stories. Reorienting research in this way, and being clear about when and how it diverges from the established interests and modes of work of our interlocutors, must of course never involve harming them in the name of a vaguely defined public or scientific principle. However, it may often involve relationships that are far from collaborative.

Conclusion

Collaboration will always be part of social research. It is an unavoidable aspect of participant observation, ensuring not just our individual access to specific research settings but equally that of future researchers. Moreover, several strong epistemic, political and moral arguments exist that support collaborative activity when studying largely powerless groups or groups with whose goals and values we closely align. However, the study of corporate managers shows that collaboration is not a virtue in and of itself. Instead, the structural differences and conflicts that exist between researcher and researched constantly force us to look for other kinds of potentially appropriate relations. These differences and conflicts should not be swept under the carpet as part of post hoc attempts to create the impression of harmony between researcher and researched (Davis 2016). They go so far as to challenge the doxic status of collaboration itself.

If anthropologists studying corporate managers do not acknowledge that their relations with research participants may often be so difficult as to preclude collaboration, they may risk being accused of complicity (Weiss 2016) or 'collaborationism', which carries the connotation of desiring to cooperate with powerful social groups that have morally questionable intentions and effects (Hoffmann 1968). Anthropology has a long history of warning us against collaborationism of this kind, not just because it fosters subjectivist fears of selling out (Tett 2021), but because in times of high inequality, imperial domination and ecological destruction, collaborating with public- and private-sector organisations is morally risky (e.g. Gough 1968). Instead, fully acknowledging the frequently detached and at times even provocative nature of social research may enable us to be explicit about our ethical choices, and allow us to work towards a more coherent ethical framework for anthropology as a whole, regardless of whether we study up or down, abroad or at home. Whether and how this diversity of relations to our research subjects affects access to future field sites remains to be seen.

Acknowledgements

I thank Patrick McKearney, Desmond McNeill, Jorge Núñez, Sebastian Stein and an anonymous reviewer for comments on earlier versions of this chapter, Elin Bergstrøm for help with finalising the text, and Katerini Storeng for general support. Finalising the text was facilitated by a grant from the Norwegian Research Council (grant number 301929) and the European Research Council (grant number 101115769).

Felix Stein is an economic anthropologist working at the Anthropology department at the University of Amsterdam and at the Centre for Development and the Environment (SUM) at the University of Oslo. His 2017 ethnography of German management consultants entitled *Work, Sleep, Repeat* won the LSE Monographs First Book Competition. His recent research has focused on the moral and political aspects of global health financing. Stein is the founder of the Open Encyclopedia of Anthropology (www.anthroencyclopedia.com).

References

Abu-Lughod, Lila. 1990. 'Can There Be a Feminist Ethnography?' *Women & Performance* 5(1): 7–27.

American Anthropological Association. 2012. 'Ethics Statement'. Ethics Forum (11 Jan.). Retrieved 27 Apr. 2024 from https://ethics.americananthro.org/category/statement/.

Asad, Talal. 1973. *Anthropology and the Colonial Encounter*. London: Ithaca Press.

Bogdanich, Walt, and Michael Forsythe. 2022. *When McKinsey Comes to Town*. New York: Penguin Random House.

Boyer, Dominic, and Ulf Hannerz. 2006. 'Introduction: Worlds of Journalism'. *Ethnography* 7(1): 5–17.

Boyer, Dominic, and George E. Marcus. 2020. 'How Do We Collaborate?' in D. Boyer and G.E. Marcus (eds), *Collaborative Anthropology Today: A Collection of Exceptions*. Ithaca, NY: Cornell University Press, pp. 22–39.

Candea, Matei, Joanna Cook, Catherine Trundle and Thomas Yarrow. 2015. 'Introduction', in M. Candea, J. Cook, C. Trundle and T. Yarrow (eds), *Detachment: Essays on the Limits of Relational Thinking*. Manchester: Manchester University Press, pp. 1–34.

Carrier, James G. 2019. 'Moral Economic Anthropology'. Delivered to the Konitsa International Summer School in Anthropology, Ethnography and Comparative Folklore of the Balkans. Konitsa, 23 July.

Cervone, Emma. 2015. 'The Promises and Conundrums of Decolonized Collaboration', in Paul Sillitoe (ed.), *Indigenous Studies and Engaged Anthropology: The Collaborative Moment*. Abingdon-on-Thames: Routledge, pp. 95–114.

Chong, Kimberly. 2018. *Best Practice: Management Consulting and the Ethics of Financialization in China*. Durham, NC: Duke University Press.

Clifford, James. 1983. 'On Ethnographic Authority'. *Representations* 1(2): 118–46.

Clifford, James, and George E. Marcus (eds). 1986. *Writing Culture: The Poetics and Politics of Ethnography: A School of American Research Advanced Seminar*. Berkeley: University of California Press.

D'Amico-Samuels, Deborah. 1997. 'Undoing Fieldwork: Personal, Political, Theoretical and Methodological Implications', in Faye V. Harrison (ed.), *Decolonizing Anthropology: Moving Further Toward an Anthropology of Liberation*. Arlington, VA: Association of Black Anthropologists, American Anthropological Association, pp. 68–87.

Davis, Dana-Aín. 2016. 'Collaboration: Provocation'. Society for Cultural Anthropology (26 Sept.). Retrieved 4 Jun. 2023 from https://culanth.org/fieldsights/collaboration-provocation.

Dullo, Eduardo. 2016. 'Seriously Enough?' in James G. Carrier (ed.), *After the Crisis: Anthropological Thought, Neoliberalism and the Aftermath*. London: Routledge, pp. 133–53.

Eriksen, Thomas Hylland. 2016. *Overheating: An Anthropology of Accelerated Change*. London: Pluto Press.

Fluehr-Lobban, Carolyn. 2008. 'Collaborative Anthropology as Twenty-First-Century Ethical Anthropology'. *Collaborative Anthropologies* 1(1): 175–82.

Freedman, Lawrence. 2013. *Strategy: A History*. New York: Oxford University Press.
Gottlieb, Alma. 1995. 'Beyond the Lonely Anthropologist: Collaboration in Research and Writing'. *American Anthropologist* 97(1): 21–26.
Gough, Kathleen. 1968. 'Anthropology and Imperialism'. *Monthly Review* 19(11): 12–27.
Graeber, David. 2018. *Bullshit Jobs: A Theory*. New York: Simon & Schuster.
Hale, Charles R. 2006. 'Activist Research v. Cultural Critique: Indigenous Land Rights and the Contradictions of Politically Engaged Anthropology'. *Cultural Anthropology* 21(1): 96–120.
Haraway, Donna. 1988. 'Situated Knowledges: The Science Question in Feminism and the Privilege of Partial Perspective'. *Feminist Studies* 14(3): 575–99.
Harris, Olivia. 2007. 'What Makes People Work?' in Rita Astuti, Jonathan Parry and Charles Stafford (eds), *Questions of Anthropology*. LSE Monographs in Social Anthropology 76. Oxford: Berg, pp. 137–65.
Harrison, Faye Venetia. 1997. 'Ethnography as Politics', in F.V. Harrison (ed.), *Decolonizing Anthropology: Moving Further Toward an Anthropology of Liberation*. Arlington, VA: Association of Black Anthropologists, American Anthropological Association, pp. 88–110.
Ho, Karen. 2009. *Liquidated: An Ethnography of Wall Street*. Durham, NC: Duke University Press.
Hoffmann, Stanley. 1968. 'Collaborationism in France during World War II'. *The Journal of Modern History* 40(3): 375–95.
Holmes, Douglas R. 2013. *Economy of Words: Communicative Imperatives in Central Banks*. Chicago: University of Chicago Press.
Holmes, Douglas R., and George E. Marcus. 2006. 'Fast Capitalism: Para-ethnography and the Rise of the Symbolic Analyst', in Melissa S. Fisher and Greg Downey (eds), *Frontiers of Capital: Ethnographic Reflections on the New Economy*. Durham, NC: Duke University Press, pp. 33–57.
———. 2008. 'Collaboration Today and the Re-imagination of the Classic Scene of Fieldwork Encounter'. *Collaborative Anthropologies* 1(1): 81–101.
Howell, Signe. 2018. 'Ethnography', edited by Felix Stein. *Open Encyclopedia of Anthropology*. Retrieved 28 Apr. 2024 from https://www.anthroencyclopedia.com/printpdf/262.
Inoue, Miyako. 2009. 'Collaboration and the Subject of Anthropology', in Matsutake Worlds Research Group (ed.), 'A New Form of Collaboration in Cultural Anthropology: Matsutake Worlds', pp. 397–99. Published in *American Ethnologist* 36(2): 380–403.
Kirsch, Stuart. 2018. *Engaged Anthropology: Politics Beyond the Text*. Oakland: University of California Press.
Lassiter, Luke Eric. 2005a. 'Collaborative Ethnography and Public Anthropology'. *Current Anthropology* 46(1): 83–106.
———. 2005b. *The Chicago Guide to Collaborative Ethnography*. Chicago: University of Chicago Press.
Lévi-Strauss, Claude. 2021. *Wild Thought: A New Translation of 'La Pensée Sauvage'*, trans. Jeffrey Mehlman and John Leavitt. Chicago: University of Chicago Press.

Mahmud, Lilith. 2014. *The Brotherhood of Freemason Sisters: Gender, Secrecy, and Fraternity in Italian Masonic Lodges*. Chicago: University of Chicago Press.
Marcus, George E., and Michael M.J. Fischer. 1996. *Anthropology as Cultural Critique: An Experimental Moment in the Human Sciences* (2nd edn). Chicago: University of Chicago Press.
Mathews, Andrew S. 2020. 'Anthropology and the Anthropocene: Criticisms, Experiments, and Collaborations'. *Annual Review of Anthropology* 49: 67–82.
Maurer, Bill, and Scott D. Mainwaring. 2022. 'Anthropology with Business: Plural Programs and Future Financial Worlds'. *Journal of Business Anthropology* 1(2): 177–96.
Mazzucato, Mariana, and Rosie Collington. 2023. *The Big Con: How the Consulting Industry Weakens Our Businesses, Infantilizes Our Governments and Warps Our Economies*. New York: Random House.
Mosse, David. 2006. 'Anti-social Anthropology? Objectivity, Objection, and the Ethnography of Public Policy and Professional Communities'. *Journal of the Royal Anthropological Institute* 12(4): 935–56.
Nader, Laura. 1972. 'Up the Anthropologist: Perspectives from Studying Up', in Dell Hymes (ed.), *Reinventing Anthropology*. New York: Random House, pp. 284–311.
Osterweil, Michal. 2013. 'Rethinking Public Anthropology through Epistemic Politics and Theoretical Practice'. *Cultural Anthropology* 28(4): 598–620.
Petropoulos, Georgios. 2017. 'An Economic Review of the Collaborative Economy'. Research Report 2017/5. Brussels: Bruegel.
Pina-Cabral, João. 2020. 'When Ethics Runs Counter to Morals'. *HAU* 10(1): 50–53.
Porter, Michael. 1996. 'What Is Strategy?' *Harvard Business Review* 74(6): 61–78.
Price, David, and Michael Kilman. 2022. 'Anthropological Inquiries: Anthropology, Spies, and War'. Lordian's Laboratory. Retrieved 5 Jun. 2023 from https://loridianslaboratory.com/tag/david-price/.
Rajak, Dinah. 2011. *In Good Company: An Anatomy of Corporate Social Responsibility*. Redwood City, CA: Stanford University Press.
Rappaport, Joanne. 2008. 'Beyond Participant Observation: Collaborative Ethnography as Theoretical Innovation'. *Collaborative Anthropologies* 1(1): 1–31.
Riles, Annelise. 2015. 'From Comparison to Collaboration: Experiments with a new Scholarly and Political Reform'. *Law and Contemporary Problems* 78(1/2): 147–83.
Smith, Linda Tuhiwai. 1999. *Decolonizing Methodologies: Research and Indigenous Peoples*. London: Zed Books.
Spittler, Gerd. 2016. *Anthropologie der Arbeit* [Anthropology of work]. Wiesbaden: Springer Fachmedien.
Stacey, Judith. 1988. 'Can There Be a Feminist Ethnography?' *Women's Studies International Forum* 11(1): 21–27.
Stein, Felix. 2017. *Work, Sleep, Repeat: The Abstract Labour of German Management Consultants*. LSE Monographs on Social Anthropology 83. London: Bloomsbury.
______. 2018a. 'Anthropology's "Impact": A Comment on Audit and the Unmeasurable Nature of Critique'. *Journal of the Royal Anthropological Institute* 24(1): 10–29.

———. 2018b. 'Selling Speed: Management Consultants, Acceleration, and Temporal Angst'. *PoLAR* 41(S1): 103–17.

Stewart, Alex, and Howard Aldrich. 2015. 'Collaboration between Management and Anthropology Researchers: Obstacles and Opportunities'. *Academy of Management Perspectives* 29(2): 173–92.

Tett, Gillian. 2021. *Anthro-Vision: How Anthropology Can Explain Business and Life.* London: Random House.

Thrift, Nigel. 1997. 'The Rise of Soft Capitalism'. *Cultural Values* 1(1): 29–57.

Verdery, Katherine. 2018. *My Life as a Spy: Investigations in a Secret Police File.* Durham, NC: Duke University Press.

Walker, Harry. 2020. 'Equality without Equivalence: An Anthropology of the Common'. *Journal of the Royal Anthropological Institute* 26(1): 146–66.

Weiss, Margot. 2016. 'Collaboration: Integration'. Society for Cultural Anthropology (16 Oct.). Retrieved 5 Jun. 2023 from https://culanth.org/fieldsights/collaboration-integration.

Welker, Marina, Damani J. Partridge and Rebecca Hardin. 2011. 'Corporate Lives: New Perspectives on the Social Life of the Corporate Form: An Introduction to Supplement 3'. *Current Anthropology* 52(S3): S3–16.

Zaloom, Caitlin. 2006. *Out of the Pits: Traders and Technology from Chicago to London.* Chicago: University of Chicago Press.

Zuboff, Shoshana. 2019. *The Age of Surveillance Capitalism: The Fight for a Human Future at the New Frontier of Power*. New York: Public Affairs.

Chapter 5

Management in the Flow of Culture

Greg Urban

This chapter focuses on management in relation to culture, particularly its flow. The common view is that culture is an inheritance from the past; it is reproduced through habit (or what I will call inertia). If only inertia were operative, a firm and its employees would proceed as they had in the past, consumers would pursue their old purchasing patterns, competitors would continue their current practices, and so on. The central proposition of this chapter is that three forces, other than inertia, are at work on culture, and that managers seek to control the flow of culture by manipulating these forces. The three forces of concern here are entropy, interest and metaculture.

Culture, in the view put forth here, is whatever is socially learnt and socially transmitted. By virtue of such transmission, it moves through space and time. For example, it is transmitted over time when employees are brought into a for-profit business firm. 'On boarding' is one small part of that transmission process. However, culture also changes as it moves, though sometimes not by as much as people might think. For example, a putatively new car model may not look so different from one that it replaced (Urban, Koh and Baskin 2007). As this suggests, change in the course of cultural motion is always a matter of degree. This chapter concerns itself with the forces that bring about those changes.

Entropy, the first force, manifests itself in two ways. One is as a disordering force emanating from outside culture, as in the early 2020s pandemic, when work and consumption patterns were disrupted and changed. The other is creativity, when innovation occurs within an existing line of cultural flow, as research into magnetism in the 1980s contributed to the development of the iPod music player early in the 2000s

(Kahney 2004; McCray 2009), which in turn fuelled development of the smartphone (Zahran 2022).

The second force, interest, manifests itself as attraction to or repulsion from the culture in question, which translates into demand and affects the price of commodities. While interest affects commodified flows of culture (that is, the sale and purchase of goods or services in market transactions), it also affects non-commodified flows (that is, those occurring in the absence of explicit sales and purchases). An example is 'The Rachel', which has its own Wikipedia entry; it is a women's hairstyle that spread in the 1990s owing to the interest it attracted when an actress wore it in a popular US television series.

The distinction between commodified (or market-based) transactions and non-commodified exchanges is relevant to understanding Coase's (1937) economic theory of the firm, which holds that firms exist to reduce transaction costs associated with market-based exchange. It is central also in research within anthropology and adjacent disciplines, where things are viewed as moving over time in and out of their state as commodities, although the term 'commoditisation' is often used instead of 'commodification' (Appadurai 1986; Kopytoff 1986).

The final force, metaculture, is the one most readily available to managers but also the one to which they are most vulnerable, as I shall argue. Metaculture moves through the world just like other culture, but it is about other culture and can impart its own force to it, as well as direct other forces to it, thereby affecting its flow. A good example is a CEO's idea of what a firm is and should be doing. It can be articulated in speech and documents directed at employees, and passed on to larger audiences through media interviews and the like. Such articulated visions are perhaps the most important tools at a manager's disposal.

Managerial control is embodied in the directives or commands the manager issues, which are quintessential metaculture and are an essential component in Weber's ([1956] 1978: 215ff.) definition of authority as the legitimate exercise of domination, which itself is 'the probability that a command with a given specific content will be obeyed by a given group of persons' (ibid.: 53). Commands are pieces of culture, but because they are also about conduct, especially habituated conduct, they impart a force to that conduct. It is important to recognise that managerial directives are not always imperative statements, even though they have that function. For managers regarded as legitimate, the most effective directives often are the most subtle.

In what follows, I first outline the position and key tasks of managers within market-based flows of culture. I then look at cases of managerial intervention in cultural flows in relation to the forces at work on them.

Managing Market-Based Cultural Flows

In a market economy, a firm exists in the context of consumers and other firms. The simplest representation of cultural flows within such a system could thus be depicted in Figure 6.1.

In that figure, arrows indicate back and forth cultural flows, both commodified and non-commodified. Solid arrows indicate cultural flows that the firm's managers can attempt to affect, between: (1) the firm and its consumers; (2) the firm and other firms; and (3) the firm and its broader environment, including governmental and non-governmental organisations and the non-human world to the extent that it reacts to the firm's activities. The dashed lines indicate flows that are only indirectly susceptible to management, as, for example, when Apple's advertising campaign portrayed PCs as 'uncool', attempting to direct customer interest away from Windows-based computers (Cox 2017). Managers also affect flows within the firm. Like the non-commodified flows between firms and customers that are the primary concern of this chapter, these flows, typically, are non-commodified (that is, they do not involve direct market-based buying and selling), and they make possible the coordination and direction necessary for the production of goods and services in the firm.

I assume that firms produce commodities that are or will be attractive to consumers. In my terms, they tap into the force of interest, which

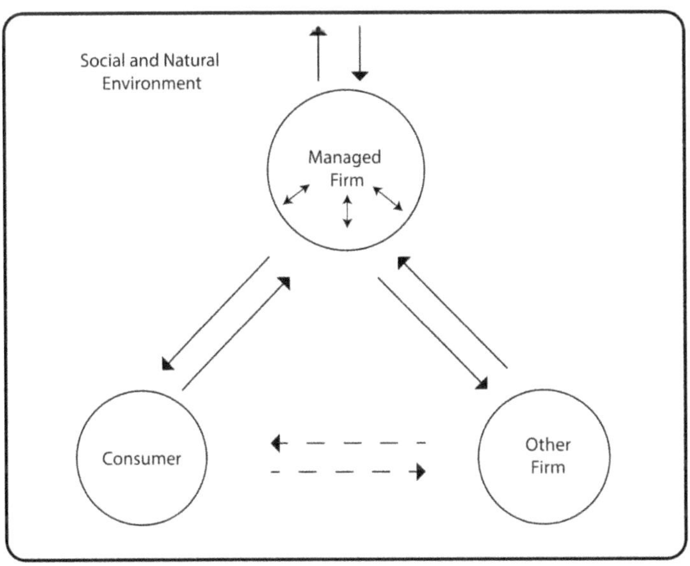

Figure 5.1. A scheme of cultural flows © Greg Urban

they use in order to modify the inertial (habitual) motion of cultural forms. Among other things, this means that management involves managing relations with competitor firms. Where competition is intense, it means directing the firm in a way that differentiates its cultural forms from those of its competitors. Lowering prices is one way of doing this. Another important one is copying the culture carried by other firms and their products in order to make use of the force of interest into which those firms have already tapped. Such copying is a form of cultural motion that generally is non-commodified.

The approach taken here treats objects, as well as cultural behaviours, as artefacts of cultural forms. Individual objects, such as the specific iPhone that I own, are artefacts of the iPhone as cultural form. In general, the goods or services produced by firms are artefacts of replicable cultural forms, and it is through interaction with the artefacts that cultural forms flow through the world.

From the perspective of this chapter, that flow takes place through replication, which occurs with greater or lesser variation. It occurs at points where interactions with the artefacts of the form produced by others take place. This happens, as I will show, when one company copies aspects of the product (viewed as a cultural form) from another company. It also happens, for example, when an individual learns from another how to use some aspect of a product (say an iPhone), whether the learning takes place face-to-face or through videos or by other means. Of course, culture also passes between people through a company's product itself – for example, when someone uses a product for a purpose engineered into the product by the company, such as taking a photograph with an iPhone.

In the following sections I take up a series of cases involving a firm's management of cultural flows. The first case, Boston Scientific, focuses on the role of non-commodified cultural flow from consumers to the company. The second case concerns a firm's innovations that undergo non-commodified replication by competing firms, the companies in this second case being Xerox, Apple and Microsoft. The third case involves the invention at General Motors of the multidivisional form of organisation or 'M-form', and its non-commodified dissemination to other companies. The final case, focusing especially on Boeing, concerns the spread of a metacultural idea, the idea that firms exist for the sole purpose of making profits that will benefit their shareholders, often referred to as 'shareholder value theory'. Everything else they do is a means to that end.

Non-commodified Cultural Flow from Consumers to Firm

John Abele is co-founder and former director of Boston Scientific and he is central to the development of the modern steerable catheter (Urban 2016, 2018). His story is a tale of two cultural flows, one commodified (the sale and purchase of catheters), the other non-commodified (the passage of information between medical doctors and Abele). The driving force behind each was interest. Doctors and hospitals wanted the catheters that Abele's company made; the company, in turn, needed the knowledge and experience of the doctors in order to develop and improve their product.

As a socially transmitted cultural form, the catheter has a venerable past, dating back to the Greco-Roman world (Moog, Karenberg and Moll 2005). Abele's own involvement with catheters dates to 1969, when he linked up with Itzhak Bentov, who had invented a device that could be steered through winding passageways such as blood vessels, and the two of them founded Medi-Tech Incorporated. It was the forerunner of Boston Scientific, which Abele, along with Peter Nicholas, co-founded in 1979. Abele's initial job in the company was project manager; in the language of this chapter that means stimulating the flow of the new steerable catheter as a commodified cultural form.

How did the new device originate? Bentov's invention built on an existing line of cultural flow, as small creatively (as opposed to randomly) entropic occurrences nudged the inertial flows in new directions. By 1968, Bentov had applied for a patent for the device, and the patent application explains the problem that it was intended to solve:

> Catheters must be introduced into blood vessels which branch out in different directions requiring some control means to direct the catheter into one of several possible passage ways after the catheter has been introduced into a straight section of the blood vessel. Uncontrolled tubes acting as catheters have been used in some applications, but misdirection of the catheter tips often occurs. (Bentov 1971)

The application mentions eleven prior US patents and two foreign ones. The oldest one is from 1878, which is for 'Improvement in India Rubber Surgical Tubes', but it says little about use, comparing the invention only to 'catheters, stomach tubes, &c.' (Lockwood 1878). However, it does mention that prior tubes were 'objectionable because of the square corners formed by cutting the eyes, causing irritation' (ibid.: 1). In other words, like Bentov's, Lockwood's invention had to do with insertion of the catheters.

Bentov's 1971 application, like the two immediately preceding patents (Edwards 1968; Almén 1970), referred to the device's use in navigating blood vessels. The innovations proposed by all three inventors were apparently in response to developments in medical practice, and in Bentov's case physicians at Beth Israel Hospital in Boston initially requested that he develop a new device. Medical practice was driving the need for a new technology.

A key event in medical practice before those three patents was the successful clearing of a blocked or severely constricted femoral artery in an 82-year-old woman who had refused surgery. Dr Charles Dotter, a radiologist, performed the procedure on 16 January 1964 (Rösch, Keller and Kaufman 2003: 841), thereby giving birth to the field called 'interventional radiology'. This was not a sub-speciality of surgery, a fact that was important for subsequent developments. This was more than four-and-a-half years before Bentov applied for his patent, and more than six-and-a-half years before it was granted (Bentov 1971).

Abele appeared on the scene just when a flood of interest had developed in this kind of procedure and, in particular, in navigating greater distances and with greater ease through blood vessels. His job, as he described it, was to talk to numerous doctors, not only to tell them about Medi-Tech's new device but also to find out problems they wanted to see addressed: the doctors 'gave an enormous amount of their time to teach me. But I reciprocated and provided them with information they might never have had otherwise' (in Urban 2018: 331). Abele was, in effect, intervening in the flow of culture, moving information between doctors and the firm, enabling the firm to improve the devices to better meet the doctors' needs.

The management of these interest-driven flows would soon become challenging, however, because the catheters were increasingly used for procedures that had been the bailiwick of surgeons. In truth, the challenge had manifested itself back in 1964 when Dotter had performed his first procedure using catheters. Although the patient had improved after the procedure, her pain easing and her ability to walk returning, Dotter's 'sceptical surgical colleagues kept the patient in the hospital under observation for several weeks, expecting the dilated artery to thrombose' (Rösch, Keller and Kaufman 2003: 841).

In other words, Dotter's new speciality, interventional radiology, and the cultural flow that it enabled, ran up against the inertial flow of medical practice within surgery. Part of the resistance from surgeons was likely bound up with issues of professional identity grounded in habitual practice (i.e. inertia). Surgeons were those who cut people open with scalpels in order to repair problems inside the body; they did not stick tubes into people, which was the province of other medical specialities.

Abele's problem was how to get the new technology that his company developed into the repertoire of surgeons. The solution turned out to hinge, again, on managing non-commodified cultural flows. That meant convincing a small set of surgeons to try it out and then spread the word (cultural flow) through conversations with other surgeons and publications. The result was something of a revolution and, indeed, Abele himself called the company's new technology 'disruptive'. Minimally invasive surgery caught on, and with it, Boston Scientific grew.

Abele's genius was in managing non-commodified cultural flows, talking to and learning from doctors, imparting what he learnt from them to others, using their insights to direct his company to build the devices they wanted and needed, and then convincing others, especially surgeons, that his company's devices could help them despite their initial resistance. That managing these non-commodified flows produced rapidly increasing commodified flows in the market seemed almost a by-product of Abele's work.

The story of John Abele and Boston Scientific is perhaps unique. The co-founder of Apple, Steve Jobs, showed little interest in finding out what his potential customers wanted, saying that they 'don't know what they want until we've shown them' (Isaacson 2011: 143). Still, Jobs was also a master manager of non-commodified cultural flow, aligning his company and products with an image of 'cool' that was itself of interest, and attractive to many potential customers. While Abele's managerial approach was listening and learning, then giving back both in commodified and non-commodified ways, Jobs's sensitivity to cultural flow may have been an embodied sensibility that resonated with many consumers.

Non-commodified Cultural Flow between Firms Affecting a Firm's Product

I know someone who had worked at Xerox headquarters early in the 1980s, a time when its offices were equipped with Xerox Star workstations. That computer had an icon-based desktop, a mouse, access to inter-computer networking, file sharing, remote printing, and more. The workstation had appeared in 1981, three years before Apple's Macintosh. According to several Xerox Star designers, the Macintosh and its predecessor, the Lisa, drew heavily on what the Apple designers had seen of the Xerox machine (Johnson et al. 1989: 26). Such inter-firm borrowing (replication with variation), in this case of the icon-based graphical user interface and the desktop metaphor, is an example of non-commodified flow between firms affecting commodified flows of a firm's product.

Xerox PARC, a research centre established in 1970, was a hub of innovation in microcomputer systems at the time. In 1973 it produced the Alto, the first microcomputer to run a graphical user interface, with the Star a later iteration. According to the Star's designers, one influence on it was Sketchpad, a computer program written by Ivan Sutherland ([1963] 2003) as part of his MIT doctoral dissertation. In their introduction to the archival version of the dissertation, Alan Blackwell and Kerry Rodden (in ibid.: 3) wrote: 'After 40 years, ideas introduced in Sketchpad still influence how every computer user thinks about computing. It made fundamental contributions in the area of human–computer interaction, being one of the first graphical user interfaces'.

The Xerox designers (Johnson et al. 1989: 21) trace the root of the inspiration for the Xerox Star to a 1945 article by Vannevar Bush, in *The Atlantic*:

> Consider a future device for individual use, which is a sort of mechanized private file and library. It needs a name, and, to coin one at random, 'memex' will do. A memex is a device in which an individual stores all his books, records, and communications, and which is mechanized so that it may be consulted with exceeding speed and flexibility. It is an enlarged intimate supplement to his memory.
>
> It consists of a desk, and while it can presumably be operated from a distance, it is primarily the piece of furniture at which he works. On the top are slanting translucent screens, on which material can be projected for convenient reading. There is a keyboard, and sets of buttons and levers. Otherwise, it looks like an ordinary desk. (Bush 1945)

It seems like the flow of culture in regard to the computerised graphical user interface had been going on for at least two decades prior to the Macintosh. As with the catheter, here we have inertial motion modified over time by creative entropic force.

The Xerox designers (Johnson et al. 1989: 21) note that the development of the Star was shaped by 'key designers changing jobs or applying concepts from their graduate research to products'. In other words, non-commodified culture moved between organisations through the movement of people, as well as by direct interactions with artefacts of a cultural form, as when Apple's designers saw the Xerox Star at a computer conference.

So how was management involved in the non-commodified flow of cultural forms between firms? The managers of the firms had at least two options: they might pay close attention to their competitors and attempt to copy aspects of what they were doing, or they might try to protect the developments in their own firm from copying by others.

During the 1970s and early 1980s, Steve Jobs was the manager who directed Apple's product development, and he did so with an eye to other firms. In 1979, Jobs and Apple engineers visited Xerox PARC. Paul Kay, a Xerox PARC engineer who worked on the Star and who was present for the visit, noted that this was nothing unusual: '[M]any people (perhaps even a thousand or more) had seen live demos of the Alto and Smalltalk before Steve [Jobs] … we were a relatively open lab for visiting colleagues and other interested people (like Herbie Hancock and Al Gore)' (Kay 2017).

The other possibility mentioned above, endeavouring to protect the firm's products from being copied, emerged later, after Jobs had been forced out of Apple in 1985. Here is a brief version of the story.

The icon-based microcomputer desktop with files and folders became, as a cultural form, identified with the Macintosh, despite the prior existence of the Xerox Star. Meanwhile, Microsoft decided to undertake its own replication (with variation) of the Xerox–Apple type of interface so that it could be run on non-Apple PCs. In 1985 Microsoft released Windows 1.0, which resembled the Mac interface so closely that it 'alarmed a number of individuals at Apple because they believed that Microsoft had stolen several design elements of the Mac operating system. Apple threatened to sue' (Thomson Reuters Legal 2019). However, the resemblance was in fact superficial, and the lawsuit never materialised.

Two years later Microsoft released Windows 2.0, which 'contained even more design elements copied straight from the Macintosh operating system' (Thomson Reuters Legal 2019). This time Apple opted to sue, focused on 'copyrights Apple held for the way information is presented and controlled on Macintosh screens', with an Apple spokesperson stating that 'Apple is serious about protecting its audiovisual display' (Pollack 1988: Section D, p. 3). The case lasted until 1995, when the US Supreme Court declined to hear an appeal of a judgment against Apple (Thomson Reuters Legal 2019). The cultural form in question was the 'look and feel' of the Macintosh visual display (US District Court 1992). All of this, of course, was long after the creation of the Xerox Star workstation, the Apple Macintosh computer and even Microsoft Windows software.

What does this tell us about the role of management in such flows of culture? It suggests that cultural forms will be copied and replicated, driven by the attractive force those forms kindle, unless that copying is constrained. Management's job is to decide in what measure to pursue inter-firm borrowing of cultural forms in order to enhance the firm's products, and in what measure to pursue lawsuits in attempts to prevent others from borrowing from it. As the Xerox–Apple–Microsoft story indicates, such cultural flows are powerful, and far from easily constrained.

Non-commodified Flow of a Firm's Organisational Form

What Alfred DuPont Chandler (1962: 42–51) called the multidivisional enterprise is a replicable cultural form. Chandler said: 'An enterprise can be said to have adopted the new form if it came to have a general office with executives whose primary tasks were general rather than functional, and if it also had at least two major multidepartmental, relatively autonomous divisions' (ibid.: 325).

In practice this meant a company with an organisational chart like that of General Motors as it had developed in the 1920s, when the company's different automobile lines came to be treated as semi-independent divisions, their interrelations coordinated under a general office. Chandler's (1962: 10) schematic drawing of a multidivisional structure has a box at the top labelled 'General Office' and a line connecting it to a horizontal segment to which are attached three additional boxes, each labelled 'Division', 'Product Line' or 'Region'. The drawing gave a highly abstract picture of GM's organisation in a form that could readily travel to other companies.

Chandler studied the historical origin of the form at General Motors and DuPont. In DuPont's case, the M-form developed in response to increasing product diversification. For its first century DuPont was a manufacturer of gunpowder, with a tightly centralised organisation that has come to be termed the unitary form (U-form). DuPont began to diversify early in the twentieth century, which created pressures on the U-form that, in Chandler's account, led to its changing to the M-form as distinct product lines were gradually given greater autonomy.

The history at General Motors ran in the other direction. Out of the decentralised holding company founded by William Durant in 1908, GM developed a multidivisional form giving direction to the separate companies that Durant had acquired. In the words of Alfred P. Sloan ([1963] 1990: 5), architect of the multidivisional form at General Motors, in Durant's early company '[t]he old companies [that Durant had bought] retained their corporate and independent operating identities in the new one, which was a holding company – that is, a central office surrounded by autonomously operating satellites'. Sloan set out to coordinate operations of the old companies under a general office while allowing them considerable autonomy.

From the perspective of this chapter, the organisational form of a company is like other cultural forms. It tends to persist through time, swept along by inertia, unless some other force deflects it from its path. At DuPont in 1919, the centralising pattern persisted despite the company's diversification. At General Motors in 1919, the individual companies persisted in their independence. In Chandler's narrative, it was the economic downturn of 1920 that led managers in both companies to implement new organisational forms. In the language of forces, the flow of inertial managerial culture was disrupted by entropy. For Chandler, it was product and geographical diversification that led most firms to adopt the M-form, rather than managers' interest in copying the success of other firms.

Chandler's work offers insights into managers who engage in interfirm borrowing of organisational form. A striking example is the Ford Motor Company, which had dominated the automobile market in the United States from 1918 to 1927, when GM surpassed it. Highly centralised during that period, Ford's managerial organisation was built around Henry Ford, and Stefan Link (2018: 88) refers to the company during that period as a 'charismatic organization' built around the aura of Henry Ford as leader. In 1945, however, leadership passed to Ford's grandson, Henry Ford II, who reorganised the company.

To do so, he turned to GM. At Ford 'in 1946, executives [hired away] from General Motors began to rebuild the company by, in *Fortune*'s words, "clapping the GM organizational garment onto the Ford manufacturing frame, trimming the garment here and filling out the frame there. Nobody around Ford makes any bones about this"' (Chandler 1962: 46, quoting Fortune 1947: 88). Henry Ford II appointed a former GM vice president, Ernest Breech, to the position of executive vice president: 'Four of Ford's newest appointees to top posts are former GM men – Harold Youngren, engineering; Lewis D. Crusoe, planning and control; Del Harder, operations; and James W. Irwin, public relations' (Fortune 1947: 88). Ford counted on their past patterns of management within GM to redirect the flow of Ford's organisational practices towards the multidivisional form.

The practices and form could also be observed at a distance, and efforts were made to replicate them. The observations might be made through materials put out by the observed firm, by media accounts or by interaction with individuals in the other firm. An example of this is the International Harvester Company. According to Chandler (1962: 371), Fowler McCormick, who became president of the company in 1941, 'had a strong interest in organisation. After a detailed examination both of the company's needs and of the General Motors experience, International Harvester shifted in 1943 from a centralized, functionally departmentalised organisation to a decentralized, multidivisional one'. Chandler does not indicate how Fowler McCormick examined General Motors, but in an archive of McCormick's papers I found a file labelled 'Organization of other companies, 1943–1951' in a series on 'Organization Research' (Wisconsin Historical Society).

Since Chandler's pioneering research, considerable attention has been paid to the M-form and its spread (Linden and Teece 2018). One of the developments relevant to my focus here is the 'imitation hypothesis', which Vijay Mahajan, Subhash Sharma and Richard A. Bettis (1988: 1188) characterise as follows: 'an innovation which offers increased profit without disproportionately increased risk, and that cannot be isolated from competitors (e.g. by patents or other barriers), will be rapidly adopted by the relevant population of firms'. The M-form has been considered such an innovation. The authors, however, provide a statistical argument that the economic version of the imitation hypothesis, based on technological innovations, may not apply to the M-form.

This brief look at the multidivisional form reveals the operation of three of the four main forces affecting its motion through time and space. Managers at General Motors and DuPont had to cope with and respond to entropic force, the random downturn in the economy in 1920. Rather than going with inertial flow, they developed the multidivisional organisational form. At Ford and International Harvester, managers were motivated by interest in emulating the market success of General Motors, and they endeavoured to copy the new multidivisional form. At Ford this happened by bringing in GM executives already habituated (inertia) in the new form. At International Harvester the copying took place through the new president's study of GM, and then implementing something similar in his own company.

A fourth force, one not yet mentioned, is metaculture or reflective force. While this force is a focus in the next section, evidence suggests its presence in the spread of the M-form. Metaculture is culture that is about other culture. In the case studied here, it is an abstract idea coded in a name (multidivisional organisation). The name is associated with a succinct description, such as Chandler supplied (1962: 335), as well as a schematic drawing or abstract organisational chart (ibid.: 10). The abstract metacultural formulation itself can attract interest and can travel independently at the behest of interest in the absence of direct inter-firm borrowing. That interest can take different forms.

Greg Linden and David J. Teece (2018: 1043) report that studies in the US and UK show that adopting M-form increases profitability, while studies in Germany and Japan do not. If not clearly leading to greater profitability, why did the M-form get adopted? One reason may be that people were attracted to it as a metacultural form. Evidence suggests that this was the case for the immediate post-Communist period in the Czech Republic. Ed Clark and Anna Soulsby (1999: 535) report that the M-form spread widely there during that period, but for reasons that 'had little or nothing to do with growth strategies such as diversification'. Rather, managers adopted the M-form idea 'because of the legitimacy and rationality with which it endowed the process of restructuring' (ibid.: 551). Correspondingly, the idea's adoption was a way to demonstrate that these managers and their enterprises 'had travelled a long way from old state Socialist management', and that they had 'established visible links with the new market-economic order, with its emphasis on decentralized, independent decision making' (ibid.: 555).

This raises the possibility that the M-form is a fad comparable to the Rachel haircut, and that it may lose popularity over time. Indeed, some saw a new form, the organisation matrix, emerging among large global corporations in the 1990s (Bartlett and Ghoshall 1993: 24). Because of that, Richard Bettis (1991: 316) argued that studying the M-form amounted to studying 'organizational fossils'. Not everyone concurs, however. Linden and Teece (2018: 1045), for example, write: 'Most indications are that the M-form organisation will continue to dominate the global landscape for the foreseeable future'. Even if some substantial portion of the M-form's spread were driven by managers' interest in a metacultural idea, the consequences of taking up that idea and endeavouring to implement it can be significant and lasting.

In comparing the inter-firm borrowing of the graphical user interface with the spread of the M-form, it is noteworthy that managers at Apple and Xerox launched lawsuits to claim ownership of the cultural form; I know of no legal claims to ownership of the multidivisional form. In the graphical user interface case, which dealt with the artefact through which the culture flowed, the lawsuits ultimately failed. The form escaped commodification.

In the multidivisional organisation case, however, a type of commodification did occur, as management consultants made money out of it. As consultants they earned fees, thereby capturing and partially commodifying the form as metaculture (see, e.g., Chandler 1962: 381–82). For example, Clark and Soulsby (1999: 548) remark that managers in the Czech Republic 'engaged the services of western and western-trained consultants, and absorbed the burgeoning literature on western management'. Outside experts, then, could suggest changes in the organisational form, for a fee. The managers would then decide whether to accept the suggested changes and, if so, how to implement them. If the suggestions involved special training, consultants would provide that training, again for a fee. The consultants thus act as teachers, purveying a metaculture that in turn shapes the purchasing firm's organisational culture. The phenomenon is one I have experienced, as a teacher acting as a consultant.

Non-commodified Inter-firm Metacultural Flow about the Purpose of Firms

The firm as form is a cultural entity made up of cultural practices. If managers generally see the purpose of a firm in roughly the same way, then 'the firm' behaves like a free-flowing, non-commodified metacultural form.

A notable influence on that form is an article written by an economist, Milton Friedman, which appeared in *The New York Times Magazine* in 1970. The article has been widely read and its central message even more widely disseminated. That message is summed up in its title: 'The social responsibility of business is to increase its profits'. In other words, it is a metacultural directive that says that managers should concentrate on making profits for the firm's stockholders. Shareholder value is distinguishable from the broader idea of a for-profit corporation. The former is an economic idea, but also a moral and ethical stance, that the best results for society ensue if corporate leaders focus exclusively on making profits for their shareholders, rather than on the corporation itself or its products or consumers, or even human life more generally.

As a metacultural form, those exposed to Friedman's message need not buy a newspaper or book, but could receive it from another individual, such as a fellow business person, a teacher or a neighbour. Such replication (with variation) can be glimpsed, for example, in an article by Chris Myers, which appeared in the magazine *Forbes* in 2016. He writes: 'When I was younger, I subscribed to the apocryphal quote attributed to famed economist Milton Friedman: "There is one and only one social responsibility of business – to increase its profits"' (Myers 2016). He calls the quote apocryphal because he searched for its source and 'discovered that it was part of a much broader statement made by Friedman to *The New York Times* in 1970: "[T]here is one and only one social responsibility of business – to use its resources and engage in activities designed to increase its profits so long as it stays within the rules of the game, which is to say, engages in open and free competition without deception or fraud"' (the first part of Myers's quote replicates what Friedman wrote, but the rest is a condensed paraphrase).

Why did Friedman's snippet of metaculture attract such interest? One factor may have been the article's rhetorical force. Amidst the charged political atmosphere of the Cold War, coupled with the countercultural movement in the US, Friedman wrote that when

> businessmen speak eloquently about the 'social responsibilities of business in a free-enterprise system', ... [i]n fact they are – or would be if they or anyone else took them seriously – preaching pure and unadulterated socialism. Businessmen who talk this way are unwitting puppets of the intellectual forces that have been undermining the basis of a free society these past decades. (Friedman 1970: 379)

The message here and echoed elsewhere in his article is that those who manage their companies with concern for the company's social responsibilities are not responsible capitalists. They are socialists, readily associated in the public mind with communism. The rhetoric behind Friedman's answer to the question 'what is the purpose of a firm' helped to catapult the message into the political arena.

Friedman (1970: 427, quoting Friedman 1962: 133) took this step himself, saying that the idea of management having a social responsibility beyond profit was '"a fundamentally subversive doctrine" in a free society'. The Soviet Union at the time was the archetype of unfreedom, symbolised by the Berlin Wall. Moreover, Friedman campaigned for the Republican candidate Barry Goldwater in the 1964 presidential election. According to Friedman's biographer, 'participation in the 1964 Goldwater campaign was his first major step in becoming a national public figure' (Ebenstein 2007: 169).

It was later, however, that, as advisor to popular US president Ronald Reagan and long-serving British prime minister Margaret Thatcher, his ideas came to affect public policy (Ebenstein 2007: 205–14). Reagan and Thatcher supported his message regarding the exclusive focus on making profits for shareholders, and it spread from them to others. The non-commodified flow of the message as a metacultural form was propelled by the interests of its political senders; business people listened to it with interest; ordinary citizens could not help but hear it.

Although non-commodified, that message had the potential to affect commodified flows, as in the case of Boeing, as told by Peter Robison in *Flying Blind: The 737 Max and the Fall of Boeing*. He says that 'from the New Deal of the 1930s to the Great Society of the 1960s', a communitarian consensus regarding the economy had prevailed in the United States (Robison 2021: 8). That 'consensus was just starting to fray when Milton Friedman, the Reaganites' favourite economist, argued what was then the contrarian viewpoint in *The New York Times Magazine* in 1970: "The social responsibility of business is to increase its profit"'.

It is worth noting that some of America's past industrialists espoused views contrary to Friedman's. Consider these quotes attributed to Henry Ford (in Anderson 2013):

> There is one rule for the industrialist and that is: make the best quality goods possible at the lowest cost possible, paying the highest wages possible.
>
> A business that makes nothing but money is a poor business.
>
> A business absolutely devoted to service will have only one worry about profits: they will be embarrassingly large.

Evidently, the cultural form that Friedman had fashioned was in competition with, and by the 1980s was displacing, others. Boeing illustrates that displacement. Once an icon of aeronautical innovation run by engineers motivated to make the best and safest products, the company's management changed its priorities in the 1990s. They decided to focus on pleasing shareholders, even if that meant ignoring their products and customers. How did this happen?

Robison tells the story, starting with the tragedies. On 29 October 2018, a Boeing 737 Max 8 passenger plane operated by Lion Air, and carrying 189 people, left Jakarta, Indonesia. Twelve minutes later it crashed into the sea, killing all those aboard. Then, on 10 March 2019, another Boeing 737 Max 8, this time operated by Ethiopian Airlines, and with 157 people aboard, crashed shortly after take-off. In both cases, software had taken control of the plane away from the pilots, angling the planes straight down.

The software involved in the crashes, in Robison's narrative, originated in cost-cutting, often despite the objections of engineers. In fact, cost-cutting was the motivation for the 737 Max in the first place. Rather than design a new plane to replace the older 737, Boeing's top managers opted for a cheaper solution: give the old plane yet another facelift. They would install new, more powerful engines on the old frame. The more powerful engines, however, interfered with the plane's aerodynamics. Under certain conditions the nose of the plane would tend to veer upward, and software was developed to solve the problem. It would angle the nose of the plane downward in order to correct for the upward veering.

The software, in place on the two crashed planes, required sensors to detect the conditions under which it should activate. If a sensor failed, the pilots would need to know what to do, which meant that they would need training. That would be expensive, and would require flight simulators, which would also be expensive. To cut costs, potential problems with the software and with the vulnerability of the sensors to failure appear to have been downplayed. In fact, reference to the existence of the software was removed from the operating manual (Robison 2021: 231).

How could a company built around engineering excellence have let this happen? For Robison, the explanation comes back to the company's focus on pleasing shareholders rather than making safe and useful products. How precisely did that mentality come about? How did the metacultural form propounded by Friedman come to colonise the minds of Boeing's managers?

Robison (2021: 8) initially links the Boeing case to Friedman's dictum, though Friedman drops out of the remaining narrative. His place is assumed by Jack Welch, former CEO of General Electric. Under Welch, General Electric aimed single-mindedly at profits for shareholders, and became the model for top management in other companies. David Gelles (2022: 6–7) says that 'Welch was the embodiment of the shareholder primacy dogma hatched by Milton Friedman'. He (ibid.: 40) says that 'whether or not Welch read Milton Friedman's original texts, there is no doubt about the source of his inspiration'. In fact, neither an earlier book about Welch (O'Boyle 1999) nor Welch's autobiography (Welch and Byrne 2001) mentions Friedman. The dictum, as metacultural form, seems to have reached Welch through the widespread dissemination of its message at the time.

There can be little doubt that the metacultural form arrived at Boeing through inter-firm copying. Just as Ford hired executives from General Motors, so Boeing hired executives from General Electric. They would embody the Jack Welch management style, which in turn made the abstract Friedman dictum concrete. Harry Stonecipher was a vice president and then division manager at GE, and was 'a driven protégé of Jack Welch' (Robison 2021: 52). Hired in 1994 as CEO by the McDonell Douglas Company, he arrived at Boeing when the two companies merged a few years later. In 1997 he became Boeing's president, and then in 2003 its CEO. He was succeeded in 2006 by James McNerney.

It was McNerney who presided over almost the entire development phase of the 737 Max. He had worked for General Electric from the early 1980s until Welch's retirement in 2001, at which time McNerney became CEO of the 3M Company and joined Boeing's board (Robison 2021: 91). McNerney's successor in 2015, Dennis Muilenberg, a Boeing insider who had led the company during the initial years of the 737 Max, was removed from office in 2019 after the second of the two crashes. His replacement was another Welch protégé, David Calhoun, who at that time was Boeing's chairman. Robison (ibid.: 242) quotes the description of Calhoun by Welch's speechwriter as 'the guy who was really the most like Jack'. Evidently, the Welch management style was the inertial culture at Boeing.

Friedman's dictum, as I have described it, is a metacultural form capable of travelling through the world via processes of replication. It tells managers how to conceptualise the companies they manage, and what to do in order to manage them. General Electric, under Jack Welch, was the Friedman dictum incarnate. Reflecting on Boeing as it exists today, Robison writes: 'Like Jack Welch's General Electric before it, Boeing became a collection of assets to be shuffled as managers saw fit to make the most beneficial combination for shareholders, not for customers or employees' (Robison 2021: 260). After reading *Flying Blind*, a former Boeing manager with whom I spoke put it this way: 'I drank the Kool-Aid'.

Conclusion

As the preceding cases illustrate, business managers negotiate a bewildering range of non-commodified cultural flows in their efforts to bring about the flow of commodities. In the case of Boston Scientific, the non-commodified flows were in the form of words exchanged with doctors and other medical practitioners. Those words shaped the company's commodities, which in turn brought about increasing commodity flows and the company's growth. The flows in the case of the graphical user interface were between firms. Apple's copying (with variation) from Xerox and Microsoft's copying (with variation) from Apple contributed to extraordinary commodity flows. Those flows in turn changed habituated practices in countless areas of daily life around the world.

For General Motors, the impact of entropic force (economic downturn) precipitated changes in the inertial organisational form of the company. Other companies, familiar with the commodity flows that came after the change in form, sought to replicate it. As the form spread, it grew more abstract, a metacultural idea that could be represented in a simple drawing and a succinct description. No longer a matter of directly copying another firm, the form took on a life of its own as metaculture that could be manifest in different companies for different purposes. In the Czech case, it became a sign of Western capitalism, distinguishing firms from their prior forms under Communism.

The cases explored in this chapter, and especially the final one, also reveal something else: the extent to which managers not only recognise cultural flows and struggle to manage them, but also are themselves immersed in and buffeted by them. The buffeting occurs because it is so difficult to gain awareness of the flows. Sometimes, in fact, it may be more appropriate to speak of having a feel for the flow of a cultural form rather than a conscious understanding of it. Having such a feel may have been true in Steve Jobs's case, when he said that potential customers did not know what they wanted until Apple showed them. This contrasts sharply with John Abele at Boston Scientific. Because Abele was not himself a medical professional, he had to rely on them to guide the development of his products. Jobs, however, was himself immersed in the technological flows he had helped to shape. He could rely on his own intuitive feel.

In the Boeing case, the cultural form was one of consciousness, an articulated idea about the purpose of business firms. It is not a form from which one can readily step back and view from the outside, the way that Abele beheld cultural flows within the medical profession as an outsider. As a form of consciousness, the articulated idea shapes how managers understand the firms that they manage and how they comprehend their own purpose in the world. The robotic application of the Friedman dictum to commodity production in the Boeing case had tragic consequences, which none of the company's managers had intended. They undoubtedly believed that making decisions in terms of what kept the stock price rising would produce desirable results for everyone in the end. In such cases, we might say that the metacultural flow shapes the manager rather than that the manager shapes the flow.

The widespread replication of linguistically articulated metacultural ideas, like Friedman's, presents perhaps the most daunting challenge for managers: how to recognise when their own understanding of the world is part of a management fad that rides a wave of popularity, crests, and then finally crashes on the shore of reality.

Acknowledgements

This chapter relies for background understanding on my interactions with hundreds of business managers over the past two decades. In some cases, this has been through research and consulting projects, as well as personal acquaintances. In others, it has been through my teaching at the University of Pennsylvania in Wharton's Executive Education programmes and in the Graduate School of Education's Chief Learning Officer programme. Over the years, numerous executives have also generously given of their time to visit my Anthropology of Corporations class at Pennsylvania. I have learnt a great deal from all of these experiences, for which I am most grateful. Special thanks go to Nancy Ameen, who conducted literature reviews and other background research for this chapter, and who was my interlocutor from the chapter's initial conceptualisation to its final editing.

Greg Urban is the Arthur Hobson Quinn Professor of Anthropology at the University of Pennsylvania. His research focuses on the motion of culture through space and time, and the forces that impel it. Through ethnographic research, he is currently exploring the modern for-profit business corporation as cultural form. He is co-author of *The Culture Puzzle: Harnessing the Forces That Drive Your Organization's Success*, and editor of *Corporations and Citizenship*, as well as being former editor of the *Journal of Business Anthropology*.

References

NB: Articles in *The New York Times* can be found by searching their website: www.nytimes.com.

Almén, Torsten Hakan Oskar. 1970. 'Medical Probe for Injecting X-Ray Contrast Medium into the Body (US Patent No. 3,500,820)'. Alexandria, VA: US Patent and Trademark Office.

Anderson, Erika. 2013. '21 Quotes from Henry Ford on Business, Leadership and Life'. *Forbes*. Retrieved 3 August 2024 from https://www.forbes.com/sites/erikaandersen/2013/05/31/21-quotes-from-henry-ford-on-business-leadership-and-life/?sh=58f30eac293c.

Appadurai, Arjun. 1986. 'Introduction: Commodities and the Politics of Value'. In Arjun Appadurai (ed.), *The Social Life of Things*. Cambridge: Cambridge University Press, pp. 3–63.

Bartlett, Christopher A., and Sumantra Ghoshall. 1993. 'Beyond the M-form: Toward a Managerial Theory of the Firm'. *Strategic Management Journal* 14: 23–46.

Bentov, Itzhak. 1971. 'Controlled Motion Devices (US Patent No. 3,605,725)'. Alexandria, VA: US Patent and Trademark Office.

Bettis, Richard A. 1991. 'Management and the Straightjacket: An Editorial Essay'. *Organization Science* 2(3): 315–19.

Bush, Vannevar. 1945. 'As We May Think'. *The Atlantic* 176(1): 101–8.

Chandler, Alfred DuPont. 1962. *Strategy and Structure: Chapters in the History of the Industrial Enterprise*. Cambridge, MA: MIT Press.

Clark, Ed, and Anna Soulsby. 1999. 'The Adoption of the Multi-divisional Form in Large Czech Enterprises: The Role of Economic, Institutional and Strategic Factors'. *Journal of Management Studies* 36(4): 535–59.

Coase, Ronald H. 1937. 'The Nature of the Firm'. *Economica* n.s. 4(16): 386–405.

Cox, Lindsay Colowich. 2017. 'Mac or PC? A Brief History of Apple & Microsoft's Ad War'. Hubspot. Retrieved 3 August 2024 from https://blog.hubspot.com/marketing/mac-pc-advertising-history.

Ebenstein, Lanny. 2007. *Milton Friedman: A Biography*. New York: St. Martin's.

Edwards, Miles Lowell. 1968. 'Catheter (US Patent No. 3,416,531)'. Alexandria, VA: US Patent and Trademark Office.

Fortune. 1947. 'The Rebirth of Ford'. *Fortune* (May): 82–89, 204, 207–11.

Friedman, Milton. 1962. *Capitalism and Freedom*. Chicago: University of Chicago Press.

———. 1970. 'A Friedman Doctrine – The Social Responsibility of Business is to Increase its Profits'. *New York Times Magazine* (13 Sept.): 379, 425–27.

Gelles, David. 2022. *The Man Who Broke Capitalism: How Jack Welch Gutted the Heartland and Crushed the Soul of Corporate America – and How to Undo His Legacy*. New York: Simon & Schuster.

Isaacson, Walter. 2011. *Steve Jobs*. New York: Simon & Schuster.

Johnson, Jeff, Teresa L. Roberts, William Verplank, David C. Smith, Charles H. Irby, Marion Beard and Kevin Mackey. 1989. 'The Xerox Star: A Retrospective'. *Computer* 22(9): 11–26, 28–29.

Kahney, Leander. 2004. 'Inside Look at Birth of the iPod'. *Wired*. Retrieved 3 August 2024 from https://www.wired.com/2004/07/inside-look-at-birth-of-the-ipod/.

Kay, Alan. 2017. 'What Was It Like to Be at Xerox PARC When Steve Jobs Visited?' Retrieved 3 August 2024 from https://www.quora.com/What-was-it-like-to-be-at-Xerox-PARC-when-Steve-Jobs-visited/.

Kopytoff, Igor. 1986. 'The Cultural Biography of Things: Commoditization as Process'. In Arjun Appadurai (ed.), *The Social Life of Things*. Cambridge: Cambridge University Press, pp. 64–91.

Linden, Greg, and David J. Teece. 2018. 'M-form Firms'. In Mie Augier and D.J. Teece (eds), *The Palgrave Encyclopedia of Strategic Management*. London: Palgrave Macmillan, pp. 1041–46.

Link, Stefan. 2018. 'The Charismatic Corporation: Finance, Administration, and Shop Floor Management under Henry Ford'. *Business History Review* 92: 85–115.

Lockwood, Rhodes. 1878. 'Improvement in India-Rubber Surgical Tubes (US Patent No. 204,905)'. Alexandria, VA: US Patent and Trademark Office.

Mahajan, Vijay, Subhash Sharma and Richard A. Bettis. 1988. 'The Adoption of the M-form Organizational Structure: A Test of the Imitation Hypothesis'. *Management Science* 34(10): 1188–1201.

McCray, W. Patrick. 2009. 'From Lab to iPod: A Story of Discovery and Commercialization in the post–Cold War Era'. *Technology and Culture* 50(1): 58–81.

Moog, Ferdinand Peter, Axel Karenberg and Friedrich Moll. 2005. 'The Catheter and its Use from Hippocrates to Galen'. *The Journal of Urology* 174: 1196–98.

Myers, Chris. 2016. 'The New "Rules of the Game": Balancing Profits and Social Responsibility in the 21st Century'. *Forbes* (30 August).

O'Boyle, Thomas F. 1999. *At Any Cost: Jack Welch, General Electric, and the Pursuit of Profit*. New York: Vintage Books.

Pollack, Andrew. 1988. 'Apple Sues Microsoft and Hewlett–Packard'. *New York Times* (19 Mar.).

Robison, Peter. 2021. *Flying Blind: The 737 Max Tragedy and the Fall of Boeing*. New York: Doubleday.

Rösch, Josef, Frederick S. Keller and John A. Kaufman. 2003. 'The Birth, Early Years, and Future of Interventional Radiology'. *Journal of Vascular and Interventional Radiology* 14: 841–53.

Sloan, Alfred P. (1963) 1990. *My Years with General Motors*. New York: Doubleday.

Sutherland, Ivan. (1963) 2003. 'Sketchpad: A Man–Machine Graphical Communication System'. PhD dissertation, Massachusetts Institute of Technology. Reprinted as Technical Report 574, University of Cambridge Computer Laboratory. Retrieved 3 August 2024 from https://www.cl.cam.ac.uk/techreports/UCAM-CL-TR-574.pdf.

Thomson Reuters Legal. 2019. 'Today in 1988: Apple Sues Microsoft for Copyright Infringement'. Retrieved 3 August 2024 from https://legal.thomsonreuters.com/blog/1988-apple-sues-microsoft/.

Urban, Greg. 2016. 'Corporations in the Flow of Culture'. *Seattle University Law Review* 39: 321–51.

———. 2018. 'The Enchantment Effect: A Semiotics of Boundary and Profit'. In Brian Moeran and Timothy de Waal Malefyt (eds), *Magical Capitalism: Enchantment, Spells, and Occult Practices in Contemporary Economies*. London: Palgrave Macmillan, pp. 321–42.

Urban, Greg, K.N. Koh and E. Baskin. 2007. '"No Carry-Over Parts": Corporations and the Metaculture of Newness'. *Suomen Antropologi: Journal of the Finnish Anthropological Society* 32(1): 5–19.

US District Court. 1992. 'Apple Computer, Inc. v. Microsoft Corp.', 799 F. Supp. 1006 (N.D. Cal. 1992). US District Court for the Northern District of California – 799 F. Supp. 1006, 10 August 1992. Retrieved 3 August 2024 from https://law.justia.com/cases/federal/district-courts/FSupp/799/1006/1379197/.

Weber, Max. (1956) 1978. *Economy and Society*, Volume I, edited by Guenther Roth and Claus Wittich. Berkeley: University of California Press.

Welch, Jack, with John A. Byrne. 2001. *Jack: Straight from the Gut*. New York: Warner Books.

Wisconsin Historical Society. 'Fowler McCormick Papers, 1878–1972'. Folder 14 in Box 5. Retrieved 3 August 2024 from http://digital.library.wisc.edu/1711.dl/wiarchives.uw-whs-mcc0000k.

Zahran, Omar. 2022. 'A Final Farewell to the iPod: The Device that Saved Apple and Made the Company What It Is Today Is Now Officially Part of the Company's Past'. *Medium*. Retrieved 3 August 2024 from https://omarzahran.medium.com/a-final-farewell-to-the-ipod-32aea71846d1.

Chapter 6

Not Every Culture Has Management, but Every Management Has Culture

Heung Wah Wong

Management scientists claim, and the public tends to believe, that management is a science that is value-neutral and objective, technical and therefore culture-free. Scientific management knowledge, not unlike the knowledge generated by the natural sciences, is claimed to be universally applicable. Such universal knowledge, as Carrier argues in his chapter in this volume, indicates the existence of what he calls a hidden realm, which is crucial in qualifying the status of professional managers who are educated in business schools, as it is believed that they can produce good results for the company they manage.

Building on my previous work (Wong 2015, 2017, 2020, 2021a, 2021b), this chapter is an argument against such universalist claims about management. One reason for this is not only that management phenomena are embedded in their cultural context, as many scholars have argued since the 1980s, but also and more importantly that those phenomena themselves are cultural facts, symbolically constituted according to a meaningful scheme that is not the only one possible. Management, thus, cannot be understood as something different from cultural fact, shaped by culture from outside, but should be conceived as internally constituted by culture, so that the knowledge generated by management science is not applicable universally. What is at issue, I argue, is how management regimes are actually structured and function according to their own cultural terms, their own concepts of what management is, rather than what it 'really is' according to Western, and especially American, management concepts.

To address this issue, one has to adopt a methodological cultural relativism. This does not mean that every management regime is as good as the others. It means, rather, that we should understand management regimes 'as positional values in a field of their own cultural relationships', so that we should 'situate [management] practices at issue in the historical and cultural order that [make] ... them possible' (Sahlins 2000: 21).

I pursue these points by exploring the cultural specificity of Chinese kinship through terms and concepts that can help us to understand the structure of the Chinese family, and consequently of the Chinese family firm. They also show that important aspects of the management of Chinese family firms are rooted in the management of personal relationships. More specifically, I argue that the management of Chinese family firms is culturally equivalent to the organisation and operation of the *jia* (household) because both *jia* and *gongsi* (companies) are the means relied upon to generate wealth. The principles underlying the management of *jia* are the same ones that underlie the management of Chinese family firms, and the Chinese not only understand but also manage firms as they do their *jia*. The implication is that we need to know how the *jia* is managed before we can understand the management of Chinese family firms. As I will show, the management of *jia* can be seen as the material objectification of Chinese kinship order. It follows that in order to understand the management of the *jia*, we should carefully consider some key terms pertinent to the Chinese kinship order: *fang*, *jia-zu* and *qi*.

In what follows I begin with the point that central to Chinese kinship is what Marshall Sahlins (2013) calls 'the mutuality of being'. The son's life comes from his father, and while the father and the son are two distinct corporeal forms, they share the same life. However, as the son's life is included in or encompassed by the father's, the father is superior to the son. This encompassing of the same but contrasting units is the basis of the hierarchy between father and son. The same is the case for the relationship between husband and wife. A daughter cannot inherit her father's life, she can only acquire life from her husband. In other words, the husband's life is the origin of the wife's, which means that the wife's life is an extension of the husband's and that her life is encompassed in his; hence, also, the husband is superior to the wife.

The values embedded in the relationship between father and son, as well as between husband and wife, are that a father and son, and a husband and wife, share what each of them has. They are also obliged to offer emotional and material assistance to each other when necessary. Further, as the life of a son or wife is an extension of the father or husband, they are understood as the alter ego, the other self, of the father or husband, and so the son or wife is required to behave appropriately. Finally, as a father or husband is the life-giver of the son or wife, the latter must submit to the former's authority. However, as son and wife share the same life as father and husband, the power of the father and husband over the son and wife cannot be absolute, which gives son and wife room to negotiate with father and husband.

The dynamics of the relationship between father and son is crucial for the study of the management of Chinese family firms. I show that the Chinese run their family firms in the same way they manage their families. One of the major features characterising the management of Chinese family firms is that although the father-founder of the firm monopolises management power in the company, he manages the firm through a group of core members, who in turn develop their own teams of core members, and they display the same social patterns as the father-founder's core members.

Core members are recruited from four categories of people. The first consists of the son, wife and others who are related to the father-founder patrilineally. The second category includes affinal relatives, including sons-in-law. The third category is usually those who are personally related to the father-founder, such as his classmates, fellow townsmen and townswomen, and former colleagues. Finally, there are those who have served the firm for a long time and have shown their loyalty to the father-founder.

The father-founder expects his core members to implement any of his orders as his alter egos, and in return he shares the fruits of the firm with them, and provides them with emotional and material support. Appropriately, core members are required to show their loyalty to the father-founder by behaving like his alter egos.

These characteristics help to explain two major features of the management of Chinese family firms. The first is that the social relations within them are personal, rather than positional or bureaucratic, and all these personal relationships need to be managed. The major management focus of Chinese family firms, therefore, lies in the management of relationships. The second is that employees of Chinese family firms are given the freedom to solve problems by themselves as they are not restricted by their formal positions or the associated authority and duties. The father-founder and the core members are willing to delegate power to their subordinates as they do not just want to know how their orders are implemented, but rather whether their aims are being achieved. Therefore, formal positions and many aspects of the activities of their occupants are not the focus of the management of Chinese family firms.

These two features constitute the major differences between Western and Chinese business management. As noted in the Introduction to this volume, the ideology of Western management is heavily shaped by

Weber's (1946: 196–244) description of bureaucracy. There, management is assumed to focus on managing the activities of the occupants of formal positions and on their conformity to, and application of, rules. Moreover, managers have authority over their subordinates because of the rules rather than because of the managers' personal authority or charisma. In sum, management is impersonal. However, as I will show, the management of Chinese family firms is always personal, and its dynamics are determined by the father-founder. It follows that the Weberian notion of management as an abstract concept cannot be taken as universal, and equally the knowledge and theories of management shaped by it are not applicable to the management of Chinese family firms.

The reader should remember that the Weberian description of bureaucracy and the management pattern associated with it are ideal-typical, which is also to say that not all Western bureaucratic organizations or their management conform perfectly to the ideal type. The same goes for the management of Chinese family firms outlined below. The family firms in the Chinese societies of Taiwan, Hong Kong and Mainland China might display different organizational patterns from that outline due to factors such as government policies, legal systems, geopolitics, and the like. In fact, in the Chinese society of Hong Kong, where the capitalist system is well developed, there are some giant Chinese family firms that closely follow the Weberian ideal type of bureaucracy and the management associated with it, while in the Chinese societies of Taiwan and Mainland China you can easily encounter some large Chinese family firms that closely follow the image of Chinese family business that I provide below.

The Chinese Kinship Order

Fang and *jia-zu* are two terms that can help us to grasp the 'native's point of view' on Chinese kinship. *Fang* means the 'bedroom of a married son and his wife' (Chen 1986: 55–56), but more often it is used to refer to 'the son himself, the son and his wife as a unit, or all his male descendants and their wives as a kin set' (ibid.: 64). *Jia-zu* is a combination of *jia* and *zu*. *Jia* has a number of meanings (Chun 1985: 127–28), one of which refers to households with an economy that 'operates on the principle of "from each [*jia* member] according to their abilities, to each according to their needs"' (Graeber 2014: 67). *Zu* is a kin set consisting of all male descendants of a common ancestor and their wives (Chen 1986: 64). Taken together, *jia-zu* is a category that includes all the male descendants of a common male ancestor and their in-marrying wives.

Several principles that are relevant to this chapter are embedded in the relation between *fang* and *jia-zu* (Chen 1990: 129–39). The first relevant principle is that *fang* is a subordinate concept to *jia-zu*, while *jia-zu* is a superordinate concept to *fang*. More importantly, *jia-zu* is inclusive; it is opposed to but encompasses *fangs*, while *fangs* are opposed to but are included in *jia-zu*.

Secondly, a man cannot have a *fang* status within his grandfather's *jia-zu*. Figure 6.1 shows a hypothetical set of kin based on A, who has two sons (B and C) and one daughter (D). A's *jia-zu* consists of two *fangs*, one based on B and one on C. From the sons' point of view, B is a *jia-zu* of E and F, but itself constitutes a *fang* in A's *jia-zu*. Likewise, C is the basis of H's *jia-zu*, but also is the basis of a *fang* in A's *jia-zu*. In any case, E, F, and H cannot be understood as forming three *fangs* of A's *jia-zu*.

Thirdly, *fang* formation is patrilineal. Only sons can constitute *fangs* in relation to their father's *jia-zu*. Hence, G and I cannot be seen as forming a *fang* in B's and C's *jia-zu*; they can only acquire membership in their husband's *fang* and *jia-zu*. For example, D can become a member of her husband's (K) *jia-zu* upon marriage.

Finally, each son's filiation with the father is unique and cannot be mixed with other brothers' filiation with the father. Hence, the number of *fangs* within a *jia-zu* depends on the number of sons the father has. For example, B has two sons, so his *jia-zu* includes two *fangs* (E and F *fangs*), while C's *jia-zu* has only one *fang* (H *fang*). I have to emphasize that each *fang* is equal within the father's *jia-zu*, while at the same time sons' *fangs*

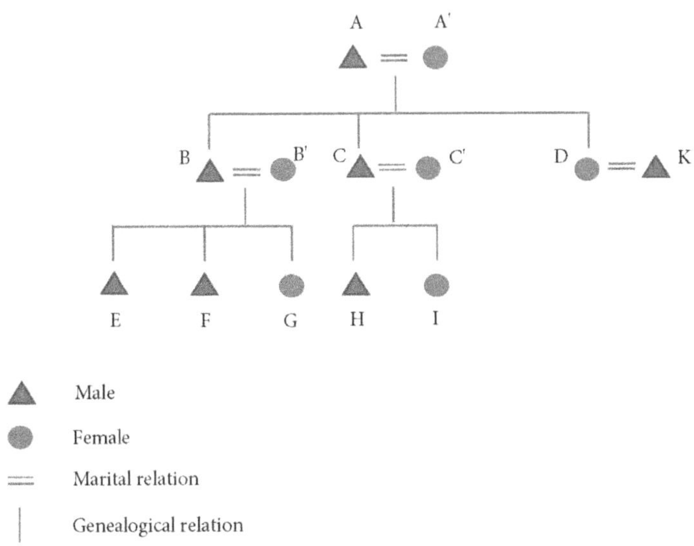

Figure 6.1. A set of kin © Heung Wah Wong

are distinct from each other as each father–son filiation is unique. Thus, B and C constitute two equal *fangs* within A's *jia-zu*, but the two *fangs* are independent of each other.

Qi

The kinship categories and relationships that are embedded in *fang* and *jia-zu* are reproduced in the Chinese notion of personhood. In it, a person is formed by *qi* (breath; sometimes transliterated as *ch'i*) and *xing* (corporeal form). *Xing* is a necessary part of personhood as it is the corporeal form of a person, but it is *qi* that determines the person's identity. *Qi* 'refers to the formless life itself, which is extended through the male reproductive function to sons and grandsons' (Shiga 1978: 123). Hence, the son inherits his life from the father, so that they share the same life. The father and son are two distinct *xings* sharing the same life (*tong qi*), which Shūzō Shiga (1967: 37) has called 'the same vital life essence between father and son'. It follows that male siblings, and by extension all those who are related to the father patrilineally, share the same life. A married woman obtains *qi* from her husband and thus shares the husband's life, through whom she also shares the same life with her husband's patrilineally related kin. In sum, the relationship between father and son, between husband and wife, and among sons of the same father, is characterised by the fact that they share the same life. Because the father, his wife and the son are members of *jia-zu* or *fang*, we can thus argue that sharing the same life defines the membership of *jia-zu* or *fang* as a genus of persons.

Jia-zu membership is the main way that the Chinese distinguish their own people from outsiders. Members of the same *jia-zu* are seen as *zijiren* (our people), while all others are usually called *wairen* (outsiders). The distinction between our people and outsiders is further reinforced by the rules of *tongxing buhun* (people with the same surname cannot marry each other) and *yixing buyang* (one cannot adopt people with different surnames) (Shiga 1967: 28–34). As this suggests, people with the same surname are supposed to be members of the same *jia-zu*. Understood as such, *tongxing buhun* and *yixing buyang* serve to maintain the social boundaries of *jia-zu*.

Recall that in Chinese societies 'the father is the origin of the son's life, while the son is the extension of the father's life' (Shiga 1967: 35), even though they are distinct bodily forms. Seen as such, Chinese kinship is what Sahlins (2013) identifies as part of the 'mutuality of being'. That phrase refers to 'people who are intrinsic to one another's existence – thus "mutual person(s)", "life itself", "intersubjective belonging", "transbodily being", and the like' (ibid.: 2). The father and the son share what each of them has, as evidenced by the fact that Chinese sons are entitled to their father's family property, especially any landed estate, and that the father can enjoy the son's honour. Indeed, the father is not the sole owner of the family property, and the son's honour is considered not just as his personal achievement but also as his father's honour.

Father–Son Relationships

Understanding Chinese kinship as mutuality of being also makes intelligible the cultural specificity of father–son relationships in Chinese societies. Firstly, the fact that the father and son share the same life implies that they are two distinct forms of the same life. Secondly, the father and son 'are people who live each other's lives and die each other's deaths. To the extent they lead common lives, they partake of each other's suffering and joys, sharing one another's experiences even as they take responsibility for and feel the effects of each other's acts' (Sahlins 2013: 28). Hence, the father and son are supposed to share what each of them has, and offer emotional and material help to one another unconditionally when a situation requires it.

Thirdly, and more importantly, the son's life is part of his father's life, while the latter is the whole of the former. In fact, the father is both part and whole. He is part, as the father is a corporeal form distinct from that of his son. He is also whole, as the father's life includes that of the son because the father is the life-giver and the son is the life-receiver. Shiga (1978) presents a hypothetical case that illustrates this. A household includes two brothers, M and A. M has a son, n, while A has three sons, b, c and d. In the event of the division of the household, the family property is not divided into six equal shares, for M, n, A, b, c and d, but is divided equally between M and A. In other words, M-n and A-b-c-d constitute two independent units, each holding half of the family property.

If A decides to pass half of the family property at a later stage, b, c, and d will equally share A's property. The same would go for M's unit if he had more than one son. Shiga argues that the principle underlying this way of dividing family property is what he calls the rule of the single father-son unit (*fushi ittai; futzu i t'i* also transliterated as *fuzi yiti*): 'It might be defined as a rule whereby during the father's lifetime the son's personality is absorbed into the father's, while after the latter's death his personality is extended into that of his son. Father and son are a continuum of the same personality, not two beings in mutual rivalry' (Shiga 1978: 119–20).

Note that the father is both part and whole, as while he is opposed to his son, his life also includes that of his son. Hence, the son's life is encompassed by or included in his father's life. This notion of encompassment implies a Dumontian idea (Dumont 1970) of hierarchical relationship between father and son. The father, as the life-giver, is superior to the life-receiver, the son. As David Graeber observes:

> Classical structuralism, according to Dumont, was developed as a technique meant to analyze the formal organization of ideas, not values. ... What most structuralists fail to realize, Dumont adds, is that these ideas are also 'values'. This is because with any such pair of terms, one will be considered superior. This superior term always 'encompasses' the inferior one. The notion of encompassment is in turn the key to Dumont's notion of hierarchy. One of his favorite illustrations is the opposition of right and left. ... In offering a handshake, Dumont notes, one must normally extend one hand or the other. The right hand put forward thus, in effect, represents one's person as a whole. ... Hence, at least in that context, the right hand 'encompasses' or 'includes' the left ... This principle of hierarchy, he argues, applies to all significant binary oppositions. (Graeber 2001: 16–17)

The above characterisation of the father–son relationship can also be applied to the husband–wife relationship in Chinese societies. Recall that a daughter is not born with *qi*; she can only obtain life from her husband upon marriage. Hence, a Chinese daughter shares life with her husband and forms a single unit with him, which Shiga (1978: 120) calls 'the rule of husband and wife as a single unit'. That is why a wife is expected to share what she has with her husband and offer him emotional and material help. The same applies to the husband. However, as the wife's life comes from her husband, her life is encompassed in her husband's. The wife, as the life-receiver, is inferior to her husband.

Jia and Its Management

The father–son relationship described above can help us to understand the operation of *jia*. According to Shiga (1978: 113), *jia* refers to the social institution of 'common living, common budget' (*t'ung chü kung ts'ai*; also transliterated as *tongju gongcai*), which can be understood as being equivalent to a 'joint account'. Members are required to surrender their income to the head of the *jia*, who then allocates them money to cover their daily expenses regardless of their financial contributions to the *jia* (Shiga 1978: 112). Those who are known to share the same life with the father are automatically members of the father's *jia*. Unmarried female descendants (daughters and sisters) and their uxorilocal husbands, and even servants, can become dependent members of the father's *jia*.

Underlying the management of *jia* are two general principles. The first is the principle of *tong qi*, mentioned above, which prescribes that people sharing the same life are expected to share what each of them has, and to offer support to one another. Secondly, the father is superior to his sons, which gives him the authority to require them to surrender their income, to distribute *jia* income, and to assign tasks to them. There are, however, constraints on the father's authority. As Francis Hsu reports:

> The father has great authority over the son, but his authority is subject to the fact that socially a father and his son are part of each other. The older man cannot abuse his power without injury to himself. The son is obliged to please and support his father, but the latter is also the provider for the son at all times. (Hsu 1971: 63)

Hence, the relationship between father and son or husband and wife cannot be reduced to simple domination and subordination: there is much room for negotiation between the dominant and subordinate parties. The father and the husband have to manage their relationship with the son and wife respectively to ensure that the latter behave like the alter ego of the former. For the son and wife, it is central to negotiate with the father and husband for some freedom to exercise their will. It is no exaggeration to say that the management of a *jia* is a matter of relationship management.

Management of *Gongsi*

There is a consensus among historians of the Chinese economy (e.g. Faure 1989; McDermott 2020) that companies (*gongsi*) are the modern version of *jia*, as both are the major means to generate wealth in Chinese societies. In fact, the Chinese not only understand but also manage firms as their *jia*, because the principles underlying the management of *jia* are the same as those that govern Chinese management, especially in family firms. I have demonstrated this ethnographically (Wong and Chau 2020, 2021), and here I would like to outline two general patterns of management within Chinese family firms that are most relevant to this chapter.

First, Chinese family firms are organised around personal relationships between the father-founder and core members (*hexin chengyuan*). Personal relationships are governed by the two principles mentioned above: the principle of *tong qi* and the principle of hierarchy based on the encompassment of the same but contrasting unit. As the father of the *jia*, the founder is the unchallengeable centre of Chinese family firms, and monopolises decision-making power. He can run the business according to his own plans; he does not need to consult with any member of the *jia*, 'while remaining completely confident that other members of the family would accept them and carry them out' (Cochran and Hsieh 2013: 2).

Under the father-founder are a group of core members to whom he delegates important business tasks. The major function of these core members is to follow the father-founder's orders, serve his needs and help him to achieve his goals. Thus, core members have to demonstrate their loyalty to the father-founder by showing that they always act as if they are his alter ego, even if doing so is against their own interests. In sum, loyalty in Chinese family firms means that one has to sacrifice oneself for the sake of the father-founder.

I said that core members are the father-founder's wife, sons and all other patrilineally related people, and his affines, including his married daughters, sons-in-law and others. I said as well that the father-founder may well recruit core members from those who have personal relationships with him, such as classmates (*tongxue*), those from the same town (*tongxiang*) and former colleagues (*tongshi*). All of these possible candidates share a sense of 'togetherness' (*tong*) with the father-founder, which is similar to the *tong qi* relation between father and son or husband and wife, and which functions to establish a reciprocal but hierarchical relationship among the parties involved (Yau and Wong, 2024).

If the father-founder is unable to secure enough core members from these three groups, he may recruit employees within the company as core members. The most likely candidates for this are employees who have demonstrated their loyalty to the father-founder over a protracted period of time within the company. Once recruited, these long-serving employees are given a special status and informal label, *laochengzi*, which literately refers to those officials in premodern China who served the emperor for a long time; in the context of Chinese family business, it means those employees who serve 'the emperor' (the father-founder) for a long time. Note that the status of *laochengzi* is based more on loyalty to the father-founder than on seniority, experience or competence.

Secondly, core members repeat the same pattern when dealing with their own subordinates. Core members expect their subordinates to be loyal to them, to accept any order from them and to implement their orders as the core members' alter egos.

Thirdly, in the relationship between the father-founder and core members, the principle of *tong qi* prescribes that the father-founder must offer them emotional and material support. This is likely to mean that the core members receive a larger share of the profits and higher social status than non-core members; and because the father-founder does not generally try to hide his favouritism towards core members, any sensible employee can recognise who are the father-founder's core members and the hierarchy in operation. Ambitious employees invariably work to cultivate a good relationship with the core members, through whom they hope to reduce their distance from the father-founder. This not only reinforces the superiority of core members among other employees but also helps core members to recruit their own circle of core members. It is important to note, though, that core members have no power in and of themselves: they 'borrow' their power from the authority of the father-founder, who remains the sole ruler of the firm.

In sum, Chinese family firms are primarily organised and governed by a web of social relationships. Those relationships are maintained by the personal loyalty of core members shown to the father-founder at the centre, who reciprocates with monetary reward, social status and prestige.

Two Relevant Characteristics of the Management of Chinese Family Firms

We have seen that authority and responsibility in Chinese family firms are governed by personal relationships and loyalty to the father-founder. Concomitantly, loyalty is particular and non-transferable. Thus, when a specific core member leaves, the person who replaces him or her will not automatically inherit his or her status as a core member or *laochengzi*.

In keeping with this logic, Chinese family firms are not organised by a stand-alone organisational chart, and indeed rarely have one. In those few that do, the chart is ignored in the day-to-day operation of the company. Equally, the father-founder does not generally think in chart-like terms of formal titles and job descriptions. Rather, he has in mind a list of people whom he would select on specific occasions for specific tasks, in keeping with how he sees what befits their character and specific relationship with him. The guiding principle here is not to put 'a right man in the right place' (Aoki 1988: 12), but to get things done by a trustworthy and loyal core member who shares some specific personal relationship with the father-founder, and this applies as well to core members and their own core members. The general rule is that a capable employee is not one who can implement his position-specific duties professionally but one who can help to solve his or her superior's problems.

Another culturally specific characteristic of Chinese family firms is that employees are given the freedom and autonomy to solve problems by themselves, unconstrained by their formal position within the firm or any set job description. Indeed, the father-founder generally encourages his core members to improvise, as he believes that the crucial factor contributing to business success is flexibility, the ability to follow and accommodate to changing trends and to bypass formal restraints that may interfere with the requisite action. Generally, the father-founder also has no interest in knowing how things are done, which is also to say that the father-founder must delegate power to his core members to get their job done, and routinely he is willing to do so. Consequently, employees in Chinese family firms enjoy a high degree of autonomy in the daily operation of their company, especially the core members.

The Nature of the Management of Chinese Family Firms: The Management of Relationships

I said that the father-founder must manage his relationships with the core members of *tong qi* to ensure that they behave like his alter egos in the company. One set of the relationships that he has to manage is with his sons. The first task of that management is to manage the conflicts among his sons, which are frequent in Chinese societies as such conflicts are built into the kinship order.

Recall that sons of the same father are independent of each other while they are equal in relation to their father, which easily gives rise to conflicts among sons. Any discriminatory distribution of material or social value among sons, no matter how minor, easily leads to conflict because sons of the same father are assumed to be equal. Conflicts among brothers can easily trigger *fen jiachan* (division of family property) and eventually *fen-jia* (division of *jia*). In that event, the father's *jia* is split into several *jia,* according to the number of sons he has. Each new *jia* as a joint account is headed by one son, while the father's *jia* vanishes. Likewise, Chinese family firms as *jia* tend to break down into several new companies, each headed by a father-founder's son. The crucial task for the father-founder is to contain the male sibling conflicts and keep all his sons working within his company for as long as possible. This requires sophisticated management of interpersonal relationships.

No matter how hard the father-founder tries, division of the *jia* is pretty much unavoidable. What the father-founder can do is to make a good arrangement for each of his sons. The ideal arrangement is that the most capable son takes over the main business of the family firm, while other, less competent sons engage in different business operations to avoid conflict among them. Such an arrangement is not easy to achieve, because the father only manages the family property and has no power to distribute it according his own will; nor can he deny his sons' succession rights to family property or *jia* management (Chen 1990: 155–56).

The fact that management of Chinese family firms cannot be achieved by those who are not *jia-zu* members makes it difficult to manage core members who are affines of the father-founders. The difficulty is due to the fact that kinship relationships are constituted by substance, *qi*, which makes Chinese kinship ascriptive, and that in turn makes it difficult to act in ways appropriate to a kinship position other than one's own. Recall that a son-in-law might stay in his father-in-law's *jia* as a dependent member, contributing financially to the *jia* and drawing resources from it. No matter how much the son-in-law contributes to the *jia* economy, he still does not have the right to any of his father-in-law's family property, for participating in the same domestic life does not qualify the son-in-law to be a member of the father-in-law's *jia-zu*.

The same is the case for the father-founder's family firm. A competent son-in-law may be recruited to serve his father-in-law's family firm as a core member, he may even play an essential role in managing the company. But he knows that he will not be allowed to succeed to his father-in-law's company. Ambitious and competent sons-in-law, then, are likely to leave the company and start their own business when they accumulate sufficient capital, which means that the father-founder has to manage the personal relationship with the son-in-law if he wants to keep him in the company.

The father-founder also needs to manage those core members who are personally related to him by a sense of 'togetherness' such as classmates, fellow townsmen and former colleagues. Unlike kinship relationships, this personal relationship is intrinsically vulnerable and has to be maintained by the endless chain of reciprocal exchanges of *li* (propriety). To maintain the personal relationship, the father-founder is expected to give and return *li* in both the private and public spheres. The content of *li* is contextually dependent: it might include the demonstration of kindness to them, such as offering financial assistance to them from his own pocket; the display of affection, such as offering a gift to their sons and daughters on festive occasions; the demonstration of favouritism, such as giving them special favours at work; the demonstration of trust, such as giving them some confidential information, and so on. The reciprocal exchange of *li* is important because the personal relationship between the father-founder and core members who are related to him through their togetherness is maintained and reinforced by that exchange. The proper ways to do the reciprocity of *li* are very complex, requiring a correct understanding of the circumstance, accurate calculation of timing, and appropriate content of *li*.

All of these points indicate that the management of Chinese family firms is the management of relationships. However, this is not relationship management in general, which is an important topic in business studies. Rather, it is the management of the specific sorts of relationships defined by the Chinese kinship order: the relationships between the father-founder and the son, between male siblings, between the father-founder and non-*jia-zu* members, between the father-founder and those with whom he maintains a relationship by the logic of togetherness, and between the father-founder and his long-serving employees. Culturally constituted, the relationships have particular properties and codes of conduct, for example that the relationship between the father-founder and those personally related to him is governed by the culturally specified dynamics of reciprocal exchanges of *li*. Like kinship, personal relationship, to invoke Sahlins (2013: 44), 'may be a universal possibility in nature, but by the same symbolic token, as codified in language and custom, it is always a cultural particularity'.

Concluding Remarks

I have argued that the management of Chinese family firms revolves around the management of relationships between the father-founder and his core members rather than the formal positions within organisations or the activities and roles associated with them. The management focus of Chinese family firms is closely related to the cultural specificity of Chinese kinship, and the principles underlying the management of *jia* are the same that underlie the management of Chinese family firms. Likewise, the principle of *tong qi* and the hierarchical relationship between the father and his core members dictate the priorities and possibilities of authority, recruitment and business operations within the firm. Personal relationships and loyalties are all-important, more important than mere merit or the kind of criteria usually viewed in the West as characterising successful organisational operations. As we saw, this imperial-style managerial system offers greater employee independence and autonomy in decision-making (albeit within the context of mutuality of being and loyalty to the father-founder) than the more highly regulated Western managerial system, in which formal positions and the functional activities of the occupants of the positions are governed by impersonal criteria of performance and managerial efficiency.

Although our study has focused upon the Chinese family firm and how it is constituted by the Chinese kinship system, the broader point that I wish to emphasize is that management phenomena are cultural facts constituted by a meaningful system, which is not the only possible one. This means that it is unfortunate that Management Studies has commonly not paid attention to culture, and when it does pay attention, culture is usually taken as an exogenous factor that is called on to explain something that cannot be understood by standard reasoning.

On some other occasions, culture is reduced to a set of dimensions measured with questionnaires, which are used to identify the pattern of different national cultures, themselves used to explain differences in management regimes across cultures. This is the approach used by Geert Hofstede (1980). As I have noted elsewhere (Wong 2015), Hofstede assumes that management phenomena are not culture, and that culture is an external force that shapes management phenomena. I have argued in this chapter that management phenomena are cultural facts, enacted as such according to a cultural scheme that is not the only one possible. In other words, management phenomena are internally constituted by culture rather than externally shaped by it.

That being so, understanding management phenomena (or any human phenomena) requires researchers to reproduce in their minds the ways that the phenomena that they observe are internally constituted by culture. In other words, management phenomena should be understood subjectively from within, as by doing so, management phenomena are made familiar and thus understandable. This is, of course, Weber's method of *Verstehen*, or empathetic understanding, which he used in *The Protestant Ethic and the Spirit of Capitalism* (Weber [1904–5] 1958).

This approach is different from that of the natural sciences, for the objectivity that is essential to guarantee the validity of scientific knowledge may not be applicable to the study of management phenomena. Given my argument in this chapter, it appears that the principle in the natural sciences that phenomena should be studied objectively from outside cannot help us to understand management phenomena. All of this speaks against the existence of what Carrier (this volume) calls management's 'hidden realm': a set of objective and general entities and forces that, it is claimed, trained and skilled management can manipulate in pursuit of organisational goals.

It is important to rectify the neglect of culture in management science. It is not that every culture has management, but every management has culture. Hence, management can only be understood and studied in a specific culture, which is also to say that management cannot be culture-free. Managers' authority and status cannot, then, be completely justified by the professional training they receive from the business schools that are dominated by the idea of management's hidden realm. Perhaps it is time to consider establishing business schools that offer culturally specific management training.

Acknowledgements

This chapter is a substantial development of Wong (2021b). Parts are adopted from it, some of them verbatim, used with permission.

Heung Wah Wong is the founder and associate professor of the Global Creative Industries Program at the University of Hong Kong. He obtained his PhD in social anthropology from Oxford University in 1996. He is the author of *Japanese Bosses, Chinese Workers: Power and Control in a Hong Kong Megastore* (University of Hawaii 1999). Wong is also a co-author of *Tradition and Transformation in a Chinese Family Business* (Routledge 2020).

References

Aoki, Masahiko. 1988. *Information, Incentives, and Bargaining in the Japanese Economy*. Cambridge: Cambridge University Press.

Chen, Chi-nan. 1986. '*Fang* and *Chia-tsu*: The Chinese Kinship System in Rural Taiwan'. PhD dissertation, Department of Anthropology, Yale University.

———. 1990. *Jiazu Yu Shehui: Taiwan Yu Zhongguo Shehui Yanjiu de Jichu Linian* (Family and Society: The Basic Concepts of the Study of Taiwanese and Chinese Societies). Taipei: Lianjing Chuban Shiye Gongsi.

Chun, Allen. 1985. 'Land is to Live: A Study of the Concept of Tsu in a Hakka Chinese Village, New Territories, Hong Kong'. PhD dissertation, Department of Anthropology, University of Chicago.

Cochran, Sherman, and Andrew Hsieh. 2013. *The Lius of Shanghai*. Cambridge, MA: Harvard University Press.

Dumont, Louis. 1970. *Homo Hierarchicus: The Caste System and its Implications*. London: Weidenfeld & Nicolson.

Faure, David. 1989. 'The Lineage as a Business Company: Patronage Versus Law in the Development of Chinese Business', in *Proceeding of the Second Conference on Modern Chinese Economic History*. Taipei: Institute of Economics, Academia Sinica, pp. 347–84.

Graeber, David. 2001. *Toward an Anthropological Theory of Value: The False Coin of Our Own Dreams*. New York: Palgrave.

———. 2014. 'On the Moral Grounds of Economic Relations: A Maussian Approach'. *Journal of Classical Sociology* 14(1): 65–77.

Hofstede, Geert. 1980. *Culture's Consequences: International Differences in Work-Related Values*. Beverly Hills, CA: Sage Publications.

Hsu, L.K. Francis. 1971. *Under the Ancestors' Shadow: Kinship, Personality, and Social Mobility in China*. Stanford, CA: Stanford University Press.

McDermott, Joseph P. 2020. *The Making of A New Rural Order in South China*. Vol. 2, Merchants, Markets, and Lineage. Cambridge: Cambridge University Press.

Sahlins, Marshall. 2000. 'Introduction,' in M. Sahlins (ed.), *Culture in Practice: Selected Essays*. New York: Zone Books, pp. 9–32.

______. 2013. *What Kinship Is – And Is Not*. Chicago: University of Chicago Press.

Shiga, Shūzō. 1967. *Chūgoku Kazokuhō no Genri* (Principles of Chinese family law). Tokyo: Shobunsha.

______. 1978. 'Family Property and the Law of Inheritance in Traditional China,' in David C. Buxbaum (ed.), *Chinese Family Law and Social Change: In Historical and Comparative Perspective*. Seattle: University of Washington Press, pp.109–50.

Weber, Max. 1946. *From Max Weber*, edited by Hans Gerth and C. Wright Mills. New York: Oxford University Press.

______. (1904–5) 1958. *The Protestant Ethic and the Spirit of Capitalism*. New York: Charles Scribner's Sons.

Wong, Heung Wah. 2015. 'Taking Culture Seriously: The Role of Culture in the Study of Business'. *Journal of Business Anthropology* 4(1): 114–50.

______. 2017. 'What is Chinese Kinship and What is Not?' in Min Han, Hironao Kawai and Heung Wah Wong (eds), *Family, Ethnicity, and State in Chinese Culture Under the Impact of Globalization*. London: Taylor & Francis, pp. 83–94.

______. 2020. 'It Is Not that All Cultures Have Business, but that All Business Has Culture', in Raza Mir and Anne-Laure Fayard (eds), *The Routledge Companion to Anthropology and Business*. London: Routledge, pp.453–72.

______. 2021a. 'Introduction'. *Journal of Business Anthropology* 10(2): 226–40.

______. 2021b. 'How the Chinese Think About the Family: The "Family" in Chinese Family Firms'. *Journal of Business Anthropology* 10(2): 241–61.

Wong, Heung Wah, and Karin Ling-fung Chau. 2020. *Tradition and Transformation in a Chinese Family Business*. London: Routledge.

______. 2021. 'No Family Company without Family: The Professionalization of a Chinese Family Business in Hong Kong'. *Journal of Business Anthropology* 10(2): 262–82.

Yau, Hoi Yan, and Heung Wah Wong. 2024. 'The Logic of "*Tong*" (Togetherness), or Why *Guanxi* Works in Chinese Societies.' *Translocal Chinese: East Asian Perspectives*, 17(2): 161–81.

Chapter 7

Life in the Head Office

Material Metaphors of Management

Emil A. Røyrvik

The world of corporate management is not only about conscious strategies, decision-making, objectives and results. It is also a social environment inhabited by real people doing concrete things in specific situations that are shaped in actual material circumstances that have social corollaries and implications. To a considerable extent corporate management is saturated and co-created by language, and the common-sense view of management focuses on language, in the form of managerial decisions and the actions that they produce, and how these influence organisations and their members. However, this view is restricted because it ignores the fact that management both reflects and shapes organisations, their members, the economy and society, and does so in ways that are not necessarily related directly to the managers' own conscious decisions and actions. These other forms of expression and enactment are important in any social setting, and the power invested in the social institution of management makes them all the more so.

Various material forms shape and co-construct managerial thinking, practice and organisational circumstances, and the key dimensions of managerial life that I want to investigate here are manifest in a number of material, non-language idioms or metaphors. I investigate them because there are expressive sides to various material objects, structures and forms, what one might call their cultural dimension, that both enact and signify different aspects of managerial work and, indeed, co-create the cultural premises of organisations and their place in, and implications for, economy and society. In this chapter I will mainly analyse how the head office building and workspaces signify such cultural processes and presuppositions in managerial, corporate worlds, and especially how, in polysemic and ambivalent ways, they reflect and contribute to constructing these worlds as spectacles of modernity, including how those worlds are made by and for men, indicating how deeply gendered modern capitalist societies are.

Based on a long-term, multi-sited ethnographic study of managerial practices in the globalised corporation Hydro (Røyrvik 2011), this chapter explores a small but key subset of what I call material metaphors of management. My focus on physical spaces and objects furthermore tries to illuminate and grasp some of the cultural premises, meanings and paradoxes of what is left out in conventional analysis of management, and also to highlight what is not said, what is possibly avoided, tacit, unconscious or even taboo among practitioners. Paraphrasing Tord Larsen (2006: 268), we might say that the time and space in which buildings and bodies are embedded are embodiments and visualisations of moral vocabularies.

Materiality has long been a central part of ethnographic analyses (Schorch, Saxer and Elders 2020), and the anthropology of space and place is a well-established and thriving field (Low and Lawrence-Zúñiga 2003). Moreover, several recent ethnographic works on corporate worlds and work touch on how physical workspaces mediate the shaping of work, organisation and culture (e.g. Chong 2018; Wilf 2019; del Nido 2021). My perspective is framed by a relational ontology that holds that relations are primary to, and constitutive of, things like material objects and individual human beings. This position is expressed, for example, in the concept that Wanda Orlikowski (2007) calls 'sociomateriality', highlighting how meaning and materiality are constitutively entangled, and how the social-human and the technical-material aspects of life are inseparable.

The Managerial Age

Management developed in the latter half of the nineteenth century as a distinct social institution in conjunction with the emergence of the large multidivision American corporation (see Urban this volume). With the creation of limited-liability joint-stock corporations, with their separation of ownership and control, management emerged in engineering as the institution that controlled the corporation on behalf of the owners. In 1932, Adolph Berle and Gardiner Means ([1932] 1991) announced the arrival of the 'the managerial revolution'.

In due course, management differentiated itself from engineering, and ideas of rationalisation, efficiency, standardisation and control were translated from the technical field that was the concern of engineers to the operation of the whole organisation. Managerial rationality permeated society during the first half of the twentieth century and has become what Yehouda Shenhav (1999: 2) called an 'unquestioned pacemaker of the modern social order'; a central function of this pacemaker has been to disseminate templates and repertoires of instrumental rationality globally.

Management quickly emerged as a leading social institution. In 1954, Peter Drucker (1954: 3), arguably the most influential management thinker of the twentieth century, wrote in *The Practice of Management*: 'The emergence of management as an essential, a distinct and a leading institution is a pivotal event in social history. Rarely, if ever, has a new basic institution, a new leading group, emerged as fast as has management since the turn of the century'. Drucker's work helped to establish management as a distinct function in society, and it can be seen as a new class that emerged between labour and capital. The emergence of management as the steward of the modern corporation and as a crucial part of 'the economy', as it emerged as an objectified and autonomous sphere of life, is a significant event in the development of capitalism as a cultural process.

Importantly, the economy, corporations and the managing of them became the domain of men. Jorun Solheim (2007) argues that our categorisation of women as caretakers and men as providers is a modern idea decisive in the development of capitalism. She argues that capitalism is a gendered and gendering process, a historical trajectory that has produced particular notions of gender. Tracing the relationships between sex, gender and capital since the Enlightenment, she maintains that the modern process of individualisation, and the emergence of the voluntary social contract between men who are free, independent and equal, had a catch to it: it entailed a sex contract, whereby women were linked to the family sphere through marriage. It was through industrial capitalist processes that the underlying connection between the family and production was broken. The result was that women became the authority in the domestic sphere, ruling the bases of morality and upbringing, but became separated from the secular economy and public life; the realm of the bourgeois male became that of the family provider, private owner and citizen. That women are seen to stand outside the economy is, according to Solheim, a bourgeois conception, subsequently exported to the working class.

In a different way, the novelist C.S. Lewis also noted that with management a new era had arrived. His satirical book *The Screwtape Letters* is a series of letters from a senior devil to his nephew on how to lure an ordinary human being into temptation. In the preface to the 1961 paperback edition, he ([1942] 2013: xxxi) told his readers that 'I live in the Managerial Age, in a world of "Admin"', and he explained that his symbol for Hell is 'something like the bureaucracy of a police state or the offices of a thoroughly nasty business concern' (ibid.: xxxii). If Lewis realised that he was living in a Managerial Age, in a world of Admin, it would not be much of an exaggeration to say that many of us feel the same way today. If Lewis's diagnosis was correct in the late 1950s, when he was writing that preface, the problem seems to have become more intense, perhaps in surprising ways, in the decades since. Hellish or not, idioms and practices of management have been adopted as ideology, sources of governance and standards of valuation throughout social life. From the new public management (Hood 1991) to the audit and metric society and culture (Power 1997; Strathern 2000; Mau 2019), concepts, tools and metrics from the world of management, including its supremely valued notions of efficiency, quantification, measurement and control, have been embedded in pretty much all areas of society (Larsen and Røyrvik 2017; Larsen et al. 2021).

I turn now to a description of the Hydro headquarters, with the goal of showing how the sociomaterial relations within it are constituted in paradoxical ways through what Tian Sørhaug (2004) calls 'managementality'. This is a pattern of power that combines Foucauldian (Foucault 2008) discipline through self-control ('governmentality') with seduction and desire. I argue that managementality reflects contemporary myths of a made-for-men modernity.

The Transparency House

The Hydro headquarters is designed to signify, but it does so in paradoxical and polysemic ways that reveal underlying cultural ideas. The most obvious thing that you notice when working there is the vast open space, combined with glass walls enclosing meeting rooms. The extensive use of glass in doors, stairs, walls and ceilings makes it easy to see in and out of rooms, and throughout the building; and Eitan Wilf (2019) notes that the extensive use of glass and the spacious, open workspaces in modern offices seem to be an effort to be perceived as new, fresh, modern and up to date, a design that is often associated with the start-up sector and the creative industries.

This open landscape is sparsely populated by neat, clean desks with docking stations for laptops, and hardly any papers, books, stationary or other office paraphernalia are visible. There is a clean-desk policy for most workstations, accompanied by a free-seating policy to enable people on the move to have a workplace, while also possibly reducing office costs. The higher-level managers have their own permanent and personal desks, with larger lamps and chairs, which together signal their status, rank and authority.

The first time I visited the head office, the building was new and Hydro staff had just moved in. While we were climbing the stairs from the entrance towards a higher-level workspace, the female manager accompanying me pointed out a female colleague working in a space on the other side of a glass wall, and noted in a humorous tone of voice that 'women here have to stop wearing skirts'. Looking up I saw that the legs of the colleague underneath her work desk were framed by the glass wall like a display reminiscent of a kind of live visual-art installation.

Due to the transparent and glass-enclosed workspace design you get a strong sense of freedom and opportunity, not least because you can see what is going on at a great distance in all directions, not only from side to side, but also to some extent upwards and downwards through the large, open staircases and hallways. Because basically the only demarcations that exist, except for the concrete floors, are glass walls and glass doors, the building provides the fascinating, ambivalent experience of being able to be part of, while not being part of, a lot of the action going on in the offices and meeting rooms. Echoing Wilf's observation, it is a visual vocabulary transmitting values and ideas of transparency, accessibility and innovation, and of being up to date and part of where the important action is going on. Transparency is one of the key terms of neoliberalised modernity, along with other important notions, such as accountability, privatisation, quality control, branding, auditing, excellence and ranking (Larsen and Røyrvik 2017), and here some of these notions are reflected and reinforced in the architecture of the building and the organisation of workspace.

However, this material metaphor of transparency, with its neoliberal connotations, coexists with its own negation, so that this Transparency House of glass can be perceived as a paradoxical space. Despite the openness, accessibility and transparency, you simultaneously experience the strict regulation of space. This begins with the reception area at the entrance to the building, which can be compared to the main entrance of the Berber house, what Pierre Bourdieu ([1973] 2003) called the threshold, a barrier between the inside and the outside as different moral and cosmological domains, one that signals and distinguishes insiders from outsiders. At the reception area guests must sign in and staff must open the gates with their access cards, which they must also use at every major door in the building. Access and lack of access are therefore intrusively present, materialised in the locked gateways, the security personnel and the door access control systems with their associated access cards. Furthermore, the interior rooms with their glass walls are sound-proofed. With that, the visual openness is contrasted with auditory exclusion, thus creating impressions and feelings of both invitation and rejection, admission and suspension. You can observe a host of activities from quite a distance – for example, who is talking to whom, how they are dressed, their body language and the like. However, the strict regulation of where you can move and who you can hear means that this arrangement highlights its paradoxical nature. It signals openness and accessibility, but also exclusivity and secrecy.

The compound effect of this contrasting or paradoxical situation, I would argue, is the emergence of a form of ethos and energy that creates various forms of needs, wants and desires, such as climbing the corporate ladder. Also, because people in the building are constantly on display, there is arguably a kind of measured voyeurism expressed and stimulated by the design. For the people being seen and watched, this can lead to behaviour based on precaution and conformity-driven self-control, as well as muted forms of tailored exhibitionism. The sociomateriality of the building thus reflects the specific constellation of trust and authority, based on both discipline and seduction, that is an integral part of Sørhaug's (2004) concept of managementality, facilitated and reinforced by this design and structuring of managerial space.

An anecdote illustrates how the signifying of the Transparency House is directed towards internal managerial audiences. I tell a version of this story in my book *The Allure of Capitalism* (2011: 136–37) and have used it to illustrate forms of power in the age of 'neoliberal simulation' (Røyrvik and Brodersen 2012), and I paraphrase it here. During my fieldwork I was invited to participate in a meeting of top management where the formal and final decision was to be made for the largest investment project ever in the history of the corporation. After I was guided through the locked and guarded gates of the company headquarters, a 'corporate assistant' accompanied me to the elevator and into the secluded office spaces where the top management meetings were held. Other managers who were to attend the meeting gathered in a large open space with stylish furniture, the space being encompassed by glass offices and, most notably, a small informal meeting room behind glass walls and doors with a large artificial open fireplace and two designer couches. That particular room, into which we could see clearly from the open space we were occupying, gave a first impression of being an intimate seating arrangement at some exclusive holiday resort. Its glass enclosure, its modern, fresh and fancy design and high-end furniture, as well as its position on a stylish, open office floor, also, however, gave the room a particular aesthetic, that of an installation or display in a gallery of modern art.

I greeted the five other people present, most of whom seemed to know each other. The corporate secretary announced that a meeting that was now taking place was behind schedule and that we would have to wait a bit longer to enter the large meeting room. People filled the time with chat about business-related matters. One male and one female manager, whom I later learned were highest-level financial managers, appeared seemingly out of thin air and went into the glass-encased 'holiday-resort' meeting room. They closed the glass doors, sat down in the adjacent leather couches and had a private conversation. It was a fascinating scene, which had a paradoxical impact on me. The combination of visual transparency and sound-proofing had the effect of broadcasting to our group in the open space some intangible conceptual categories, like disclosure, secrecy, importance and exclusivity, that made us want to be on the inside rather than the outside.

This example illustrates how sociomaterial relations can constitute management through power and seduction, mediated by material structures communicating transparency, openness and accessibility on the one hand, but demarcating an exclusive space that we can see but that is out of our reach because we cannot hear. We were, then, non-participating participants, a kind of voyeuristic audience made up of people who are both insiders and outsiders at the same time. The building design works in this way as a mediating, material metaphor in expressing and performing managementality's modes of power, which include forms that create wants and desires. Some aspects of such paradoxical forms of material mediation are taken up by Wilf (2019) in his study of creativity and innovation consultants. He describes some of the practices and consequences of how material artefacts, as well as communicative practices, mediate ideas and ideals about things such as expertise, flexibility, speed and creativity. These mediations in people's workspaces come with unintended consequences, often producing effects opposite to the ideal notions of smooth and innovative flows of people and ideas. The mediations also clutter up the work processes by creating rigidness, opacity and stasis. In general, it might thus be argued that material metaphors, like linguistic metaphors, are inherently polysemic expressions that reflect complex cultural processes.

The mediating metaphor of the Transparency House echoes work on the domestic house, for instance by Suzanne Blier (1999: 43) in her discussion of the Batammaliba in West Africa: 'The house translates cosmogonic narratives into a material, spatial form. The architectural representations of cosmological themes work both as mnemonic aids and as permanent and concrete expressions of the underlying principles of Batammaliba cosmological order' (other work on the house and its symbolic functions includes Carsten and Hugh-Jones 1995; L'Estoile and Neiburg 2020). Classic work of special relevance here is Mary Douglas's (1991) exploration of the home as a particular kind of place with moral and aesthetic dimensions, and especially something that I have mentioned already, Bourdieu's ([1973] 2003) study of the Berber house. He sees that house as a material manifestation of Kabyle cosmology and social structure, and says that the layout of the house expresses and organises social relations through the valuation, categorisation and hierarchisation of classes of people, and the distinction of insiders and outsiders. Although both Douglas and Bourdieu, like Blier, focused on people's homes, their analytical approach applies more generally.

Kimberly Chong (2018) has made a comparable argument, showing the hierarchisation and valuation of two classes of a firm's employees, in the organisational vernacular bluntly described as 'revenue-generator' or 'billable' versus 'cost-generator' or 'nonbillable' employees. She says that these valuations are reflected in the office workspace design notions 'front office' and 'back office', and how the distinction between the two classes was reinforced by highly unequal wages and differential access to material resources like telephones, stationery and photocopiers.

The moral vocabulary of the Hydro headquarters building is polysemic, but as I will describe, it is similar to the Berber house in the way that it spatially manifests visions of divisions (Bourdieu 1990) that enact sociomaterial relations that are valorised and hierarchised by gender and seniority (as illustrated by the lamps and chairs above).

Bodies in Black

How physical bodies and their uses are shaped in the head office is relevant to the working of material metaphors and their reflection and reinforcement of cultural processes. The sociomateriality of clothing and how it affects the bodies that people see and display can signify aspects of social values and institutions, and vice versa, in a variety of ways (Barthes 2006), and the ritual use of bodies establishes facts of experience and transmits knowledge (Barth 1975). Further, bodies mediate objects, language, subjective perceptions and shared symbols. As such, the body serves as a mediating metaphor for the relationships between parts and wholes on various scales, which include the relation between individuals, organisations and society. For example, managers' plans and designs enable and enforce by various means the standardisation of bodily use to fit notions about corporate values and the quality of work, and to support goals and norms of health, environment and safety.

The Transparency House architectural design works in intimate relationship with the shaping of corporate bodies. This appears in matters such as decorum and appropriateness, the regulation of work rhythms, rituals of deference and demeanour, the projection of status and power, and several other aspects of work life. In practice this means observing, shaping and moulding the body in interplay with abstract values and ideas about culture and morality, formed discursively by the larger corporate body. Yet, these processes are far from straightforward.

When traversing various Hydro spaces, it is difficult to avoid noticing that both the employees and managerial bodies in the company largely constitute, to borrow from James Brown (1966), 'a man's world'. Only 23 per cent of its global employees, and 20 per cent of its leaders, were women in 2023. This is an increase from about 14 per cent women employees in 2016, but a decrease from about 25 per cent women leaders (top 50 and top 200 leaders) from the same year (Hydro 2024). Since the first systematic theory of gendered organisations appeared (Acker 1990, 1992), several feminist scholars have analysed gender inequality and patriarchy in organisational worlds (Benschop 2021). The clothing of professional bodies is a way of looking at this from the perspective of materiality and the head-office workspace.

Men in power, be it heads of states or of corporations, routinely wear suits, as do men who dress for success to embody confidence, control and potency in a variety of situations. The suit is the costume par excellence of the manager. Wearing a suit in Hydro is strongly associated with managerial or corporate work, while suits are seldom worn in the production plants themselves, or even in the office buildings at the plants. As one would suspect, though, it seemed that the degree of formality of clothing was a reflection of a person's age and position in the hierarchy: the older and higher placed, the more formally dressed. This, however, is complicated by the fact that people in different occupational groups tended to dress differently. Economists and those in finance dressed up more systematically than did those in engineering, and projects people were more informal than traders, even though both groups had their main offices at the company headquarters.

Women commonly wear a female version of the suit, but often with creative modifications. They construct numerous variants of coats, blouses, tops, sweaters, skirts and trousers, ranging from the more formal to the more casual. Female managers are always dressed neatly, properly and elegantly, so that they are visible but they do not show off. One interesting distinction between men's and women's clothing is that there is more of a one-to-one relationship between the male suit as a work costume and as a ceremonial or celebratory costume than is the case with women, whose suit is arguably more restricted to the workplace and contrasts with their various dresses and costumes worn elsewhere. Moreover, women dress up at work with a range of accessories to complete their costumes: bracelets, rings, nice belts, earrings, scarves, make-up and perfume. It seems as though women seek to avoid imitating the male suit too closely, possibly to avoid being labelled 'men in skirts', while at the same time referencing and translating the dominant male, managerial suit into their female work costumes.

Anne Hollander (1994: 5) explains why the suit has survived a myriad of fashion trends over the last two hundred years. In a nutshell, she argues that the male suit embodies the fantasy of the modern form as a vehicle of power, beauty and positive sexuality. The symbolic power and appeal of the suit links the man and the manager to some of the most durable conceptions underpinning modern social life, such as cars and planes, as well as to the efficiency, elegance and powerful forces of nature and animals. Even if female dress in some respects tries to imitate the male suit, it has never succeeded in emulating its 'sign of power in the world, and potency in the head', nor its 'fundamental aesthetic superiority, a more advanced seriousness of visual form' (ibid.: 40).

The symbolic significance of the dominance of the Hydro male manager in a suit is also, I would argue, another expression of the authority pattern of combined discipline and seduction characteristic of Sørhaug's concept of managementality. While Foucault's ([2004] 2008) governmentality is largely concerned with control through self-control, managementality includes the notions of 'mimetic desire' and seduction to help explain the motivation for and force of self-control or self-management. Mimetic desire is desiring what you think others desire (Girard 1977), and Sørhaug argues that mimetic desire is integral to managementality as it makes 'its men *want to want*' (Sørhaug 2004: 104; all Sørhaug quotes are my translations).

Given Hollander's arguments, it is understandable that the suit is the preferred managing uniform. The Hydro corporate culture, as expressed by some of its key members, is characterised by a rational and sober, quiet-going but confident and powerful seriousness (Røyrvik 2011). The male suit is thus a perfect idiomatic enactment of such forms of authority and cultural expressiveness, while simultaneously reinforcing the modern myths of management, and the domination by men of the economy and public life.

Polyoptic Power: Surveillance from Below and Within

Extending the discussion of power and seduction at the headquarters, we can say that the moral vocabulary of the Hydro house of glass evokes notions of a workplace version of Erving Goffman's (1961) 'total institution' (Røyrvik and Brodersen 2012). The two differ because membership in Hydro is voluntary, which is not the case with the mental hospitals or prisons analysed by Goffman. But there are some striking similarities: for example, that much of your life is conducted while being visible and in the presence of a large number of other people, and that there is no place to hide from the surveillance of others. An interesting influence of the Transparency House on social relations is that Goffman's famous distinction between frontstage and backstage seems to dissolve. With no opaque office door to close behind you, only surface frontstage spaces are available throughout the day. No wonder that in movies and television programmes people in office spaces are often depicted as spending quite a bit of time being frustrated, crying, sulking, making out, or using their phones in the (at least partial) privacy afforded by bathroom toilets. Another similarity is that life in the head office, as well as in total institutions, is governed by formal and rational planning and rules that demand conformity, and perhaps a more surprising parallel is that managers, like people in total institutions, are not free to choose how they spend their time. For example, meetings are the main mode of managerial work, and many managers in Hydro say that they do not control the scheduling of meetings very much. Management scholars like Henry Mintzberg (1973) say that managers have little control over their own time and activities, while Sørhaug (2007) argues that managers are infantilised by this situation.

For Bourdieu ([1973] 2003), the Berber house expressed a strong distinction between the private, indoor sphere of women and the public outdoor life of men. With the Hydro Transparency House, we might argue that an idea of the outdoor, public life of men has travelled indoors and come to occupy a kind of modernist, corporate and quasi-public space enacting the paradoxes described above. Furthermore, the insider–outsider distinction is strongly expressed, but at the same time blurred, as shown with the example of the 'mountain resort installation' above.

The visibility and surveillance of these frontstage spaces is also akin to Foucault's (1980) well-known discussion of panoptic power as a metaphor of modern disciplinary societies. Foucault's disciplinary society is based on the new techniques of industrial management that created control through taken-for-granted self-control, significantly working through and shaping the body and the self by regulating and directing bodily energies into productive activities. An example of such panoptic surveillance is included in Juan del Nido's (2021) ethnography of taxi drivers in Buenos Aires, and shows how the design of the union office building organises and monitors taxi drivers' bodies and actions.

The design of the Transparency House is, however, very different from the Panopticon prison design, where there is a central place from which an authority can observe everyone without itself being observed. In the headquarters, however, everybody can be observed and watched more or less all of the time by one or more others, and, like the Panopticon, they will usually not be aware of whether or not they are being watched. Moreover, the building design is different from the Panopticon because it stimulates a degree of monitoring upwards in the hierarchy, a degree of surveillance of people in higher rank and authority.

Together with Marianne Brodersen (Røyrvik and Brodersen 2012), I suggest calling this type of decentralised and more reciprocal surveillance a 'polyopticon'. In our development of the idea of the polyopticon, we suggested that the headquarters amounts to a material expression of complex and to some extent heterogeneous cultural values and forms of power in the postmodern era of simulation and simulacra. It could be argued that the polyopticon also signifies and manifests more democratic and egalitarian forms of surveillance and discipline, in line with the history and self-perception of Hydro corporate culture as part of the 'democratic capitalism' of Norway (Røyrvik 2011), though it resembles the Panopticon in terms of self-monitoring and self-discipline. Furthermore, the democratic elements of the polyopticon design of the building might be said to work in tandem with the material vocabulary that signifies and enables processes of mimetic desire and seduction that co-create managementality, that make people want to want certain things: a higher-level job, the visible legs beneath the table, inclusion in the private conversations of top managers behind closed glass doors, having access to the larger and more exclusive offices of the top people, and other signs and symbols of status, position and wealth.

The Things among Modern Managing Men

The polyopticon headquarters is thus a material expression of complex cultural values, which when taken together can be in tension with each other. Like the Kabyle house, however, it is a material metaphor that expresses and shapes notions of hierarchy and value based not least on gender. In the masculine, although officially gender-neutral, atmosphere of industrial work life and managementality, as Sørhaug (2004) argues, women are perceived not only as lacking the interests and rationality that corporate life requires, but also as representing the opposed values of emotion, passion and care. The corporate spaces co-constructing managementality are spaces that, following Sørhaug (ibid.: 101), comprise largely 'things and men': 'Everything in this space can be said to be concerned with the thing, or the things between men'. He argues that work life in general suppresses sexuality and gender, which it has turned into a negative category. Moreover, this negativity has been projected onto women: 'Men have no sexuality in industrial production, because they are the ones there, and they are the ones who should be there. It becomes relevant that women are women, but not that men are men. In working life human beings are men' (ibid.). The #metoo campaign revelations have provided interesting illustrations of the mechanisms that help to bring this about.

It follows that women could be perceived as a threat to the male community, and that male managers who are too much in alliance with women could be looked upon with suspicion by other organisation members. Symbolically, men may get infected by the power and myths of both the 'the mother' and 'the mistress'. In both cases, passions and emotions conquer objectivity and rationality. In Sørhaug's analysis, this infection challenges male managerial bonding, and the manager could go so far astray as to transgress the limits of the male-management community, and thus face the possibility of symbolic and social isolation.

While male homoerotic communion is an understudied phenomenon, Sørhaug (2004: 103) argues that in the private sphere women may be perceived as people, but as women in capitalism symbolically have 'moved out of the world of work, and into the family', in the context of corporate life, work and management they are unconsciously seen not as people, but rather as objectified and fetishised things, or 'even *the* thing, among men'. In this analysis seduction is at the root of power. While, of course, women in work life are never simply objectified positions between men, they present a potential force of destruction of the homoerotic community, and thus are often kept at a distance. As with the Berber house, by relegating the female powers of reproduction implicitly to the private sphere, those in the male managing community can believe themselves to be self-sustaining and self-perpetuating in their pursuit of organisational, technological and economic production.

Conclusion

My discussion of the material metaphors enacted in the head office have shown, often in paradoxical ways, some of the things that common analyses and perceptions of management leave out. Focusing on decision-making, running the company, and the plethora of leadership concepts that fill the curricula of business schools worldwide – such as 'strategic management', 'transactional' and 'transformational' leadership – largely ignores the fact that management involves whole people who think, act and feel in real situations constituted in complex sociomaterial relations and environments. Attending to this broader context and assemblage of connections that include the physical and material surroundings, as this chapter has done, is merited not only because it is vital for understanding management as a social institution. Perhaps even more important is that such an analysis focuses on how management ends up seeing and shaping the world. This is because, through its relations and repertoires, management reflects and reinforces particular cultural patterns, and it projects and propagates forceful templates of thought and practice throughout social life.

Focusing on real people in real situations, and particularly how their relations are constituted in material structures such as office spaces, building design, material artefacts, clothing and bodies, illuminates how 'life in the head office' is classified, valued and hierarchised. This involves highlighting ontological issues of how the world is and how it works. Management is situated in a long tradition of the continuous development of modern capitalism, strongly characterised by instrumentalism, economism, individualism, and hierarchical and gendered relations. The forms of power and the visions and divisions of the world projected by managementality, as expressed through the moral vocabulary of the material metaphors investigated here, show how it reflects the historical development of modernity and capitalism, but nevertheless includes and reinforces new modalities of power and classification.

In the seemingly sterile and professional world of the 'transparent' head office, a single building perpetuating myths of modernity and the categorical, gendering entanglements of men and modern economy and work life, we also find paradoxical expressions of power that include seduction and the shaping of passions, as well as more egalitarian forms of surveillance (the polyopticon). Shorthand notions such as neoliberalisation can be helpful, but as we have seen, a sociomaterial analysis can highlight the complexities of power in and beyond corporate worlds involving notions such as transparency, surveillance and self-control. The polysemic vocabulary of the material metaphors includes as well ideas related to openness and aspiration, inclusion and involvement, beauty, desire and the changing relationships between the public and the private.

Emil A. Røyrvik is professor at the Department of Sociology and Political Science, the Norwegian University of Science and Technology (NTNU). His focus of research is on ethnography and anthropological theory in the context of political economy, organisational worlds, and economic and cultural transformations. Some recently published articles include 'Traveling, Translation, Transformation: On Social Responsibility and the Nordic Model in China' (2023); 'Sacralizing Finance, Sacrificing Society' (2021); and 'The Stable Stranger: Constructing the Roma within the European Neoliberal Culture Complex' (with Marianne Blom Brodersen, 2022).

References

Acker, Joanne. 1990. 'Hierarchies, Jobs, Bodies: A Theory of Gendered Organizations'. *Gender and Society* 4(2): 139–58.

———. 1992. 'Gendering Organizational Theory', in Albert J. Mills and Peta Tancred (eds), *Gendering Organizational Analysis*. Newbury Park, CA: Sage Publications, pp. 248–60.

Barth, Fredrik. 1975. *Ritual and Knowledge among the Baktaman of New Guinea*. Oslo: Universitetsforlaget.

Barthes, Roland. 2006. *The Language of Fashion*. Oxford: Berg.

Benschop, Yvonne. 2021. 'Grand Challenges, Feminist Answers'. *Organization Theory* 2(3): n.p.

Berle, Adolf A., and Gardiner C. Means. (1932) 1991. *The Modern Corporation and Private Property*. New Brunswick, NJ: Transaction Publishers.

Blier, Suzanne Preston. 1999. *The Anatomy of Architecture: Ontology and Metaphor in Batammaliba Architectural Expression*. Chicago: University of Chicago Press.

Bourdieu, Pierre. 1990. *The Logic of Practice*. Cambridge: Polity Press.

———. (1973) 2003. 'The Berber House', in Mary Douglas (ed.), *Rules and Meanings: The Anthropology of Everyday Knowledge*. London: Routledge, pp. 98–110.

Brown, James. 1966. 'It's a Man's Man's Man's World'. Cincinnati, OH: King Records. Retrieved 4 August 2024 from www.youtube.com/watch?v=IvlioQ2Ot2c.

Carsten, Janet, and Stephen Hugh-Jones (eds). 1995. *About the House: Lévi-Strauss and Beyond*. Cambridge: Cambridge University Press.

Chong, Kimberly. 2018. *Best Practice: Management Consulting and the Ethics of Financialization in China*. Durham, NC: Duke University Press.

del Nido, Juan M. 2021. *Taxis vs. Uber: Courts, Markets, and Technology in Buenos Aires*. Stanford, CA: Stanford University Press.

Douglas, Mary. 1991. 'The Idea of a Home: A Kind of Space'. *Social Research* 58(1): 287–307.

Drucker, Peter F. 1954. *The Practice of Management*. London: Heinemann.

Foucault, Michel. 1980. *Power/Knowledge: Selected Interviews and other Writings 1972–1977*, ed. and trans. by Colin Gordon. Brighton, UK: Harvester Press.

———. (2004) 2008. *The Birth of Biopolitics: Lectures at the College de France, 1978–79*, ed. by Michel Senellart. New York: Palgrave Macmillan.

Girard, René. 1977. *Violence and the Sacred*. Baltimore, MD: The Johns Hopkins University Press.

Goffman, Erving. 1961. *Asylums: Essays on the Condition of the Social Situation of Mental Patients and Other Inmates*. New York: Penguin.

Hollander, Anne. 1994. *Sex and Suits: The Evolution of Modern Dress*. New York: Kodansha International.

Hood, Christopher. 1991. 'A Public Management for All Seasons?' *Public Administration* 69(1): 3–19.

Hydro. 2024. 'Integrated Annual Report 2023'. Oslo: Norsk Hydro. Retrieved 4 August 2024 from https://www.hydro.com/Document/Doc/Integrated%20Annual%20Report%202023_ENG.pdf?docId=594088.

Larsen, Tord. 2006. *Den Globale Samtalen: Om Dialogens Muligheter* [The global conversation: On the possibilities of dialogue]. Oslo: Scandinavian Academic Press.

Larsen, Tord, and Emil A. Røyrvik (eds). 2017. *Trangen til å Telle: Objektifisering, Måling og Standardisering som Samfunnspraksis* [Craving to count: Objectification, measurement and standardisation as social practice]. Oslo: Scandinavian Academic Press.

Larsen, Tord, Nigel Rapport, Kalpana Ram, Ted Porter and Michael Blim (eds). 2021. *Objectification and Standardization: On the Limits and Effects of Ritually Fixing and Measuring Life*. Durham, NC: Carolina Academic Press.

L'Estoile, Benoît, and Federico Neiburg. 2020. 'Governing the House: An Ethnographic Approach (Introduction)'. *Etnográfica* 24(3): 655–64.

Lewis, C.S. (1942) 2013. *The Screwtape Letters. Annotated Edition*. New York: HarperCollins.

Low, Setha M., and Denise Lawrence-Zúñiga (eds). 2003. *The Anthropology of Space and Place: Locating Culture*. Malden, MA: Blackwell Publishing.

Mau, Steffen. 2019. *The Metric Society: On the Quantification of the Social*. Cambridge: Polity Press.

Mintzberg, Henry. 1973. *The Nature of Managerial Work*. New York: Harper & Row.

Orlikowski, Wanda J. 2007. 'Sociomaterial Practices: Exploring Technology at Work'. *Organization Studies* 28(9): 1435–48.

Power, Michael. 1997. *The Audit Society: Rituals of Verification*. Oxford: Oxford University Press.

Røyrvik, Emil A. 2011. *The Allure of Capitalism: An Ethnography of Management and the Global Economy in Crisis*. Oxford: Berghahn Books.

Røyrvik, Emil André, and Marianne Blom Brodersen. 2012. 'Real Virtuality: Power and Simulation in the Age of Neoliberal Crisis'. *Culture Unbound* 4(4): 637–59.

Schorch, Philip, Martin Saxer and Marlen Elders (eds). 2020. *Exploring Materiality and Connectivity in Anthropology and Beyond*. London: UCL Press.

Shenhav, Yehouda A. 1999. *Manufacturing Rationality: The Engineering Foundations of the Managerial Revolution*. New York: Oxford University Press.

Solheim, Jorunn. 2007. *Kjønn og Modernitet* [Gender and modernity]. Oslo: Pax Forlag.

Sørhaug, Tian. 2004. *Managementalitet og Autoritetens Forvandling: Ledelse i en Kunnskapsøkonomi* [Mangementality and the transformation of authority: Management in a knowledge economy]. Bergen: Fagbokforlaget.

———. 2007. 'Først og Sist'. Oslo: NRK TV (2 March). Retrieved 4 August 2024 from https://tv.nrk.no/serie/foerst-og-sist/2007/OUHA39000807/avspiller.

Strathern, Marilyn (ed.). 2000. *Audit Cultures: Anthropological Studies in Accountability, Ethics and the Academy*. London: Routledge.

Wilf, Eitan Y. 2019. *Creativity on Demand: The Dilemmas of Innovation in an Accelerated Age*. Chicago: University of Chicago Press.

Chapter 8

Venture Capital Investors as (Asset) Managers

Johannes Lenhard

Asset managers are one of the core forces in an increasingly financialised economy, turning companies into temporary manifestations of capital rather than organisations focused on doing or making something. They are distinct from other kinds of managers depicted in this volume because what they manage is firstly capital, which they receive from asset owners like pension funds, insurance companies, university endowments and state funds, as well as wealthy individuals and family offices (Preqin 2022; Christophers 2023). The biggest asset managers are Blackrock, Vanguard and Fidelity, and together they manage more than $US 20 trillion, almost as much as the GDP of the United States.

I spent the better part of the last five years with a specific sort of asset manager, venture-capital investors (VCs). Because readers are not likely to be familiar with venture-capital investors, I will present a simplified sketch of how they operate before diving into the kind of management they do.

A VC firm raises money from what are called limited partners (LPs), who are either asset owners themselves or represent yet another layer of asset management; LPs are 'limited' because they have no formal say in the operation of the investor whom they engage to make investment decisions. Typically, VC investors, on behalf of LPs, seek out young enterprises (start-ups) that have been established by a set of entrepreneurs (founders) who need money to develop their idea into a product or service. In return for its investment, the VC firm gets a minority of shares in the start-up company and often a seat on its board of directors. It is expected that within 6–12 years the start-up will be bought by another company or will issue shares to the public, in what is called an initial public offering (IPO). At this exit event, the VC firm will sell its shares. The proceeds of the sale are returned to the LPs, less the VC firm's carried interest fees (usually 20 per cent of any profit made on its investment).[1]

On the face of it, then, 'venture capital firms groom start-up companies' (Braun 2022: 632; see also Cooiman 2023) on behalf of asset owners, mostly investing in technology and biotech enterprises. VC investors are, after all, financial investors, and as such are focused on making above-market-rate returns on their investment. While analyses of VCs often focus on the way that the management of their assets increases financialisation and economic inequality, here I focus on a potential tension surrounding VCs' involvement in what I argue are two different types of management: managing capital for asset owners and simultaneously managing the growth of the start-up companies they invest in. Those types of management are quite different: one implies knowledge of finance and investment, the other of how to scale up a large variety of differently focused young tech companies. Venture-capital investors fluctuate readily between both management realms. The justification for the VC investors' involvement in both types of management stems from the sort of abstract management knowledge that Carrier describes in his chapter, and from the simple minority ownership the investors have of the start-up companies. The two types of management do not necessarily have to be aligned, and if they are not, tensions arise.

Venture-capital investors invest capital in exchange for small stakes (under 20 per cent) of early-stage start-up companies. This distinguishes them from buyout (sometimes called private equity or PE) asset managers, who commonly buy a *controlling* stake in small and medium-sized companies, and from those who invest in large firms that have shares traded in public markets. Because they take minority stakes in start-ups, VC firms need less capital and smaller teams. Despite not owning controlling stakes, a number of VCs sit on the boards of start-ups as they grow in size, giving them a certain level of formal power over the start-up. In addition, VCs often act as mentors, strategic advisors and what are called value-add partners for the entrepreneurs. In other words, VCs' management activities go beyond financial asset management and extend into company management and corporate governance.

Prominent recent crises at Uber (Issac 2019) and WeWork (Brown and Farrel 2022) demonstrate this power of VC investors. In both cases, decisions by the investors, who together held a majority of seats on the boards of the two companies, led to the firing of both of the start-ups' founders. With slightly less explosive consequences, many VC firms are involved in start-up management and what they often call value-add activities, from fund-raising support to marketing and recruiting for the start-ups, with the goal of steering them towards a successful IPO or sale, and hence a successful exit and financial return for the VC firm. The active management involvement is, then, in the name of financial return.

In theory, the two VC management activities, managing money and helping to manage the start-up, are aligned. As asset managers, VCs work to achieve outsized financial returns for the asset owners; as portfolio company managers they use their power and influence to make the company a success, and their exit from it profitable. This appears to be different from what happens with large asset managers. Benjamin Braun (2022) says these big asset managers could be as active as I observed venture capitalists to be, but in fact they tend to avoid getting involved in shaping the companies in which they invest (see also Christophers 2023: 39). Instead, they try to increase the financial assets that they manage, and hence their management fees (which are paid annually independent of the investment's success); they also focus more on lobbying to influence government regarding things like monetary policy, taxation and regulation in ways that will benefit their investments. In other words, Braun observes, big asset managers focus on policy and increasing fees rather than active involvement in the companies in their portfolio.

What I observed of venture-capital investors reveals a slightly different practice: many, including some of the most prominent VCs, claim to be, and often are, actively engaged in being value-add investors involved in company management. This involvement leads to the tensions that concern me in this chapter. One tension stems from the possibility that the value-add investors will over-manage or under-manage the start-up; the other tension arises from weak company management as a source of poor financial returns on the asset owner's money.

Those tensions between managing asset owners' capital and managing a company in which the VC has invested may be heightened with venture capitalists, but in fact are common in corporations, being an instance of the principal–agent problem, something that I address later.

Research Background

I started working in venture capital in 2011, part-time and as a consultant, first at a corporate venture fund in the UK and afterwards at an early-stage VC family office and at a healthcare VC firm in Germany. I was involved in almost all parts of VC work, from deal sourcing (finding suitable start-ups for investment) and due diligence (understanding the quality of a possible investment), to preparing investment decisions (writing investment memos), portfolio management (reporting) and fundraising for the VC itself (preparing presentations to potential limited partners). My research on VCs began in 2018, during my time as a postdoctoral fellow at the Max Planck – Cambridge Centre for Ethics, Economy and Social Change. With my industry experience I was able to gain long-term access to an unresearched part of the finance sector, which has so far been difficult for social scientists (Souleles 2018).

The first interviews I conducted in the UK and Germany were with my former colleagues and contacts, as well as co-investors whom I had encountered in my work, and since then I have spoken with many of them repeatedly. Many of them have introduced me to VCs in their own networks, allowing me to extend my research to include the United States. I have since conducted close to one thousand interviews with over two hundred VC investors and almost fifty LPs in Silicon Valley, New York, London and Berlin. Moreover, my industry experience allowed me to conduct more than one year of participant observation. This included involvement in several dozen industry conferences in Europe and the US; I visited start-up pitch competitions (including so-called demo days), conducted due diligence on companies, wrote investment memos and took part in investment committee meetings. Everyone I encountered consented to my research and I have obscured people's identity, except for those who said that I could use their names.

Value-Add Investing and Its Tension

Over the last ten years a lot of capital has flowed into venture capital (Willhelm 2021), in spite of earlier criticism of the sector, especially its weak overall financial performance (Kedrosky 2009). This influx of capital was driven by changing external factors (Janeway 2018), especially the low central-bank interest rates that made more risky investments attractive to asset owners. Since 2012 the promise of venture capital, which is concerned with investments that are not liquid or traded on public markets but which have the potential for outsized returns, led to the influx of many 'tourist investors' – people investing in the sector for the first time or without any specific expertise.

One consequence of this influx appeared among start-up companies. Following a winner-take-all mentality, companies like Netflix, LinkedIn and Doordash, and recently many web3 and crypto companies, raised bigger amounts of money to expand quickly, intending to beat their competitors simply by spending more on marketing to attract customers. This has led to what Reid Hoffman (2018), a venture-capital investor in Silicon Valley, called 'blitscaling'.

A second consequence, more relevant for this chapter, appeared among VC investors. That influx of capital produced a more competitive VC sector, and VCs, driven by fear of missing out (FOMO), competed for access to promising start-ups. At times winning this competition against another investor[2] became more important for the investment decision than the actual business value of the start-up, and it led to bidding wars among investors.

This led to the need for VC funds to position themselves in contrast to and in competition with each other by offering something to the start-up companies that went beyond money. Enabled also by the increasing assets under management and the resulting higher income from management fees, VCs started to brand themselves as 'value-add' investors[3] (Gyllander 2017). In one of my interviews in 2019 with a Silicon Valley VC partner whom I call Jason, he describes this approach in detail:

> What I enjoy most is working with the teams building the company. … When we get involved – maybe they have a million in revenue and so … there would be an investment of $5–10 mio and [we] would also be the first board member. … At the stage we invest, it's expensive money for the entrepreneurs – so what is value add? Typically, if they are dealing with us, they are not just looking for the highest valuation; they are entrepreneurs that [are] really looking for somebody who brings something … perhaps somebody [who] has been in the business for twenty years or so. First that often involves building the team; we are helping them with hiring the head of sales, head of product … we would build that team, help them build out the sales team, professional sales people, scale that … with metrics that are attractive to your [next] investors … helping founders to think through on the gas pedal.

Jason describes his fund as a value-add investor, and himself and his fellow investors not only as active board members involved in decisions about the start-up's overall strategy, but also as hands-on, experienced co-entrepreneurs, managers involved on the inside of the company, such as strategy, hiring and team expansion. Especially in the United States, where the VC sector has been bigger and attracted more capital than in Europe, VCs have been positioning themselves explicitly as value-add investors, also sometimes called a type of 'platform venture capital' (Lacy 2015; Hartnett 2017). Based on industry interviews, Louis Coppey (2016) says that such VC firms 'offer resources to entrepreneurs in addition to money and their partner's time and expertise. To do so, VC firms hire functional experts who do not work on investments but focus entirely on supporting portfolio companies. They help entrepreneurs on several topics such as recruiting, marketing, design or data science'.

The best-known and most widely copied example of this model is the Silicon Valley VC firm a16z.[4] They raised an additional $US 9 billion in

2022 from limited partners to further expand the platform they started in 2010. By 2016 they already had more than 150 specialist staff to support portfolio companies, and that number has grown significantly since then, including teams focused on 'go to market', 'fundraising', 'talent', 'technical talent', 'people practices', 'marketing' and 'operations' for their start-up portfolio companies.

***

I have said that value-add VCs act as advisors and are involved in company oversight, including via board seats. More than that, they are actively involved in the day-to-day management and operation of the start-ups in which they invest. This model produces tensions, however, which I want to explore.

Following persistent debate, even in the industry itself (e.g. Feld 2015; Maxwell 2015), Kjartan Rist (2019) describes one of the problems with the value-add model of venture capital:

> [W]hile a lot of VCs say they offer this value-add support with their portfolio companies, very few get it right. Sit back too much, and portfolio companies could miss out on valuable contacts and experience. But take it too far, and you're interfering where you're not wanted, and, in a worst-case scenario, could break the relationship.

While value-add management can have positive financial effects (Teten et al. 2013), it is the dangers of the 'too little' or 'too much' of management that I will illustrate and analyse in the remainder of this chapter, based largely on cases from my own research.

Two Cases of Bad Management

As Rist indicated, there are two directions of the possible management tension between a VC and its portfolio companies, both of which can lead to bad management: too much or too little influence and oversight. I illustrate these with the examples of Nish, a VC in the UK with twenty years' experience, and Tom, a seasoned Silicon Valley investor.

Case 1: Over-Management

I met Nish through one of my longest connections to VCs in London. We met in front of his office and walked to an Indian restaurant to have lunch. When I meet a VC for the first time, my first question is always a very open one, and I asked Nish to introduce himself and his fund's approach to VC investing. Very quickly, he got from the fund's set-up (started in 1999; fifth round of funding, £250m raised in 2020; 95 per cent of capital from institutional investors) and performance (top 10 per cent of VCs, on average achieving 5-fold returns per fund) to their 'value-add focused strategy':

> We create opportunities. If you look at our history, for instance in 2008 we bought eight companies from Philips and built them and sold them ... We invested in [Delivery start-up] when they did £7m [in revenue], built it with them, IPOed it and now the market cap[italisation] is £2.2bn. ... We believe that you need to do it in order to know it. We bring twenty years of experience from things that have gone well and that have not gone well: how to hire a VP Sales, open an office in Mountain View. We have done all that with companies in the last two decades. We get involved in this because we know a lot of the answers because we have seen this before.

Nish strongly believed in his and his fund's influence on 'building companies', a common phrase used in the world of start-ups that means the management, expansion and operation of companies. In their case, their experience as VC investors qualified them to guide and support their portfolio companies with, for instance, hiring or international expansion.

He also explained his personal involvement as a board member with oversight function and as a manager in his portfolio companies:

> I sit on six boards and see myself as a resource for the CEO. They call me. I don't call them. Once a month I have a board meeting. With some companies I am involved in projects beyond that. I think a third of my time is spent with portfolio companies. We help them with advice, introduction, strategic decisions.

From what Nish explained, his involvement was multifaceted and varied among his portfolio companies, far beyond simple board oversight. All the same, towards the end of our lunch he said: 'In the end, it is the CEO who runs the company. I have confidence in the CEO or I have to replace the CEO. I want a CEO who knows how to do all these operational things'.

In this, Nish acknowledged that the founders run the start-up, but that investors like him have influence on, and even power over, hiring and firing. It is this power that start-up founders fear, ultimately being fired by investors who have lost confidence in their leadership and end up treating the start-up not as a site of production or group of people doing something, but as an asset that needs to generate a return.

***

This example brings to the fore two possible issues connected to VCs' over-management. First, we need to take into account the consequences of VC influence on the level of the start-up. The incentives of the investor as an asset manager with a specific investment and exit schedule can be misaligned with the start-up founders' schedule. Financial success for the investor only comes with an exit, the sale of their shares; the influence of the investor, their management of the portfolio company, is aimed at producing such an exit. Removing the founders, as was the case with Uber and WeWork, is the most intrusive form of this type of management, and the one most feared by founders (Jackson 2019). Other examples could involve making or vetoing decisions to open a new office in a new country, launch a new product, make a specific hire or use a particular marketing approach.

When VCs try to align the management of the portfolio company with the VC's interest as an asset manager, the result can look like bad management to the founders. For them, working towards building a sustainable and profitable company could well be more important than the investor's desire for a successful exit after a few years. In fact, for most founders, VC management influence should be limited; while they might be dependent on VC money to build their company, they do not necessarily trust the investors' ability to help execute their vision, especially given the investors' focus on the eventual exit.

In addition, founders can have doubts about the VC's ability to manage a start-up: What if the VC's management and influence is in fact misguided? From the perspective of founders, the benefits that come from the influence of VC investors on their portfolio companies' management are doubtful, especially when it comes to anything beyond fundraising (see Fritjofsson 2022). In other words, for many founders it is questionable whether VCs should be doing what Nish's firm seeks to do.

Statistically speaking, only one particular kind of investor is reliably good at going from the initial investment decision to the successful exit. That is people who became VCs after having successfully set up a company of their own, and they are good because their value-add is better than that of VCs who were unsuccessful founders or who were not founders of companies (Gompers and Mukharlyamov 2022). Given that more than 90 per cent of VC investors in Europe do not have a background as successful founders (Diversity VC 2019), the idea of the value-add investor becoming standard practice seems like a recipe for (financial) disaster. This is not only true when it comes to building new sustainable companies but also for achieving the VC's first management goal, which is to be a successful financial asset manager who pays high returns to their asset owners.

Case 2: Under-Management

Tom is one of the leading partners in one of Silicon Valley's most lauded VC firms, and he and I have been speaking regularly since 2019. Our conversations have been open right from the beginning, and we have naturally talked about many problems, both for the VC industry generally and for Tom's firm. In one of our earlier conversations, when I was sitting in his Sand Hill Road office with my research assistant, he described the issues surrounding one of his former portfolio companies, which I will call 'Bottle'.

Bottle was engaged in selling a software service to businesses, but due to the highly regulated nature of the specific service and the differences in the regulations across US states, issues arose when expanding the company. Tom explained:

> We came to know over time that there were issues with licensing. … I can imagine that the board had a reasonably informed decision and said, okay we're going to go into some states where it's not really clear whether we're in the right bounds legally. Maybe I'm too morally loose on this, but for me, that's a reasonable risk to take as a business. … I think we asked: we as a company, as a board, are we willing to take risks that might have downstream legal or regulatory issues? But we've talked about them, we understand them, and we may be wrong or right on it but consciously we decided that it's a risk we're willing to take.

What Tom describes is a situation that he sees arising regularly in management and board decision-making, in start-ups and established corporations alike: After considering the known facts and risks, including regulatory and legal ones, what do we think is the right thing to do, especially given the experimental nature of the start-up sector overall? In an attempt to avoid over-managing, the company was initially allowed to proceed with their rapid expansion, despite entering a grey legal area.

In the case of Bottle, this decision ended up being the wrong one, and eventually led to the writing off of the company as an investment. Tom explained that ultimately

> the board brought out an outside law firm, did an investigation; what we didn't know, but maybe what we should've known, was that there was also this separate issue of the manipulation of testing. And look, that's just blatantly illegal. There's no risk-based or market-based argument you could make for something like that … there were activities that were illegal – what happened

> with [Bottle] around manipulating test results – and those were done without consultation with the board.

When public pressure on Bottle and its board grew because variations in state regulation meant that licensing was problematic and potentially illegal, Tom and his fellow board members demanded an external audit, which revealed blatantly fraudulent activities, with the manipulation of test results that he mentioned, similar to the kind of fraud that occurred at Theranos and for which the head of that company was recently convicted (Griffith 2022).

From the perspective of management as oversight, a question arises: Could and should Tom and his fellow investors and board members involved with Bottle have seen this kind of fraud developing over time? Continuing our conversation, we talked about companies that are not in Tom's portfolio but that led him to conclude that they should. Regarding the investors in the ride-sharing firm Uber, he explains:

> Where I think it's harder for me to let the board off the hook is – you know the culture of the company because it's built early on – so, at some point you know that there's a culture of like, 'move fast, break things, ask for forgiveness later', whatever it is. And those could be innocuous, but at some point … you have to believe that, with a company growing at that rapid pace with more and more people coming on, the likelihood of that culture being misinterpreted is high. So, where I would fault the board in these cases is that at some point you probably have a duty to ask questions based at least on what you know of the culture, that you may not have otherwise asked had it been a different culture.

***

Bottle, like Uber, WeWork and most recently the crypto-exchange company FTX, was under the oversight of venture-capital investors who had seats on the board of directors, and all of those firms ran into enormous problems under that oversight (Issac 2019; Brown and Farrel 2022; Ryan 2022). As Tom explained with reference to Uber, a company's culture develops early on, and a board made up of investors is responsible for preventing dangerous developments, the sort that can become visible in the form of sexual harassment claims or the lack of an HR department (on Uber, see Issac 2019). Arguably, VCs were failing to ask the questions that they should have asked, closing their eyes and trusting the founders in an attempt to avoid over-managing (or be seen as 'founder-friendly'), until scandal hit and the damage is done, both to the company on whose board they sat and to their own investors hit by the write-off of the investment.

Were these risks worth taking? For Uber, the result was an under-performing IPO and less profit for the investors who had invested in the company and for the asset owners whose money they had used: for WeWork the initial IPO was cancelled, and FTX went into liquidation. In these and comparable cases, venture-capital investors seem to have under-managed the companies and so failed in their duty to produce the greatest returns for their limited partners. Tom said that in the case of Bottle his limited partners were similarly unhappy: 'I was on the phone with LPs for days'.

A second problem with VC under-management can be described as 'over-promise and under-deliver'. In the spirit of what Stefan Leins (2018, 2020) calls the narrative economy, in their pitch to start-up founders as they seek to get the deal, VC investors present a narrative that portrays their various management credentials and experiences, and their commitment to being a value-add investor. They do not, however, necessarily deliver on their promises. A recent report (Pratty 2021), based on data from five hundred European founders and investors, showed that the majority (92 per cent) of VCs see and present themselves as value add. However, the majority of founders (61 per cent) rated the VCs value-add activities as below average (similar findings based on US data are in Fritjofsson 2022), and over a third of founders said that VCs failed to deliver on their promises. There are several possible reasons for this under-management, an obvious one being that VCs often do not have enough qualified staff to support all their portfolio companies post-investment. While this aspect of under-management may not be as dangerous for the start-up as the lack of oversight described previously, it can create tension between founders and VCs, and harm the investor's reputation.

Learning from VCs About (Asset) Management

> If you think about it on a rational level … What are you in business to: if you are in business to maximise the competitiveness of your [VC] firm, you could maximise short-term profit maximisation, but they would have downstream implications. We should have a model in our head what these implications are.

With these words, Tom explained to me what I think is the tension involved in the two kinds of VC management. On the one hand they are financial asset managers who are in business to maximise profits for the asset owners whose money they manage. On the other hand, however, VCs are also managers of and in start-up companies, as value-add investors and board members. This is in contrast to the asset managers Braun (2022) describes, as I mentioned before.

Recently, however, VCs have opted to become company managers as well as asset managers. This involvement in the strategic and day-to-day running of the business can lead to both over-management and a systematic tension between the founders focused on building a company and VCs focused on exiting a company and paying their limited-partner investors. When they fail to deliver on their promised value-add activities, however, VCs might under-manage and under-deliver; they might also neglect their oversight responsibility as managers and board members, and so fail to spot possible risks. In cases of both over- and under-management, tensions can arise and the consequences can be negative, both for the company and for the financial returns that investors and asset owners will receive. In the case of both too much and too little management, then, VCs might not be able to be successful asset managers.

***

Seeing VCs as having two different management responsibilities helps us to understand venture capital and its systematic tensions; it also helps us to provide a different perspective on management more generally. In conventional corporate settings, the company as an entity is usually distinct from the managers as individuals, which creates the potential for a conflict of interest that is often called the principal–agent problem (Jensen and Meckling 1976). The conflict can arise when managers exert their influence in a way that increases their own reward without regard to the long-term benefit of the company. Treating the company's share price as a proxy for the well-being of the company, and connecting managers' pay to that share price, was originally seen as a way to tackle this problem by aligning the interests of the managers with those of the company (Garen 1994), but this has come to be seen as insufficient (Carberry and Zajac 2021).

For VC investors, this conflict is structured differently and is further complicated through their double role as a manager of the money that asset owners have invested and as a manager involved in the portfolio companies. Remember that a VC's primary goal as asset manager is to exit the company in 6–12 years, either through an IPO or a sale. Their management involvement should be focused on this goal even if it conflicts with any vision that the founders might have of the future of their company.

As asset managers, VCs could be described as agents of financialisation, turning people, things and companies into financial assets and seeking to increase their value, sell them on and use the proceeds to restart the cycle. However, VCs are not a monolithic group and are much less focused on simple financial return than this. Usually, they are influenced less by calculations of the present net value of their investments than they are by idiosyncratic, personal values such as who they are friends with, what the hot topics in the market are, or what products they personally care about and find exciting. In fact, the average VC fund is a poor asset manager, and does not produce good risk-adjusted returns to its limited partners (Kedrosky 2009).

I want to close this chapter with a question: Could the tensions that I have described in this chapter, which seem inherent in the different kinds of management in which VCs are involved, be resolved by obliging VCs to adjust to a plainer asset-manager role? Why not divide the double job that I have described, so that the investors can stick to being financiers and the founders can be the (sole) managers of their companies? Current macro-economic and commercial changes, notably less available capital and less competition among VCs, could lead in this direction by reducing the pressure on investors to deliver more than just capital. Instead, they could limit themselves to being asset managers. Is not mastering one type of management enough?

What a UK angel investor[5] with thirty years' experience and hundreds of portfolio companies presented to me as a criticism of VCs, retrospectively in fact sounds like a fitting description of the original (and perhaps new) VC model. This investor explained that VC funds

> are more likely to treat investment in new ventures as though they were like a stock trade; they put money in, and they want to take money out. They do very little to help the venture to grow. ... Say this company, they give you money, they come to board meetings but don't say a word, and [then] they want to get their money out.

Unlike the fear that Brett Christophers (2023: 48f.) voices about asset managers having come to own and charge for usage of 'core physical systems of social functioning and reproduction', such as housing and infrastructure, VCs might in fact do better with a single management focus. Instead of struggling with the tensions created by being two kinds of managers, of assets and of companies, VCs might want to focus on the management of money. The (temporary) assetisation (Birch and Muniesa 2020) of start-up companies by VCs, and VCs and asset owners benefiting financially from the (occasional) successful product commercialisation, seems much less problematic societally than asset managers owning and profiting from (scarce) housing and infrastructure.

Johannes Lenhard is affiliated with the Minderoo Centre for Technology and Democracy at the University of Cambridge and St Edmund's College, Cambridge. His doctoral research was on the survival practices of homeless people in London and Paris, published as *Making Better Lives* (Berghahn Books, 2022), and he is currently finishing a monograph on the ethics of venture-capital investors (under contract with Columbia University Press). He recently published a book on diversity and inclusion in venture capital and tech, *Better Venture* (with E. Brodnock, Holloway, 2023). He also writes journalism for outlets such as Techcrunch, Prospect, Sifted, Aeon, the Conversation and Crunchbase, and now predominantly runs the non-profit organisation VentureESG.

Notes

1. Limited partners also pay VC firms an annual management fee, usually around 2 per cent of the VC's fund size. This fee is used to pay salaries and other costs associated with running the fund (e.g. office, travel).
2. Many VC investors in the last decade of almost 'free money' had issues accessing certain highly sought-after deals; competing against (and winning over) other investors, especially big brand names from Silicon Valley, became a driver in itself, at times independent of or as important as the business proposition of the start-up. In other words, FOMO between VCs was a major factor in VC decision-making.
3. This is also sometimes called a type of 'platform venture capital' (Lacy 2015; Hartnett 2017).
4. a16z stands for Andreessen Horowitz, the names of the two founders of the firm, and 16 is the number of letters between the A and Z of their two names (www.a16z.com). Their model is described in Coppey 2016.
5. In contrast to venture-capital investors who act on behalf of limited partners, angel investors invest their own money; often they have previously been entrepreneurs or executives from big tech firms.

References

NB: Articles in *The New York Times* can be found by searching their website: www.nytimes.com.

Birch, Kean, and Fabian Muniesa (eds). 2020. *Assetization: Turning Things into Assets in Technoscientific Capitalism*. Boston: MIT Press.

Braun, Benjamin. 2022. 'Exit, Control, and Politics: Structural Power and Corporate Governance under Asset Manager Capitalism'. *Politics and Society* 50(4): 630–54.

Brown, Eliot, and Maureen Farrel. 2022. *The Cult of We: WeWork and the Great Start-Up Delusion*. New York: HarperCollins.

Carberry, Edward J., and Edward J. Zajac. 2021. 'Unpacking the Dynamics of a Contested Practice: The Case of Executive Compensation and the Shareholder Value Orientation in the USA'. *Socio-Economic Review* 19(1): 157–87.

Christophers, Brett. 2023. *Our Lives in Their Portfolios: Why Asset Managers Own the World*. London: Verso.

Cooiman, Franziska. 2023. 'Veni vidi VC – The Backend of the Digital Economy and its Political Making'. *Review of International Political Economy* 30(1): 229–51.

Coppey, Louis. 2016. 'Why Do VC Firms Become Platforms? (Or why A16z is Successful)'. *Medium* (5 July). Retrieved 31 Jan. 2023 from https://medium.com/startup-grind/why-do-vc-firms-become-platforms-or-why-a16z-is-so-successful-be12b2d7ce2e.

Diversity VC. 2019. 'Diversity in UK Venture Capital 2019'. Retrieved 8 June 2023 from https://drive.google.com/file/d/1iYnF8hQwK8N9uqVFlbn-4oNqhGkW6e-9/view.

Feld, Brad. 2015. 'The Paradox of VC Value-Add'. Retrieved 31 May 2023 from https://feld.com/archives/2015/04/paradox-vc-value-add/.

Fritjofsson, Carl. 2022. 'Do VCs Add Value?' Retrieved 31 May 2023 from https://blog.creandum.com/do-vcs-add-value-4-years-later-the-answer-remains-sometimes-49c53a8865b4.

Garen, John E. 1994. 'Executive Compensation and Principal–Agent Theory'. *Journal of Political Economy* 102(6): 1175–99.

Gompers, Paul A., and Vladimir Mukharlyamov. 2022. 'Transferable Skill? Founders as Venture Capitalists'. Working paper 29907. Cambridge, MA: National Bureau of Economic Research.

Griffith, Erin. 2022. 'Elizabeth Holmes is Set to be Sentenced on Sept. 26.' *The New York Times* (12 Jan.).

Gyllander, Jenny. 2017. '"Dear VC, Now It's Your Turn to Pitch" – An Exploratory Study on Venture Capital Firms' Brand and Reputation'. Archive no. 16034. Espoo, Finland: Aalto University.

Hartnett, Heather. 2017. 'The Rise of "The Platform" for Venture Capital Funds'. *Forbes*. Retrieved 31 May 2023 from https://www.forbes.com/sites/heatherhartnett/2017/09/28/the-rise-of-the-platform-for-venture-capital-funds/?sh=69db83264484.

Hoffman, Reid. 2018. *Blitzscaling: The Lightning-Fast Path to Building Massively Valuable Companies*. New York: HarperCollins.

Issac, Mike. 2019. *Super Pumped: The Battle for Uber*. New York: W.W. Norton.

Jackson, Tim. 2019. 'How to Get Fired as a Startup CEO'. *Medium*. Retrieved 31 May 2023 from https://medium.com/lessons-from-startup-ceos/how-to-get-fired-as-a-startup-ceo-2cc064881f0b.

Janeway, William H. 2018. *Doing Capitalism in the Innovation Economy: Markets, Speculation and the State*. Cambridge: Cambridge University Press.

Jensen, Michael C., and William H. Meckling. 1976. 'Theory of the Firm: Managerial Behavior, Agency Costs and Ownership Structure'. *Journal of Financial Economics* 3: 305–60.

Kedrosky, Paul. 2009. 'Right-sizing the US Venture Capital Industry'. Kansas City: Ewing Marion Kauffman Foundation.

Lacy, Kyle. 2015. 'Value-add VCs Are Not Bullshit – Here's Why'. *VentureBeat*. Retrieved 31 May 2023 from https://venturebeat.com/entrepreneur/value-add-vcs-are-not-bullsht-heres-why/.

Leins, Stefan. 2018. *Stories of Capitalism: Inside the Role of Financial Analysts*. Chicago: University of Chicago Press.
———. 2020. '"Responsible Investment": ESG and the Post-Crisis Ethical Order'. *Economy and Society* 49(1): 71–91.
Maxwell, Scott. 2015. 'The Truth about VC Value-Add'. Retrieved 31 May 2023 from https://openviewpartners.com/blog/truth-vc-value-add/.
Pratty, Freya. 2021. 'VCs Don't Add as Much Value as They Think, Say Founders'. *Sifted*. Retrieved 31 May 2023 from https://sifted.eu/articles/vcs-value-add/.
Preqin. 2022. '2022 Preqin Global Venture Capital Report'. London: Prequin. Retrieved 31 May 2023 from https://www.preqin.com/insights/global-reports/2022-preqin-global-venture-capital-report.
Rist, Kjartan. 2019. 'How to Add Value as a VC: The Fine Line between Support and Interference'. *Forbes*. Retrieved 31 May 2023 from https://www.forbes.com/sites/kjartanrist/2019/10/31/support-or-interference-how-to-add-value-as-a-vc/?sh=2f21c431a3eb.
Ryan, Aidan. 2022. 'What the FTX Crash Means for VCs and Startups'. *The Information*. Retrieved 31 May 2023 from https://www.theinformation.com/articles/what-the-ftx-crash-means-for-vcs-and-startups.
Souleles, Daniel. 2018. 'How to Study People Who Do Not Want to be Studied: Practical Reflections on Studying Up'. *PoLAR* 41(S1): 51–68.
Teten, David, Adham AbdelFattah, Koen Bremer and Gyorgy Buslig. 2013. 'The Lower-Risk Startup: How Venture Capitalists Increase the Odds of Startup Success'. *The Journal of Private Equity* 16(2): 7–19.
Willhelm, Alex. 2021. 'In 2020, VCs Invested $428M into US-based Startups Every Day'. *TechCrunch*. Retrieved 31 May 2023 from https://techcrunch.com/2021/01/19/in-2020-vcs-invested-428m-into-us-based-startups-every-day/.

Afterword

For an Anthropology of Management

Stefan Leins

As Michael Prentice states in his contribution to this volume, there is no anthropology of management. Why so? With this volume, that question becomes even more puzzling. Management, as the authors illustrate, is a core technique of current capitalism, a practice that needs to be studied thoroughly when trying to understand our current economic regime. Managers govern people, goods and money, and, in doing so, become influential actors in economy and society. It is no coincidence that some people, when unhappy with a service, ask to 'speak to the manager'. Usually, this is both a request and a threat. On the one hand, these customers hope to get hold of someone who is in charge and can handle their wish or complaint. On the other hand, it reflects the fact that the manager is in a position to chastise the worker who caused the customer's dissatisfaction. As this indicates, management means the ability to govern and to exert power.

The volume at hand presents a broad range of ideas about how to think about management from an anthropological perspective, in chapters that approach management in terms of conceptual (Carrier, Prentice), empirical (Lenhard, Orta, Røyrvik, Urban, Wong) and methodological (Stein) issues. We learn about different forms of management practices and discourses and about economic and political issues linked to them. All of the chapters succeed in making explicit the practices and discourses that, as James Carrier notes in his introductory chapter, are often taken for granted and invisible.

This volume thus offers a promising start to what Prentice says is missing: an anthropology of management. Such an anthropology can build upon scholarly work that has been published within recent years and that, unfortunately, has not been able to count on the support of its own subfield. For instance, there is *Work, Sleep, Repeat: The Abstract Labour of German Management Consultants*, by Felix Stein (2017). This ethnography of management consultants did not get the attention it deserved, probably because it was not enough about finance to attract anthropologists working on financial markets, and not enough about 'real' work to attract those in the anthropology of work. Another attempt to start an anthropology of management is *Allure of Capitalism: An Ethnography of Management and the Global Economy in Crisis*, by Emil Røyrvik (2011). It is conceptually and empirically strong, an ethnography that allows readers to step into an opaque and seemingly mysterious world. A third example is Kimberly Chong's (2018) *Best Practice: Management Consulting and the Ethics of Financialization in China*, a careful ethnography of management practices that addresses the question of why they are so central to current capitalism.

After this volume, what can we say about management as an anthropological subject? I think that there are four very broad lessons to be drawn. First, the popularity of management has something to do with the way capitalism currently works: things not only have to be produced, circulated and consumed, but also managed. This means that some person or institution must oversee how particular operations are executed so that they help the organisation to operate as intended. Second, management is ideologically charged. As Orta describes in his contribution, this is particularly visible when looking at the way managers are educated in MBA programmes. It also becomes visible, as Røyrvik illustrates, in the way that managers present themselves and in how they talk. Third, as mentioned above, management has something to do with hierarchy. Managers exercise power through the decisions they make. As Carrier describes in his chapter, this is interesting because managers' power seems to contradict Marxist analysis of how capitalism works: managers may be powerful, but they are employees rather than capitalists. And fourth, even though management seems to be so important, the legitimacy of management practices is shaky. This was the case for the financial analysts I studied (Leins 2018), for managers often ran the risk of becoming scapegoats if things did not work as planned. In these cases, a picture of a 'real economy' is evoked, in which economic actors are evaluated based upon their 'productive value', and managers are portrayed as non-productive and somehow shady economic free-riders (see Muniesa 2014; Neiburg and Guyer 2017).

Is 'Management' 'Bureaucracy' Repackaged?

One thing that is striking in many of the contributions to this volume is the proximity of management and bureaucracy. 'Management' is usually used in commercial contexts, while 'bureaucracy' is primarily used when describing government activities, but the parallels between the two are obvious. The fact that some of the chapters in this volume use Weber's notion of bureaucracy to conceptualise management shows that 'management' and 'bureaucracy' can be used almost interchangeably when referring to institutional practices.

Similar to studies of management, a body of anthropological literature on bureaucracy has emerged recently (e.g. Ferguson 1994; Gupta 2012; Bierschenk and de Sardan 2014; Mathur 2016). Most importantly, the work of David Graeber has inspired scholars to think about bureaucracy as an anthropological field of interest. Two points that Graeber makes seem critical to understanding bureaucracy. First, he argues that historically it is linked to the rise of capitalism. A lot of bureaucratic state practices, he claims, have emerged to secure things like private property. The idea that bureaucracy stands in opposition to economic practices thus seems wrong (Graeber 2015). Second, Graeber (2018) introduced the concept of 'bullshit jobs', types of professional work that are meaningless and do not produce societal or economic value. To Graeber, management is a typical example of such jobs. He says that we live in the 'age of managerial feudalism', which resembles classic feudalism in terms of its hierarchical structure and redistributive function (ibid.: 175–89).

While reading the chapters in this volume, I asked myself whether Graeber's critical view and other anthropological literature on bureaucracy could help to strengthen our view of management. An obvious way to start is to ask if management practices could be understood as bullshit jobs. Take, for example, the role and the practices of venture capitalists that Johannes Lenhard describes in his chapter. Their management activities help to provide capital and to turn business endeavours into financial assets. However, without the existence of these venture capitalists the businesses could still operate, albeit perhaps on a smaller scale. What could we gain if we understood venture-capitalist operations as forms of bullshit jobs? The same applies to Røyrvik's 'men in black suits'. What exactly is their actual impact on the economy? Can the gendered discourse that he analyses be understood as a form of what Graeber calls 'professional bullshitting'?

Linking the anthropological literature on management and the literature on bureaucracy could potentially be fruitful and lead to greater insights into the nature of these cultural practices. Could we maybe even agree that management is just the neoliberal term to describe the same thing that scholars working on the state call bureaucracy? Let us get these fields into conversation!

Management beyond the Realm of Economy

In 2019 I defined management as 'a mode of governing people or things in accordance with economic ideas and rationales' (Leins 2019: 91). I thus see economic thinking as being at the heart of management. This does not, however, mean that management as practice is limited to the frankly economic. The influence of economic ideas on society in general is apparent when phrases such as 'lean management' and 'evidence-based management' are found in all kinds of professional fields.

In development agencies, for example, concepts of management and people trained in management have become increasingly influential. The works of Arturo Escobar (1995) and David Mosse (2005) illustrate this ethnographically. In Escobar's case, an economic ideology of how poverty is to be 'managed' entered the realm of development professionals late in the twentieth century. Mosse's work points to the same trend towards an increasingly economistic perspective on development aid. Similarly, ideas and practices of management have entered the field of health. Medical anthropologists have called this a 'neoliberal governance' in healthcare (e.g. Keshavjee 2014; Kehr, Dilger and van Eeuvijk 2018). How does management play out in these fields? Are the practices similar to or different from management practices in the more purely economic realm?

The contributions to this volume exclusively deal with management in the economic context. Authors therefore use phrases such as 'corporate management' (Stein), 'business management' (Orta) and 'company management' (Lenhard) when talking about their cases. Such a focus seems only natural in a book such as this, in which the authors are interested in similar empirical fields. In the future, however, it would be beneficial to integrate findings from studies of management beyond the economic realm into the emerging field of the anthropology of management. I think that anthropologists working on corporations and on development, health, state-based practices and other fields could learn a lot from each other.

In the early 2000s, when the anthropology of finance emerged as a subfield, it benefited a lot from the anthropology of science. The work of scholars such as Bruno Latour and Steve Woolgar (1979) and Karin Knorr

Cetina (1999) helped anthropologists to think about how knowledge is constructed, substantiated and defended against challenges posed by other knowledge claims. In the anthropology of finance, questions of knowledge production, expertise and epistemology thus became a key point of interest. Even though the empirical fields were different, with science on one hand and financial markets on the other, each side benefited from the other's perspective. I think that the anthropology of management could similarly take inspiration from other fields, and use their conceptual frames to strengthen the study of management.

Management, Concretely

In the Introduction to this volume, Carrier explains that he takes thinking about management abstractly to mean looking at it 'free of the assumptions and elisions that adhere to it and that make it seem familiar, ordinary'. The chapters in this volume indeed succeed in this, allowing us to look at management from a new perspective. They do so by sharing intriguing conceptual thoughts, ethnographic material and methodological considerations.

All the same, the anthropology of management needs to become concrete. Anthropology has always been particularly good at relating the abstract to the empirical, the nitty-gritty of everyday practices and discourse. Books by Røyrvik (2013), Stein (2017), Chong (2018), Andrew Orta (2019) and others have laid the foundation for this, but there are still many aspects of management that can and should be studied empirically. And as management is so central to current capitalism, such future studies will be of relevance not only to scholars interested in management, but to economic and political anthropologists.

To substantiate such current and future studies, a closer look into the work of what is called 'critical management studies' might be helpful. That is an interdisciplinary research field that is particularly popular in the United Kingdom and in Scandinavia. It has its own division in the Academy of Management, holds regular conferences, and appears in special sections in renowned academic journals.

Those in critical management studies subscribe to a critical evaluation of management practices, and use philosophical concepts from the Frankfurt school, poststructuralism and feminist theory as a basis for their work (Alvesson and Willmott 2003). While some of that work is conceptual, an increasing number of scholars have started to work empirically, many of whom use ethnographic approaches (e.g. Smets et al. 2014; Lehn 2019). They differ somewhat from the way that anthropologists do ethnography, but their results are very interesting and there is considerable conceptual and methodological common ground that we should capitalise on to learn about management beyond the studies produced in our own scholarly networks.

***

I see great potential in an anthropology of management, to which this volume so helpfully contributes. To strengthen this emerging subfield, I have suggested four steps. First, the anthropology of management should think about the relationship between management and bureaucracy, and integrate the recent work on bureaucracy into its conceptual frames. Second, it needs to integrate anthropological studies that analyse managerial practices and discourse that take place beyond the realm of the economy. Third, anthropologists working on management should establish contact with scholars from critical management studies in order to exchange ideas and strengthen their conceptual frameworks. And fourth, the anthropology of management needs to enhance its empirical foundation. Such a growth can be achieved best by showing other scholars how important management is, not only for the subfield but for anthropology in general. And I have no doubt that the volume at hand represents a convincing first step in this.

Stefan Leins is professor of Social Anthropology at the University of Bern. He works on commodity trading, management practices, supply chains and financial markets with a focus on valuation, morality and narratives. His *Stories of Capitalism: Inside the Role of Financial Analysts* was published by the University of Chicago Press in 2018. He has had articles published in *Anthropology Today*, *Economy and Society* and *Ethnos*.

References

Alvesson, Mats, and Hugh Willmott (eds). 2003. *Studying Management Critically*. London: Sage.

Bierschenk, Thomas, and Jean-Pierre de Sardan. 2014. 'Studying the Dynamics of African Bureaucracies: An Introduction to *States at Work*', in Thomas Bierschenk and Jean-Pierre de Sardan (eds), *States at Work: Dynamics of African Bureaucracies*. Leiden: Brill, pp. 3–34.

Chong, Kimberly. 2018. *Best Practice: Management Consulting and the Ethics of Financialization in China*. Durham, NC: Duke University Press.

Escobar, Arturo. 1995. *Encountering Development: The Making and Unmaking of the Third World*. Princeton, NJ: Princeton University Press.

Ferguson, James. 1994. *The Anti-Politics Machine: Development, Depoliticization, and Bureaucratic Power in Lesotho*. Cambridge: Cambridge University Press.
Graeber, David. 2015. *The Utopia of Rules: On Technology, Stupidity, and the Secret Joys of Bureaucracy*. Brooklyn, NY: Melville House.
______. 2018. *Bullshit Jobs: A Theory*. New York: Simon & Schuster.
Gupta, Akhil. 2012. *Red Tape: Bureaucracy, Structural Violence, and Poverty in India*. Durham, NC: Duke University Press.
Kehr, Janina, Hansjörg Dilger and Piet van Eeuvijk. 2018. 'Transfigurations of Health and the Moral Economy of Medicine'. *Zeitschrift für Ethnologie* 143(1): 1–20.
Keshavjee, Salmaan. 2014. *Blind Spot: How Neoliberalism Infiltrated Global Health*. Oakland: University of California Press.
Knorr Cetina, Karin. 1999. *Epistemic Cultures: How the Sciences Make Knowledge*. Cambridge, MA: Harvard University Press.
Latour, Bruno, and Steve Woolgar. 1979. *Laboratory Life: The Social Construction of Scientific Facts*. Beverly Hills, CA: Sage Publications.
Lehn, Dirk vom. 2019. 'Phenomenology-based Ethnography for Management Studies and Organizational Analysis'. *British Journal of Management* 30(1): 188–202.
Leins, Stefan. 2018. *Stories of Capitalism: Inside the Role of Financial Analysts*. Chicago: University of Chicago Press.
______. 2019. 'Management', in James G. Carrier (ed.), *A Research Agenda for Economic Anthropology*. Cheltenham, UK: Edward Elgar, pp. 80–104.
Mathur, Nayanika. 2016. *Paper Tiger: Law, Bureaucracy and the Developmental State in Himalayan India*. Cambridge: Cambridge University Press.
Mosse, David. 2005. *Cultivating Development: An Ethnography of Aid Policy and Practice*. London: Pluto Press.
Muniesa, Fabian. 2014. *The Provoked Economy: Economic Reality and the Performative Turn*. Abingdon, UK: Routledge.
Neiburg, Federico, and Jane I. Guyer. 2017. 'The Real in the Real Economy'. *HAU: Journal of Ethnographic Theory* 7(3): 261–79.
Orta, Andrew. 2019. *Making Global MBAs: The Culture of Business and the Business of Culture*. Oakland: University of California Press.
Røyrvik, Emil A. 2011. *The Allure of Capitalism: An Ethnography of Management and the Global Economy in Crisis*. New York: Berghahn Books.
Smets, Michael, Gary Burke, Paulo Jarzabkowski and Paul Spee. 2014. 'Charting New Territory for Organizational Ethnography'. *Journal of Organizational Ethnography* 3(1): 10–26.
Stein, Felix. 2017. *Work, Sleep, Repeat: The Abstract Labour of German Management Consultants*. LSE Monographs on Social Anthropology 83. London: Bloomsbury.

Index

www.ingramcontent.com/pod-product-compliance
Lightning Source LLC
Chambersburg PA
CBHW071248180926
51613CB00002B/164
9781805396925